TWO OLD INDIANS

Jagjiwan Sohal

Black Rose Writing | Texas

©2024 by Jagjiwan Sohal
All rights reserved. No part of this book may be reproduced, stored in a retrieval system or transmitted in any form or by any means without the prior written permission of the publishers, except by a reviewer who may quote brief passages in a review to be printed in a newspaper, magazine or journal.

The author grants the final approval for this literary material.

First printing

This is a work of fiction. Names, characters, businesses, places, events, and incidents are either the products of the author's imagination or used in a fictitious manner. Any resemblance to actual persons, living or dead, or actual events is purely coincidental.

ISBN: 978-1-68513-457-0
PUBLISHED BY BLACK ROSE WRITING
www.blackrosewriting.com

Printed in the United States of America
Suggested Retail Price (SRP) $21.95

Two Old Indians is printed in Garamond Premier Pro

*As a planet-friendly publisher, Black Rose Writing does its best to eliminate unnecessary waste to reduce paper usage and energy costs, while never compromising the reading experience. As a result, the final word count vs. page count may not meet common expectations.

To our elders who still have many miles left in the tank.

TWO OLD INDIANS

CHAPTER 1

The year is 1977 and Morris "Mohawk" Jones stands in the corner, waiting patiently for Jack Stanhope to start the intros. He should be stretching, like his Hungarian trainer Ervin constantly tells him when they're pumping iron together, but Mohawk is too busy checking out the hot redhead in the third row. She's looking right at him, cute freckles spattered all over her nose and upper cheeks and wearing a tight green t-shirt and blue jeans, barely paying attention to the pimply and pudgy boyfriend beside her, who Mohawk can see is excitedly yammering about something as he holds up the show program.

She's gotta be twenty, Mohawk thought, wondering if he could get some backstage peon to tell her where he'll be hanging out after the matches. *Hope she's at least eighteen. Chick like that can get me in trouble if she's not...*

Mohawk cracked his knuckles, adjusted his wrist tape, and glanced down to see if his new red boots with the suede trim were still neatly tied up. He had problems with them a few nights ago in Pittsburgh against some local masked jobber named Pulverizer and didn't want to stumble around the ring in a tough wrestling town like Chicago. Tonight was a big one and Mohawk knew he had to bring his best. Even so, he couldn't help but give the redhead a quick wink and a smile. He even flexed his pecs for her and waited a few seconds to see if she would blush as bright as her hair color. She did and immediately looked away, all flustered and pink.

"Got her," Mohawk said to himself before he began wandering around the ring. He wasn't the most popular wrestler on the card but was getting there. Just a few more years of working the circuit and he might be in the main events. Maybe even becoming world champ...

That would be something.

Mohawk looked around at the crowd. They were mostly teenagers, bell-bottomed with brown boots and ringer tees. Many of them had poofy hair and big sunglasses even though it was indoors and quite dark in the arena. Cigarette smoke wafted all around and Mohawk hated this. The smell bothered him when he was wrestling, especially if it was a long match and he was breathing heavy. Mohawk very much preferred outdoor shows in the summer, at a county fair or carnival. The best wrestling experience he ever had was in a baseball stadium in Memphis. The fresh air was invigorating and he had performed great that day. Unfortunately, it was December right now so an outdoor show wasn't happening anytime soon.

"Nice house tonight, eh, Mo?" a powerful voice asked above the excited din of the audience. Mohawk looked over at the ring announcer, the legendary Jack Stanhope, a handsome and impeccably dressed former wrestler. Jack was fit and in his late fifties but a bad knee injury had ended his quest for the heavyweight title almost two decades ago. He still hung around the business because he loved it and even though Mohawk liked Jack, he didn't want to end up like him. All the twenty-five-year-old Mohawk Jones wanted to do was to make a million dollars, get out of wrestling and, if possible, break into acting. And why not? He was handsome enough, the ladies loved him, and maybe he could change Hollywood as the first Native American leading man. And there was no way he was going to let some tubby white guy he could crush with one hand push him around on a movie set in a cowboys and Indians picture.

"Mo? You here?" Jack said, which startled Mohawk out of his thoughts. He then grinned at the older man.

"I'm here, Jack," he said, adding, confidently, "Just waiting for the show to start."

Heavy boos rained down from the crowd, which got both men's attention in a hurry. The jeers were directed at Mohawk's opponent, the fearsome-looking Cobra Tara Singh. A sinewy and hairy-chested grappler from India, Cobra was the same age as Mohawk and wore a turban and sequined cape to the ring, twirling his evil villain mustache while glaring around the arena with his wild eyes. Mohawk didn't know Cobra very well but was excited to lock up with the man. This was going to be their first match together and Mohawk had heard Cobra was a legit shooter, a top-ranked Greco-Roman amateur in Asia who might have been Olympic material if he chose that path. Cobra's athletic background was a warning not to take liberties with the man in the ring. It wasn't Mohawk's style to do so, anyway. He preferred being booked to win more than lose, as did most wrestlers, but most of all, Mohawk wanted to be known as a wrestler who other guys could trust in the ring to make them look good and keep them uninjured.

The fans' harsh reaction intensified as Cobra sauntered down the aisle to the ring. He sneered at Mohawk and then made more nasty faces at the crowd, showing his disdain for them. Mohawk couldn't believe the hatred Cobra was generating and even though he was the babyface good guy, he was a bit envious of the reaction.

Once Cobra climbed into the ring, he shouted something rude in his native language at Mohawk, who had to bite down hard to not crack up laughing. *What a heel*, Mohawk thought, that twinge of jealousy creeping up in him again. *He's gonna be a superstar and make a ton of money...*

The two combatants faced off in opposite corners with ol' reliable Jack standing between them. He had a thin microphone in his hand, similar to the one Bob Barker held on The Price Is Right. It didn't look like enough to get the attention of over six thousand fans but Mohawk knew that Jack's authoritative voice would quiet everyone down.

It was time to get going and Mohawk took several deep breaths to calm himself. After about four years in professional wrestling, working matches several times a week, he rarely got nervous before a show now. This was different, though. He really needed a great performance tonight.

"IN THIS CORNER!" Jack boomed. "WEIGHING IN AT TWO HUNDRED AND TWENTY POUNDS...THE FIGHTIN' BRAVE... MOHAAAAAAWK JONES!"

Mohawk always loved how Jack did the Mohaaaaawk part of his name. To distract himself, he waved to the crowd and did a shortened version of his Indian war dance. Mohawk dipped into his heritage only during a show and it was a gimmick that worked for him, even though there were a bunch of other Native American wrestlers out there. The fans loved his dance and cheered him. Mohawk was glad to see that he was going into this big match with a ton of support.

Jack then turned to Cobra, standing arrogantly as he leaned on the ring ropes, like he was Indian royalty too noble to be in a city full of American peasants.

"AND HIS OPPONENT! WEIGHING IN AT TWO HUNDRED AND EIGHTEEN POUNDS ... THE SINISTER PUNJABI ... COBRA ... TARA ... SINGHHHHH!!!"

The boos, catcalls and hisses were deafening and they got louder and louder as Cobra screamed at the fans. The bell then rang and, just like they had planned backstage, Cobra dashed across the ring and sneak-attacked Mohawk with hard forearms shots to the head and back. This quieted the fans down immediately, many watching in stunned silence as the evil foreigner pummeled the courageous young hero.

Mohawk dropped to the mat from the onslaught and Cobra stomped him relentlessly with his shiny black boots. Mohawk was pleased by this. He could tell that Cobra was a real pro since the blows barely made an impact, glancing harmlessly off his shoulders and chest. Even so, Mohawk sold them like he was getting beaten down by a sledgehammer.

"C'mon, Mohawk, baby!" Mohawk heard a young woman scream at him. He looked through the ropes to see that the hot redhead was standing on her seat, waving her fists in the air. Her boyfriend wasn't too happy about this. Probably because of the "baby" part.

"Let's go, my friend," Cobra whispered in his heavy East Indian accent as he pulled Mohawk up to his feet, so imperceptibly that no one could detect their conversation, as they had been trained. "Keep your head in the game, eh? The redhead with the tits will be there for after. Your turn now..."

This meant it was time for Mohawk to make his comeback. As Cobra put his hands around his throat in a fake choke and the spectators gasped and gaped in horror, Mohawk summoned up his strength and forced his way free, using his powerful arms to shove the stunned Cobra aside. Mohawk then looked up, shrieked to the heavens for assistance from the Indian spirits, and exploded with lightning-quick chops to Cobra's torso. The fans exploded and Cobra's chest reddened with each blow.

"Easy, easy," Cobra said quietly, trying to calm Mohawk down so he wouldn't hit him so hard. "Do the dance now..."

"Got it," Mohawk nodded.

As Cobra wobbled on his feet, dazed from the babyface's heroic attack, Mohawk went into his full-on war dance, firing up the crowd even more. Cobra then begged off and fell to his knees, now playing the intimidated heel character, supremely frightened of Mohawk's righteous fury. Cobra backed away into the corner and Mohawk followed him, throwing a sweet dropkick where he leaped high in the air and delivered two flying boots to Cobra's face.

"The best dropkick in the game!" Mohawk had gloated to some of his wrestling buddies while they downed beers at the bar the night before.

After getting dropkick-ed, Cobra dropped like a stone and Mohawk bent down to pick him up again to deliver more punishment. In reality, he was checking on the guy as he thought he might have kicked too hard, hoping he hadn't busted Cobra open in the nose or mouth.

"You good?" Mohawk whispered, pulling Cobra by the hair. "Too stiff?"

"Not stiff at all," Cobra said. "Nice dropkick."

"Best in the game, brother."

Cobra beamed and the two wrestled for another frenzied seven minutes, going back and forth on offense. One particular highlight was Mohawk dragging Cobra around the ring by his mustache, the fans squealing in delight. Unfortunately, it wasn't to be Mohawk's night as Cobra cheated to win by "hitting" him with his "mystical brass knuckles forged in the Himalayan mountains" (actually just a piece of harmless rubber painted gold). The referee, a new kid named Ed Goins who had come in from the Portland territory, counted the pin and the boos rained down. Mohawk would have preferred to win in front of a hot crowd but he knew he had done well. That was almost as satisfying as a victory.

As the pompous Cobra strutted up the aisle and teased the fans, Mohawk lay down in the middle of the ring until his opponent disappeared behind the curtain. Mohawk then slowly stood up, painfully shaking off the cobwebs from Cobra's dastardly cheap-shot. The audience applauded him, which confirmed to Mohawk that his match had been a good one. They were cheering him in defeat.

"Great match," Ed said in Mohawk's ear as he "helped" him out of the ring.

"Thanks, bud," Mohawk said. "You were great, too."

"Yeah?"

"Definitely. Do me a favor?"

"Okay…"

"Go tell that redhead the hotel we're staying at tonight."

"The one with the tits?"

"That's the one."

"What a fucking match, brother!" Cobra exclaimed when Mohawk joined him backstage. Mohawk was pleased that Cobra had waited for him behind the curtain to check on him and share his thoughts on the match. The guy was a real pro.

"Nah, you did the work," Mohawk said. He appreciated Cobra's enthusiasm but knew that without Cobra's ability to get heat with the crowd, and, by extension, get them on Mohawk's side, the match would have been average at best. Cobra was a good wrestler but most of his act was his theatrics. If it was a straight-up wrestling match based on athleticism, there was no way he could keep up with Mohawk.

Even so, matches based on emotion and story got more of a reaction from the fans so who was Mohawk to judge how Cobra wrestled? Especially since, in a real fight, he could probably hand Mohawk his ass.

Mohawk wouldn't make it easy, though. He was a tough Indian boy. He could handle himself.

"We both did the work!" Cobra said, slapping his hand on Mohawk's shoulder in a friendly way. Mohawk smiled. He liked this guy.

The two walked down the corridor together, past various backstage workers on their way to the locker room. They chatted about the match and how into it the crowd was. Mohawk saw that this was all Cobra cared about, which was fine. They were performers in the very sense of the word.

"I am telling you, brother," Cobra continued. "We do that match anywhere in the world and it is box office! Main event cash!". Mohawk could see that Cobra also cared a lot about the money and as they finished showering off the sticky sweat from their bodies and dressed, he could see why. Cobra had expensive tastes, wearing tailored clothes and designer shoes while flashing a gold watch.

How does a guy my age have that kind of dough? Mohawk thought enviously. He was doing okay himself but during the lean months, he was living match to match sometimes.

As Mohawk pulled on his slacks and buttoned up his polo shirt, the sleeves tight around the biceps, he took a glance around the locker room. It was filled with wrestling misfits of all kinds, every shape and size and background. There was Kenya, the African giant who weighed almost four hundred pounds. He was actually Joe Jackson from Harlem and one of the nicest guys in wrestling, having once saved Mohawk in a bar fight by taking out three dangerous-looking bikers with ease. Then there was Buddy Blaze, a good-looking and well-muscled white guy from Tampa who Mohawk didn't like very much, mostly because he was always bullshitting and liked to walk around the locker room butt naked (and he really shouldn't have since he had nothing to brag about). There were a few others, laughing as they changed for their matches or played cards. Mohawk and Cobra had been the fourth match on the card so there was still a bunch of wrestling left in the show. Mohawk could even hear the roar of the crowd during the semi-main event as he finished combing his hair.

Cobra was still blabbing about their match when a powerful grunt was heard. Mohawk looked up to see that Mr. Sanada, a legendary Japanese wrestler and Mohawk's trainer, was staring down at him with his piercing black eyes. Mr. Sanada was probably the most respected wrestler in the industry, a stocky former world champion in his mid-forties.

Mohawk had trained in Mr. Sanada's "dojo" for a full year before having his first match. Mr. Sanada was a brutal teacher and the training was almost abusive...but Mohawk appreciated and loved the man for it. The Japanese are the best pro wrestling trainers in the world and Mr. Sanada taught Mohawk valuable lessons how not only to protect himself in the ring but also his opponents.

"Mr. Sanada," Mohawk said, bowing his head slightly in respect. Mr. Sanada's presence was so intimidating that even Cobra had hushed up, now standing at the side with wide eyes. Mohawk then asked, almost hopefully, "Good match?"

Mr. Sanada continued to glower...until he finally nodded.

"Good match," the man said gruffly, his Japanese accent still as forceful as ever despite decades spent in North America. He then turned away, nodded to Cobra, and headed to the ring for his match.

"Brother!" Cobra exclaimed, leaping forward. "A 'good match' from Mr. Sanada! Wow!"

Mohawk felt a wave of pleasure he had never experienced before. If he was alone, he might have broken down in joyous tears.

Mr. Sanada's praise meant everything to him but he wasn't going to cry in a locker room of meaty and manly wrestlers. No way.

"Gentlemen," a suave voice said as Mohawk and Cobra stood together to speak to the promoter of the show. Stan Victory was a retired wrestler and one of the biggest stars ever in professional wrestling. He portrayed the All-American hero and even though he was from before Mohawk's time, Mohawk knew him as not only a wrestling star but someone who did television commercials and other endorsements. The guy was a household name and Stan Victory's striking blue eyes, cascading blonde hair, and outfits wrapped in the red, white and blue of the American flag were well-known to everyone from giddy little kids to adoring grandmothers.

Now Stan operated the Chicago wrestling territory, one of the most profitable in the business. He was one of Mohawk's many bosses as he toured the country but probably the most important of his employers.

Mohawk and Cobra said nothing as Stan Victory appraised them. He then broke out in a big grin and clapped excitedly.

"These two!" he shouted, gesturing to the others in the locker room. "These two are young guns who know how to work! All of you should be paying attention because they're coming for your spots!" Stan turned back to Mohawk and Cobra. "I've got big plans for you two. Big, big plans!"

And with that, Stan left the locker room, leaving the astonished Mohawk and Cobra in his wake. They received some congrats from Kenya and a sneer from Buddy Blaze and as Mohawk and Cobra made their way to the parking lot together to their cars, Cobra stopped and got in front of Mohawk. Mohawk could tell the man had something he desperately wanted to say.

"We had them today," he began softly. "In the palm of hands."

"I know," Mohawk said.

"I do not think you do."

Cobra put his hands on Mohawk's shoulders, staring deep into his eyes.

"I am so glad to have locked up with you today," he said. "You and me...we are both Indian..."

Mohawk rolled his eyes slightly.

"Not really," he said. "You're from India and I'm..."

"Both of us! Indians!" Cobra interrupted. He then sighed happily. "My friend, I am positive we will make lots of money together! All the money! I promise you!"

Cobra put out his hand and Mohawk shook it warmly.

"Will you eat at a restaurant with me tonight?" Cobra asked.

"Maybe some other time," Mohawk replied.

"Very well. I will see you soon. Have a good night, my brother."

"You too, Cobra."

Cobra then saluted Mohawk and strolled off. Mohawk watched him climb into a sleek black Trans Am and wave goodbye before roaring out of the parking lot.

"Damn," Mohawk said out loud. "Wish I had a ride like that…"

He headed over to his own car, a battered but reliable sedan he bought off a wrestler in San Antonio. As he slid behind the wheel, Mohawk took a moment to collect himself.

"A good night," he smiled as he put the key in the ignition.

And it was about to get better.

He had a sexy redhead waiting for him at his hotel.

CHAPTER 2

The year is 1986. Mohawk Jones is now thirty-four years old and although he wished it had come sooner in his career...tonight is his night. After leaving Stan Victory's company in 1978 for a few big money years in Japan, he toured around Mexico, the Florida panhandle and then western Canada, making decent coin and having a fucking great time while doing it. He improved his skills and persona and now Mohawk confidently feels he's one of the best wrestlers in the world. He signed up again with Stan just a year ago and from there, went on a tear of great matches and main events. Stan's wrestling federation has grown massively in the years since Mohawk first left, now the top pro wrestling organization in North America, and with the company's promotional power behind him, Mohawk Jones is poised to become Stan Victory's next top star.

And tonight, Mohawk is booked to win the world championship.

From Cobra Tara Singh.

Making his way down the aisle for his first pay-per-view main event, Mohawk is fired-up as he slaps the hands of excited fans. His theme music, a collection of traditional Native American sounds mashed with heavy metal, rocks throughout the arena. Mohawk has leaned into the Native American stuff a lot more recently, wearing a feathered head-dress and some "war paint" on his face. The gimmick tweaks seemed to work since he's now more popular than ever.

There's twenty thousand people in attendance here in Kansas City and hundreds of thousands, maybe millions, watching at home, theaters and in sports bars all around the world. It's the biggest moment of Mohawk Jones' career...fuck, his life...and he can't help but feel guilty that he's going to take the world title, and the big money spot, from his best friend.

But I deserve it, Mohawk thought, leaping over the top rope into the ring and firing up a fist in the air to a loud ovation. Just three years earlier, his career was threatened because of a terrible knee injury, a landing to the outside of the ring gone wrong, but Mohawk fought his way back. Now the knee's stronger than ever and he feels like he's in the best shape of his life. Mohawk's at the age where the aches and pains of a pro wrestling career are supposed to start catching up to you but he still feels good. It doesn't hurt when he rolls out of bed although many veterans have warned him that those mornings are coming.

Then Mohawk remembered the guy who helped him get to this very moment. The man who called to check up on him as he was healing up, visited him whenever he was in town, and was always there for an encouraging word or lame joke to cheer him up.

Cobra Tara Singh.

Fuck.

To distract himself, Mohawk looked out at the audience as he strolled around the ring, running his hand across the top rope. Pro wrestling had taken off in the eighties, mostly because of Stan Victory's stellar salesmanship. The crowds were bigger, mostly filled with little kids now that wrestling aired on Saturday mornings, right after cartoons. There were toys, t-shirts and merchandise in the stores and wrestlers were like rock stars now, often booked on TV talk shows to promote themselves and upcoming shows. Mohawk himself was scheduled to go on Johnny Carson later this week to celebrate his title win.

First things first, though. He had to get through tonight.

Mohawk stayed locked in as the smiling babyface hero, waving to the kids and their parents in the stands, although on the inside, he was nervous, the butterflies having a battle royal in his stomach. He saw some women he wouldn't mind to get to know better after the show but it also made him feel very lonely. Mohawk was reminded that he had no one waiting for him at home after the match. The few relationships he had generally ended since the women couldn't handle the hardships of him being on the road all the time, as well as the affairs he couldn't resist having.

Mohawk wished that his parents, Ted and Barbara Jones, who had adopted him as a toddler, had made it out to see his moment of triumph. They didn't like to travel and both were initially unsure of their son's foray into professional wrestling, Mohawk's dad hoping he would have gone on to play college ball and make it to the NFL instead. They had come around, though. When his mother and father were more interested in road trips a few years back, Mohawk had brought them to one of his big matches against Cobra and he took them backstage where Cobra was nothing but a gentleman, taking all of them out to a fancy dinner after. His mom even sent a Christmas card to Cobra that year.

Dammit, Mohawk thought. *Stop feeling guilty! It's business! Cobra'll understand...he's the one who taught you that it's a business...he's a good man...the best man...*

"Head in the game, Mo," Ruth whispered to him, a slight giggle in her voice. She was Stan Victory's top ring announcer with Jack Stanhope passing away from cancer not long ago. Many of the older wrestlers didn't like a woman like Ruth in their ring, with her bright red lipstick, sequined mini-skirts and high heels, and they grumbled non-stop about it. Mohawk ignored the complaints because he liked Ruth (as did many of the horny fans...Ruth's bathing suit posters sold very well). The two had dated briefly upon her being hired, keeping it very hush-hush, and it was rumored that she was now dating Stan Victory after his wife divorced him. Or maybe she ended the marriage because of Ruth.

"I'm fine," Mohawk said curtly. "Don't worry about me." Usually, he and Ruth would have had some playful banter before a match but Mohawk wasn't into flirting right now. He nodded at Ed Goins, who was the referee for the match. This was a cue for Ed to come over and they both went over the finish sequence, just so they were on the same page, their hands casually running over their mouths so no fan would be the wiser. This was just

Mohawk being overly cautious. Ed was such a trusty pro now and didn't require any coaching.

Suddenly, the somber sounds of a sitar sprinkled throughout the arena followed by the crash of thunderous Indian drums, a menacing theme song for the top heel wrestler in the world. Cobra Tara Singh was a hated bad guy when Mohawk first met him but now he was downright despised. As soon as he appeared at the top of the stage leading to the ring, the fans were on their feet, booing him with every ounce of energy in them. It was deafening and Mohawk couldn't even hear Ruth and Ed as they spoke to him. So he just nodded and pretended that he could.

Dressed in a robe of gold with a matching gold turban and long tights (Mohawk wore his customary red tights and fringe boots although he had added some white stripes to his trunks), Cobra slunk his way to the ring, hissing at everyone around him. However, Mohawk could tell the man was laboring, although the fans might not have noticed. Mohawk had heard Cobra had suffered a back injury during a match in Portland but he still made his dates. He had to...he was the world champion.

Mohawk's eyes went to the sparkling world title which was worn around Cobra's waist. *That's all I've ever wanted,* he thought hungrily. *To be the world champ...even if I lost it tomorrow...at least I could say I had it once...*

Ruth did her ring introductions and to Mohawk's relief, his cheers overtook Cobra's boos. That meant the fans had paid to see him beat Cobra and take his title, which filled Mohawk with more confidence.

Time to shine.

The bell rang and Ed jumped out of the way to let Mohawk and Cobra do their thing. They locked-up and Mohawk moved his lips close to Cobra's ear.

"You hurt?" he asked. He hadn't had a chance to speak with Cobra before the show. They chatted on the phone a week ago to go over what they were going to do in the match but then both were booked on separate coasts so their communication was minimal.

"Fine," Cobra said tightly. Mohawk winced. He could tell that Cobra was gutting it out. He was in a lot of pain but still showed up to do the deed.

For him.

Mohawk pushed Cobra to the ropes. The fans cheered, reacting to everything that was happening.

"We can have an easy one," Mohawk offered. "They're only here for the title switch. They don't care about the match..."

He saw the anger flash in Cobra's eyes and right after, Mohawk received a hard slap on his chest. It stung like hell and Mohawk's knees almost buckled, the boos raining down on Cobra for the dastardly cheap-shot.

"Fuck you, motherfucker!" Cobra said in his thick East Indian accent. Mohawk had insulted the man's pride. "Let us fucking go!"

And they did. They had a twenty-minute non-stop affair, with some of the sweetest wrestling ever seen to that point. Since the early eighties, professional wrestling had gotten more intense and the moves had become flashier, the audience wanting to see more than just two sweaty guys in their underwear struggle over a headlock for thirty minutes. Both Mohawk Jones and Cobra Tara Singh were up for the task, though. They had traveled the world and improved their craft against the best grapplers in the world.

Backdrop suplex. Flying clothesline. Top rope splash. The dreaded piledriver.

Mohawk and Cobra could do it all.

Mohawk was surprised that as injured as he was, Cobra was staying with him every step of the way. The pace of the match was incredible, to the point that Ed himself was drenched with sweat as he slid around the mat to count pinfalls.

"You guys are incredible," he wheezed, wiping his forehead with the back of his hand.

The crowd was whipped into a frenzy and it was time to go to the finish. Cobra hit his awesome shoulderbreaker move but Mohawk kicked out at two, causing the fans to gasp in surprise. Mohawk could hear a murmur go through the crowd as they knew something huge was going to happen. No one had ever kicked out of Cobra Tara Singh's finishing move before.

Now Mohawk was on his feet, glaring at the bewildered Cobra before pointing at him. He then did his war dance and the place went unglued. Mohawk hit Cobra with a dropkick...and another...and then hoisted him up for his running powerslam move. He executed it perfectly in the middle of the ring, covered the prone Cobra for the pin and Ed got ready to slap the ring canvas with his hand.

One.

Two.

Three.

"Thank you, brother," Mohawk said to Cobra, as he rolled off his opponent. He then closed his eyes to soak everything in. Although the fans were screaming at the top of their lungs, over his theme music and Ruth's official declaration of the new world heavyweight champion, he could only hear silence.

He did it.

Mohawk opened his eyes and found himself exhausted and exhilarated at the same time. He was on his feet, trying to control his heavy breathing, just as Ed was shoving the world title into his hands, a big grin on his face.

"Take your bow, champ!" he shouted giddily before leaving the ring.

Mohawk then triumphantly held up the title for the crowd, who cheered and cheered and cheered. It was never-ending and Mohawk didn't want to leave the ring. All the work, on the mat and in the gym, all the cuts and bruises, all the broken bones and torn muscles, all the endless travel, the loneliness and heartache, it had culminated in this moment, the greatest of his life.

Mohawk hugged the title belt to his chest and then remembered to look for Cobra. The man had put him over like a million bucks in the match, which he knew immediately was a classic, and he hoped to see his best friend's face somewhere, smiling proudly at him.

He couldn't find Cobra, though. And although he did his best to perform the post-match interview in the ring with Stan Victory, his concern started to grow. Mohawk did eventually spot Cobra, getting helped to the backstage area by Ed and the ringside doctor. He looked like he was in really bad shape.

Fuck.

Mohawk was greeted by a standing ovation from the other wrestlers as soon as he stepped through the burgundy backstage curtain. He had worked hard his entire career to be respectful to everyone, from the opening match guys, the jobbers (the wrestlers who were only around to make the real stars look good), the aging veterans, and the other main eventers. Mohawk Jones was known as a good dude in the wrestling business so the whole crew was excited to see him win the big one. He got a ton of handshakes, high-fives, and even a hug from an excited young rookie who he traveled with from time to time.

"You're awesome, Mohawk!" the rook, a kid named Steve, hollered.

Mohawk smiled at this, playfully giving Steve a noogie, before he noticed that Cobra wasn't among the wrestlers congratulating him.

Maybe he's getting patched up at the doctor's station, Mohawk thought, heading for the locker room. Aside from his back injury, Cobra had suffered a slight cut from a glancing blow that had bled a little during the match.

Once in the locker room, Mohawk reluctantly put the world title down and headed for the shower. He wanted to feel refreshed and more like himself again after rinsing off and scrubbing the dirt and grime from the mat canvas off him. When he stepped out and headed back to the dressing area in a towel, Mohawk had another small group waiting for him.

"There's my champ!" Stan Victory shouted proudly, flashing his pearly-white grin. He was holding the world title and slapped it against Mohawk's chest for him to hold. Some photographers flashed their cameras at him and Mohawk was glad he had styled his hair before coming out. The shower water glistening on his admirable physique would help his appearance and these photos would definitely look good in the wrestling trade magazines.

Kenya and Buddy Blaze were also there. They had been part of the crowd who had congratulated Mohawk before his shower but he was glad to see them here now, particularly Kenya.

"Nice work," Buddy said, chewing his Juicy Fruit furiously. "Hope you got some left in the tank when we're booked together. It's happening soon."

"It is?" Mohawk asked.

"That's right," Stan Victory chimed in. "Buddy's your first feud coming out of your title win. I'm sure you boys'll tear the house down!"

"We will," Buddy added confidently. "Maybe I'll be the one to take that belt off you, Mo!"

He chuckled a little, sounding like a hyena, and walked off to his locker. Mohawk knew Buddy was being a prick on purpose so he wasn't too put off by the man's joke. He was surprised that Buddy would be his next opponent, though. Mohawk had hoped for some rematches with Cobra around the normal touring loop first.

"So proud of you, brother," Kenya said, giving a heavy backslap like he always did. It stung but it was how the big man showed affection. Mohawk could take the pain for his pal.

"Thanks, Ken," Mohawk said. "Thanks for everything."

Kenya was the one Mohawk had beaten to "earn" his title shot against Cobra. Kenya had made Mohawk look like a superhero when he allowed him to powerslam him. Kenya was a giant in wrestling and rarely went off his feet. To slam the man was the sign of ultimate respect and professional courtesy.

The crowd began to disperse, with more congrats sent Mohawk's way from onlookers. He noticed he was still hugging his title.

Mohawk didn't ever want to let it go.

He then heard a familiar grunt. Mr. Sanada, who had traveled specifically on Mohawk's dime to attend the show, wanted to speak to his student. He gestured to a bench and the two sat down.

The recently retired Mr. Sanada had knee surgery himself not too long ago and was walking with a cane. His face was more weathered now, some scar tissue visible around the forehead, but he remained an imposing figure.

Mohawk waited patiently as Mr. Sanada took a moment to gather his thoughts.

And then the man did something Mohawk had never seen before.

He smiled.

"Good match," Mr. Sanada said simply. He then stared deeply into Mohawk's eyes. "Good wrestler." Finally, Mr. Sanada jabbed the title belt on Mohawk's shoulder with a finger. "Good champion!"

Mohawk had nothing to say to this and he knew to say something, like thanking Mr. Sanada profusely, would embarrass the man. So he bowed deeply instead and Mr. Sanada nodded in approval. He said nothing else and then got up to leave. Mohawk rushed to the door to hold it for the man out of respect and as Mr. Sanada exited, Cobra Tara Singh entered.

Mr. Sanada gave Cobra a nod as he left but Cobra ignored it. This was an insult that Mohawk noted but Mr. Sanada didn't seem to mind. He gave another nod to Mohawk on the way out and soon disappeared around a corner. Mohawk then turned his focus back to Cobra. His face was bandaged near the eyebrow and he held a big ice pack on the small of his back. The man looked to be in terrible shape and the concerned Mohawk rushed over to him.

"Cobra, let me help you, man," he said.

"Get off me!" Cobra shouted. This immediately got the attention of the others in the room. Stan Victory had left but Kenya and Buddy still stuck around.

Mohawk was stunned. Why was Cobra acting like this? He then saw that Cobra was glaring at the title belt before he looked up and snarled at Mohawk.

"Don't forget," Cobra said menacingly. "The man who make you to be the champion. Me. I make you."

Mohawk's jaw dropped. He couldn't believe what he was hearing. Neither could anyone else.

"Cobra, c'mon," Kenya said gently, trying to diffuse the situation. "Ya'll two are friends."

"Friends?" Cobra said, rolling his eyes. He then pressed the knuckles on his fist to Mohawk's chest. "Remember...I make you."

He then scooped up his clothes and exited the locker room, still wearing his ring gear. Mohawk was frozen in shock until Buddy, of all people, broke the tension with an encouraging word.

"Forget him, Mo," he said. "He's just mad he's not the champ anymore."

At this, Mohawk couldn't help but smile. It was true. Cobra wasn't the world heavyweight champion anymore.

He was.

A couple of hours later, Mohawk was in his hotel room. He could have easily gone out and partied it up with Kenya and Buddy to celebrate his victory, or at least picked up a lady or two from the bar to bring to his room…but he didn't want to. Instead, he bought a six-pack of beer and some burgers and watched an old Western on TV. It was bliss.

When the movie ended, Mohawk lay on his bed, the world title beside him, stationed on its own pillow. The gold plating glittered and Mohawk couldn't help but bend down to kiss the belt.

I'm the world champion.

So fuck you, Cobra Tara Singh.

CHAPTER 3

The year is 1998 and Mohawk Jones feels like he's in the fight of his life. The match is in a grimy high school gym in Philly and every part of his body is screaming in pain. Mohawk's forty-six now, a very old forty-six, and although his days as a world champion in the big promotions are long gone, he can main event an independent show for a smaller company. He's lucky to still have that kind of name value.

The problem is that Mohawk is a shell of the wrestler he was and he knows it. Too many miles on his body and too many hard bumps in the ring. He can't throw a dropkick anymore and his wrestling arsenal is limited to slow punches, kicks, chops, and if his shoulders aren't hurting him too badly, his patented powerslam. Even working out, which Mohawk loved to do so much before, is a bitch now, especially cardio workouts. Luckily, his physique isn't too bad but that's mostly because of the steroids.

What Mohawk can do, and do well enough to sell tickets, is bleed.

A lot.

"Hardcore" matches have become the hottest thing in wrestling in the late nineties and Mohawk has now become a "brawler", a wrestler who relies on heavy violence to get over with crowds. He uses steel chairs and wooden sticks on his opponents, sometimes barbed wire and thumbtacks, and receives the same kind of blows in return. Now his body is full of scars and every night, he cuts himself with a small concealed blade on the upper forehead to get the blood flowing. The fans howl with glee when they see him wear the "crimson mask".

Mohawk is still very popular and is making a decent living but he hurts all the time and he doesn't like what he's been reduced to. He's never home, can barely get a few hours of sleep a night due to the aches and pains, is drinking more than ever, and, for the first time, Mohawk loathes what he does for a living.

"Take my sign!" a fan at the guardrail screams as Mohawk wipes the blood around his eyes. The kid has to be sixteen at the most and holds a sign that says "Die Cobra Die". Mohawk is disgusted by this but takes the sign anyway, which he's glad isn't too heavy. He then lightly whacks Cobra in the head with it.

The small but exuberant crowd of two hundred fans erupts as Mohawk mugs for them and looks down at the prone Cobra. The man wasn't hurt in the least and had also "bladed" for his own bloody mess of a face. Sadly, the years had not been kind to Cobra, either. He now had a big beer belly that sagged over his tights, his muscle tone was gone, and his hair had receded to a long ponytail in the back. He still had his prodigious mustache but Cobra moved very gingerly around the ring now, nowhere close to the incredible athlete he had been in his youth.

Like Mohawk, all Cobra could do was brawl and bleed now. They were both considered legends in the sport, former world champs who were still "draws", and could command solid fees for their appearances on independent events. The storied feud between Mohawk Jones and Cobra Tara Singh had lasted decades and both had made a lot of money from it.

They still hated each other and things had gotten progressively worse in their relationship since the night Mohawk won the world title. So even though they were booked together quite often, they didn't take it easy on each other in the ring. Every third or fourth shot, whether it be a punch or a kick, was laid in for real, with full force, but neither confronted the other about it. Whoever won or lost was up to the promoter but both men were going to be feeling the effects of their match later.

If he didn't need the money for his retirement, whenever the hell that would be, Mohawk would never do these matches with Cobra. He would prefer to be away from "The Sinister Asshole" as much as he could.

Mohawk pulled Cobra up to his feet but his opponent was ready for him. Cobra hit him with a punch to the stomach and then shoved him into the ring post. Mohawk protected himself but some of his blood still splashed onto the steel.

"He is nothing!" Cobra yelled at the crowd, the Indian accent still very thick. He then pointed at Mohawk. "I will break your body!"

Cobra ran at Mohawk, who caught him with an ugly clothesline move. Mohawk knew it was terrible: awkward and fake-looking. It was the best he could do, though.

Mohawk threw Cobra into the ring and brought a steel chair in with him. The match was contested under "no holds barred" rules...which meant there were basically no rules. There was only a referee to count the pin and this guy was no Ed Goins, just some skinny trainee punk who seemed nauseated at the sight of blood.

"Take it and hit me on the back," Mohawk whispered to Cobra as he prepared to swing the chair at him. Cobra nodded and hit Mohawk with a "low blow", a phony punch to the balls. Mohawk appropriately buckled to his knees, writhing in pain and discomfort, and Cobra Tara Singh eagerly picked up the chair. He gleefully danced a little, Bollywood-style, and waved his weapon at the crowd. They booed him mercilessly so he danced some more, allowing Mohawk to get in position to take the blow on his back, which wouldn't hurt too bad. However, Cobra was getting into his act and before Mohawk could hiss at him to focus, the man swung the chair down onto Mohawk's head.

Hard.

Mohawk saw flashes of light and dropped to the mat like a stone as the audience gasped. They knew it was a legit shot.

Mohawk wasn't knocked out but was close to it.

He also couldn't move.

"Shit!" Cobra said, seeing what he had done. "Your back...I should have hit your back!"

Mohawk didn't say anything. He couldn't.

"Should we go home?" Cobra asked nervously. This was the code phrase for ending the match and this was a no way/no how for Mohawk. He was booked to win and he wasn't going to let this motherfucker hit him for real and then get the satisfaction of a victory over him.

No way.

No how.

Mohawk willed himself up to all fours. He looked up at Cobra, who didn't seem remorseful at all.

"Hit me again," Mohawk spat out. "On the fucking back!"

Nodding quickly, Cobra did what he was told.

Th-wack!

Mohawk dropped again but this time, the chair attack didn't hurt. He had actually asked for Cobra to do so to keep the match going so he could recover. He nodded at Cobra to hit him once more, this time on the back of the thighs, giving him even more time to get his head right.

By the time Cobra was about to unload with the next chair-shot, Mohawk could feel himself ready to continue. He knew he was in bad shape, and was probably concussed, but he was well enough to finish the match. At least he hoped he was.

Mohawk crawled away from Cobra, who missed with the chair, hitting the mat and comically jarring his fingers, causing him to screech and release his grip on the chair. During this, Mohawk made it to the ropes and used them to pull himself to his feet.

He was very unsteady and it was dangerous for him to continue on…but he could also hear the fans chanting for him.

Mo-hawk!

Mo-hawk!

Mohhhh-hawwwwwk!

The chant was something that was added to Mohawk's comeback routine when he was in his late thirties. The fans would fire him up and then he would go into his war dance.

C'mon, body, he thought, shaking himself up, as if the adrenaline was coursing through him. *Work so I can do the fucking dance…*

It was probably the most painful Indian war dance that Mohawk had ever done but it did the job. The fans were rocking in their seats as Cobra played his role in the sequence, landing punches to Mohawk's shoulders that had no effect and then looking bewildered about it. It was like, "Why can't I hurt this guy anymore?!"

Mohawk was gaining steam and now it was his time to vanquish the bad guy.

He blocked a big punch from Cobra and peppered him with jabs and chops. The fans were going even more nuts. This was what they paid for: two older legends playing the hits. Cobra was now knocked "loopy" and Mohawk went to the finish. He grabbed the chair to show everyone that turnabout was fair play, and nailed Cobra, safely, in the butt with it.

Mohawk then scooped up Cobra with the best powerslam he could possibly do in the circumstances, which was still quite awful with Cobra basically jumping into the move without Mohawk muscling him up, and the geek of a ref counted the pinfall.

One. Two. Three.

Mohawk had won but could barely move. Something was wrong with his ankle, his elbow, one of his fingers had to be broken, but most of all, Mohawk was worried about his head. It ached like crazy and he felt like throwing up.

Mohawk still had the strength to get back to his feet and do a wave in appreciation for the fans, many of whom were already filing out to beat the traffic now that the main event was over. Cobra was holding the lower part of his back and this enraged Mohawk.

Fucking faker...I didn't hit you that hard.

He tore after Cobra, ready to confront him after the chair shot that could have damn near ended him.

Having it out with Cobra was a long time coming. Sure, they disliked each other and took some small liberties in the ring but never to legitimately injure the other.

This was too fucking far.

"Cobra!" Mohawk screamed, as he tore through the curtain. There were some people around but Mohawk didn't care. He spotted Cobra talking to the promoter, a super wrestling fan who owned a used car dealership and mostly just wanted to hang out with the wrestlers.

"What the fuck you want?" Cobra fired back.

"This!"

Mohawk reared back and punched Cobra right in the face as hard as he could. In their athletic primes, Mohawk might have been able to hang with Cobra in a street-fight for a short while but eventually, Cobra's amateur wrestling background would have smothered him. Those days were gone, though. Cobra wasn't nearly in good enough shape to out-grapple Mohawk now.

Cobra fell backward, landing on the stunned promoter, both stumbling about before they fell to the floor. To Mohawk's surprise, Cobra was a lot spryer than he thought. He hopped back to his feet in a hurry, holding his bruised jaw.

"You still hit like a weakling!" Cobra roared, punching Mohawk right in the chest. It hurt like hell but Mohawk was thankful Cobra hadn't hit him in the head, which was throbbing.

Now the adrenaline was pumping and both men were ready to go for it. Cobra leaped at Mohawk with a double-leg takedown, hooking him under the knees. Cobra didn't have the strength to put Mohawk on the ground so the two stood there in a stalemate, wrestling with each other and flailing their arms, trying to land punches.

"You hit me with that chair on purpose!" Mohawk shouted.

"It was payback, man!" Cobra yelled back. "You hit me with big sign! And a chair to the bum!"

"Those were soft and you fucking know it!"

Cobra growled and was finally able to drag Mohawk down to the dirty cement floor. They rolled around together, exchanging some weak slaps, and Mohawk was aware that a crowd was gathering. No one was stepping in to break the fight up although there were calls for them to stop immediately, especially from the petrified promoter, who probably feared a lawsuit of some kind.

Mohawk was beginning to regret the whole thing. With how pro wrestling was now, with the newsletters and the internet stuff, this skirmish was definitely going to be big news in the industry and not in a favorable way.

Regardless, Mohawk refused to give an inch to Cobra Tara Singh. He now had him in a chokehold and wanted to put him out. Not kill the guy, of course, but at least choke Cobra to sleep for a few minutes so he would know that Mohawk Jones was no pushover and he didn't put up with any bullshit. Unfortunately, Cobra's wrestling instincts kicked in and he easily got out of the move, reversing to a weak full nelson, and the two continued to pathetically try to conquer the other.

"Squash this shit!" a thunderous voice bellowed out and everyone froze, even Mohawk and Cobra. They looked over to the still-imposing Kenya, who rolled in on his wheelchair. Weight gain and diabetes had cost Kenya his career, and his foot, but he still attended independent wrestling shows for appearances and autograph signings to make ends meet. Kenya and Mohawk were still very close but there was nothing friendly in the man's eyes at the moment. With his bald head and heavy black beard, Kenya was scarier now than when he was a monster bad guy in his prime.

Mohawk and Cobra broke apart but didn't dare get up to their feet unless they thought it was safe to, Kenya continuing to glower at them.

"Years of this shit!" Kenya shouted. "Ya'll two have been fighting for too long...and for what? Pro wrestling? This shit don't matter!"

"You don't get it, Ken," Mohawk said lamely. "He shot on me..."

Kenya turned to Cobra, pointing a thick finger at the cowed wrestler.

"Unprofessional!" Kenya roared.

He waved to the others who had been watching the brawl, younger guys who were just trying to learn and hopefully get a break in the wrestling business someday.

"What kind of example are you setting for these rooks?" Kenya continued, on a real roll now. "You're both legends...goddamn act like it!". He then turned his rage on the wrestlers and other spectators. "And you little bitches...let this be your lesson today from Papa Kenya: you see a fight like this, you break it up! Doesn't matter who it is, a main eventer or an opening match guy! We're a brotherhood!"

Kenya's forehead had little beads of sweat on it now. He spun around on his wheelchair to face Mohawk and Cobra again.

"Now shake hands and be done with it!" Kenya demanded.

Without hesitation, Mohawk and Cobra shook hands. They didn't look each other in the eye but this seemed to be enough for Kenya.

"T-thanks so much, er, for that," the promoter stammered.

"Shut the fuck up, bitch!" Kenya said, wheeling off with the promoter. "Give me my money…I wanna go home…tired of this shit…"

The backstage area emptied and Mohawk and Cobra stared at each other for a few seconds longer, as if waiting to see if the other was ready to continue on with their fight. Mohawk didn't want to as every fiber of his being was screaming in agony, especially his head. Thankfully, Cobra spun away and headed off to the showers and Mohawk went to the locker room, grabbed his stuff, and rushed off to his shitty hotel. He lay on the bed, taking inventory of his injuries. The ankle was definitely sprained, the elbow banged-up, his knees and hips were in agony and his back and shoulders would need some kind of treatment. Nothing was worse than his head, though and Mohawk got no sleep that night. And when he got home and was checked out by his doctor, his suspicions were correct: a big-time concussion and no wrestling for a few months, at the very least.

This was fine with Mohawk. After that disastrous match in Philly, the last thing he wanted was to get in the ring again. If his career was over, so be it.

Mohawk was also certain about one other thing. He never wanted another match with Cobra Tara Singh as long as he lived.

He never wanted to see the guy again, either.

CHAPTER 4

The year is 2022 and Mohawk Jones' knees are fucking killing him. So is his back. His hips aren't doing too great, either.

Even so, Mohawk didn't want to take the chair that was offered to him, preferring to stand proudly in front of his teenage audience, trying to radiate some kind of presence. COVID wasn't in the news as often now so no one was masked-up although they did have to be vaccinated to meet with The Fighting Brave, Mohawk Jones.

Mohawk couldn't understand why so many were had complained about getting vaccinated. The last thing he wanted, as a man who was now a senior citizen, was to be taken down by a virus from China.

They didn't even have pro wrestlers there.

As an older gentleman, Mohawk tried his best to stay in good shape, training a few times a week and still having a somewhat straight back, although he did lose a bunch of muscle mass over the years. Despite this, Mohawk Jones was a fit geezer, although he had a ton of aches and pains from his years in the wrestling ring, ones that would probably require surgery eventually. Mohawk rarely thought about the future like that, though, more annoyed that he had to wear his reading glasses so often now, that his hair was all gray and receding (although he still rocked a braided ponytail) and that he couldn't hear as well.

He was wrestling a sixty-minute Broadway against time and he was definitely being booked to lose this one.

Due to the pandemic, Mohawk hadn't made any real public appearances in almost two years and since things had started opening up again, he wasn't sure he wanted to do that many more signings or wrestling convention shows. He had retired as a wrestler in the early 2000s and even though he would never say so aloud, Mohawk actually enjoyed being locked down in his home, no one bothering him, and being able to just relax and watch television. Groceries and toiletries were delivered to the house and it was actually a nice little existence, although his roommate could be a real pain in the ass. Still, after decades of grinding on the road, running from town to town, country to country, if Mohawk never stepped foot in an airport again, he would die a happy man.

He didn't plan on dying anytime soon, though.

Despite his reservations of leaving the house, Mohawk had recently started venturing out again, especially if the money was right. For some reason, he found himself in demand as a "pro wrestling legend" and even got offers to do TV commercials or in-depth interviews, retrospectives on his career on something called a podcast. These new requests definitely took some getting used to, especially after the wrestling world had seemed to forget him as soon as he finished up as a performer. And Mohawk himself didn't feel like following the current-day wrestlers, either. The youngsters were flashier and less interesting (as least to him) than the grapplers of his era.

On this day, Mohawk had woken up with sorer knees than usual and his lower back was killing him, having tightened up overnight. Mohawk had tried lifting weights heavier than he should have and now he was paying the price. So he really didn't want to do an appearance today, especially this one, which was unpaid.

And what the hell was he supposed to talk to "Indigenous Youth" about anyway? Being an Indian? They knew who they were.

James Gagne, the friendly social worker in his forties who helped run some programs for inner-city Indian kids, had called him to ask if he could speak talk to a small group of students. James came across as a good guy and he had even shown up at Mohawk's house to drive him into the city and bring him to a small community center for Natives. The center wasn't located in a nice part of downtown, more a neglected and battered district full of thrift stores, grungy coffee shops, a sports bar or two, and not much else. Mohawk was astonished by what had seen outside of the center, the drunk and drug-addled Indians who were scattered around the neighborhood, some speaking to themselves in gibberish or just lying down on the sidewalk, pedestrians stepping over their bodies on their way to wherever. Mohawk had always known things were bad for his people but it was different seeing it up close.

Hmph, he thought, grunting a little. *My people...I don't even know what tribe I am...*

It was true. Mohawk had been adopted by a white couple who raised him...white. Sure, he looked different from the other kids at his suburban school, his skin more tanned, his hair jet-black and facial features unique (compared to the Caucasians around him), but all his young life, Mohawk didn't acknowledge his "otherness" and truth be told, no one really gave him guff about it, either. Probably because he was a star athlete in football, baseball and track in high school and that cemented him among the popular kids. In fact, Mohawk had only acknowledged his heritage to lock down a winning gimmick for his professional wrestling career after a year or so of floundering as a nondescript rookie on the circuit. Otherwise, it didn't matter to him and Mohawk truly did not feel that connected to his culture at all. He had meant to look deeper into his ancestry after he retired but just never got around to it.

Then he got older and it felt even less important.

Now he was standing in a brightly-colored room that usually functioned as a daycare center with little stuffed animals, toys, and picture books piled into one corner. Mohawk cleared his throat, looking out to the bored teenagers who did not seem that impressed with him. Apparently, James had lied, saying that the youngsters had been excited to meet him but this didn't bother Mohawk. He was a former world heavyweight champion...he would win these kids over.

There were about ten of them, many with long hair, tattoos, piercings, hats on backwards...all looked like tough customers, actually. Mohawk couldn't help but pick out one or two with heavier frames and think that they might make good pro wrestlers.

Mohawk glanced over at James, who stood by the back wall, a cheesy smile on his face. The man had told him he was a massive Mohawk Jones fan. He was even giving Mohawk a thumbs-up right now.

Time for the show.

"Hello," Mohawk said. "I'm Mohawk Jones. I used to be a professional wrestler a while back. I even won the world title."

No real reaction to this and this disappointed Mohawk a little. He hoped that some of the kids would at least crack a smile. It was a big-time achievement, wasn't it?

"I traveled all over the world as a wrestler," Mohawk continued. "I've wrestled in Puerto Rico, Japan, Germany, Australia..."

Again, Mohawk got nothing from the kids and he was starting to feel uncomfortable. He forgot the next part of his presentation, which was to talk about his training and his biggest matches but instead, a long awkward pause ensued, which was thankfully broken when a hand went up. Mohawk nodded at the boy, who had a fuzzy mustache and some wiry black hairs on his chin.

"Yeah?" he said, grateful that one of these punks was showing some damn interest.

"You ever wrestle John Cena?" the kid asked.

"Or The Rock?" another added.

Mohawk shook his head.

"No," he replied. "I wrestled The Rock's father, though. And his grandfather...High Chief and I had this great match in San Francisco back in the..."

Mohawk continued on, telling what he thought was a fantastic story of how he and Peter Maivia had beaten the shit out of each other in front of a hot crowd. Unfortunately, the kids didn't seem to care. Mohawk could see some yawns coming out of their mouths. He glanced over at James, who shrugged helplessly, as if not understanding at why this group of "at-risk" youth weren't as delighted as he was with a legend like Mohawk Jones visiting them.

"Mr. Jones, why don't you show the tape you brought with you?" James suggested.

Mohawk nodded, also believing this to be a good idea. The kids chattered among themselves as he fed the tape into the VCR with shaky hands. Mohawk pressed PLAY and after a few seconds of static on the TV, early footage of his wrestling career appeared on the screen.

Mohawk couldn't help but smile at seeing his younger self and was especially glad to notice that some of the kids had leaned forward in curiosity. They watched as Young Mohawk Jones, so handsome, muscular, and full of energy, threw standing dropkicks, flying forearms, and his big powerslam, shown at different angles and with slo-mo instant replays. The fans in the arenas went crazy and even Mohawk marveled at how great he once was.

Then Young Mohawk did his war dance and the entire room burst out in snickers.

Mohawk was confused. This was mocking laughter.

"Yo!" one kid yelled. "Check out the Fightin' Brave!"

Roaring laughter at this as fingers pointed at the television screen followed by catcalls of slang that Mohawk didn't understand. Some of the teens even got up and did the war dance themselves, parodying Mohawk as they moved around the room, gleefully knocking into each other or the small desks used by the daycare kids.

"Settle down!" James commanded as the teens took their seats again, mischievous smirks on their faces. The sharp stabs in Mohawk's knees had begun to ache even more, a red haze of pain that he had to grit his teeth against. He needed to sit badly, the strain of standing so long having an awful impact on his joints...but he also didn't want to show weakness in front of these rude little bastards.

Mohawk switched off the VCR, unsure how to continue on. He then spotted a studious-looking young woman raise her hand. The girl was around the same age as the others but came across as more mature and thoughtful. At least Mohawk thought so due to the big-ass glasses she wore that seem to cover up most of the girl's face.

"Yeah? What is it?" he said, maybe too gruffly.

"How does it feel to see that stuff now, Mr. Jones?" the girl asked politely, a genuine lilt in her voice.

"What do you mean?" Mohawk asked back.

The young woman straightened up in her seat and all eyes turned to her. It was clear the others in the classroom respected the spectacled girl.

"I mean, when you did a dance like that…came out with a feathered headdress…did all that stereotypical Indian stuff…" she said, building her statement. "Don't you feel bad about it today?"

Mohawk frowned, not understanding at all.

"Bad?" he said. "Did you hear those fans on the videotape? All those things I did helped me become a star."

"And made Indians look like a joke," another teen said bitterly.

"Like we're all just backward-ass "noble" savages," another chimed in.

Mohawk's stomach dropped. He felt trapped, his mind going blank and incapable of defending himself. Luckily, James was there and he rushed in to save him.

"Alright, that's enough for today. Why don't you all go for a snack?" he said. "Go to the cafeteria and Ronalda will set you up, okay? But first let's thank Mr. Mohawk Jones for taking the time out of his busy schedule to spend the afternoon with us."

Some half-hearted clapping. Most of the kids were more excited about snack-time so they filed out quickly and thankfully didn't linger. However, the young woman with the huge glasses stayed behind and made her way over to Mohawk, who still felt slightly shell-shocked.

"I'm sorry if I insulted you, Mr. Jones," she said. "That wasn't what I was trying to do."

Mohawk couldn't do anything but stare blankly at the girl. He did eventually nod and James gestured for the young woman to leave. Both he and Mohawk then took a seat together. This was a relief for Mohawk, as sitting instantly helped ease the discomfort in his legs and back. He still felt awful, though. Like a complete chump.

"I'm sorry, too, Mr. Jones," James began earnestly. "Please don't hate me for bringing you in today. I truly didn't know it was going to go down like that."

Mohawk smiled a little for James. No need to make the man feel worse than he was already feeling.

"It's fine," Mohawk said.

"Don't take to heart what they said," James continued. "You really were a role model to a lot of Indian kids like me. You were the only one on television who wasn't getting shot down by white cowboys. You were a good guy who did what was right. A hero. Really."

Mohawk didn't believe James for one second and just wanted to go home. James said that he would drive him back and as they walked to the parking lot, Mohawk glanced around at some indecipherable but clearly Native-inspired graffiti on the building walls. Animals, landscapes, some Indian symbols...it was all striking and beautiful but Mohawk was saddened he felt no real connection to it.

As they were about to get into James' small Toyota, the social worker paused, looking uneasy.

"What?" Mohawk asked. He knew what James wanted. Better to get this stuff over with.

"Can, I, uh...er...maybe..." James stammered.

"Get one of those selfie photos with me?"

"Yes! If it's not too much trouble."

"No trouble at all."

Mohawk had figured a request like this was coming and the two posed for the photo, Mohawk putting up a fist, trying his best to look like a tough customer.

"Could you also..." James trailed off.

"Sign some merch?" Mohawk offered.

"Yes!"

Mohawk obliged, spending a few minutes autographing some old posters and boxed action figures from decades ago that were probably worth a small fortune. He had definitely made James' day, who then drove Mohawk to his townhouse on the outskirts of the city. James was now fully comfortable to "fanboy" over his childhood hero and Mohawk tried his best to be entertaining to the man, answering his questions as best he could. Mohawk's memory of the old days was decent but super fans like James were tough to cater to since they had an encyclopedic knowledge of pro wrestling. Unfortunately, a lot of that stuff was all a blur to Mohawk.

Would I have done things different? Mohawk thought. *If I could go back and do it over?*

Probably not. Things probably would have ended up the same for Mohawk Jones, which made him feel slightly bitter.

Still, Mohawk had always tried to be nice to fans like James, something that had been drummed in him by Mr. Sanada.

"If you are good guy," Mr. Sanada said roughly in that Japanese accent that Mohawk missed hearing. "You be nice guy to fan. If bad guy, you be bad."

Mohawk had never played a heel in his career. He was always on the side of good.

However, now he actually felt like a real asshole. The young woman with the glasses and her friends' words about him being a stereotype wasn't anything he had considered before. Sure, he knew he was playing a role but it was always a proud portrayal of a Native American hero.

Wasn't it?

Or was he just acting like a clown for money, selling out his culture?

Mohawk didn't really know the answer.

CHAPTER 5

After James dropped him off in front of his townhouse, while floating the notion of having brunch together on Sunday, Mohawk waited patiently for the man to drive away. It seemed to take forever as James just waved and smiled for what seemed like an eternity. When James finally left, Mohawk stood on his porch and looked around the neighborhood. He wanted to savor these few quiet moments before he faced what was lurking inside his home.

His neighborhood was a middle-class one, full of teachers, construction workers, some blue-collar factory workers, and their families. Lots of kids rode their bicycles around on the sidewalks or shot hoops on driveway basketball nets mounted on their houses. It was a relatively quiet place to live, which is how Mohawk liked it, the laughter of the children reminding him of the days when young people loved him. The neighborhood wasn't quite the suburbs but close enough to the city where you could take a bus or drive in yourself. Of course, Mohawk didn't really drive anymore but that was fine with him. Years of being a "wheelman" for a group of rowdy, hard-partying wrestlers wasn't something he had fond memories of.

Mohawk looked around the exterior of his house. It was well-maintained, which he took pride in, the driveway clear of stones and dirt and the garage door still looking fresh after being painted two years ago.

The windows looked clean and there were a few simple flowers he had bought from a supermarket's garden center planted by the front door. The teenager Mohawk had paid to mow his lawn did a good job this week, too. It was a modest home, although a famous retired wrestler should probably have done better for himself. Mohawk had made a ton of money in his career but hadn't always invested the best. Some real estate opportunities had shit the bed and Mohawk paid the price, although he lived comfortably enough in this simple life that he didn't have to worry about money that much.

Mohawk watched as a young mother pushed a stroller by his house. The sidewalk was close enough to the front door so he could see the child inside, a small white baby fast asleep. Mohawk surmised the mom had recently given birth, still carrying some of her pregnancy weight and dressed in comfortable sweats, but she was radiant, clearly enjoying motherhood. For some reason, Mohawk felt a twinge of jealousy, which surprised him.

"Hi there," the young mom smiled at Mohawk as she walked past him with the stroller in her New Balance sneakers.

"Hello," Mohawk said politely. "Have a nice day."

The mother nodded and Mohawk watched mother and child as they rounded a corner, probably off to the park that was nearby. He then turned around and put his key into the lock. He was just about to turn it when he heard from within the townhouse:

"Mohawk, you bastard!" the shrill accented voice screeched. "Is that you, brother?"

Oh god, Mohawk thought. *Why couldn't this motherfucker be napping?*

He opened the front door and stepped inside. Right away, the pungent aroma of grilled onions and hot mirchi peppers hit him like a boot to the face.

He's fucking cooking, too...

Mohawk's stomach twisted as although his roommate was a decent enough cook, the smells of his food were very strong. The odors clung to clothes, hair and everything in the house and Mohawk had constantly complained to the man, telling him repeatedly to turn on the fan above the stove and to open the windows while cooking. Mohawk had hoped that maybe the neighbors would complain about it but they loved sniffing the Indian flavors, jokingly hoping for an invite to dinner as they jogged or biked by.

"Mohawk!" the voice called out from the kitchen at the back of the house. "You come now!"

Mohawk sighed. He just wanted to go up to his bedroom, take a piss, and lie down but Cobra Tara Singh was going to keep on bellowing for him until he made an appearance. So he followed the scent and found the old man dancing in front of a frying pan although there was no music playing. The guy always had a tune in his head, though, mostly Bollywood pop music, which Mohawk was thankful wasn't playing from the radio on the counter. Usually, that shit was blaring through the house at all hours. At first, Mohawk didn't mind it, even enjoying the joyful melodies and singing along, despite not knowing what any of the words meant. However, a few years of this stuff would be enough to drive anyone insane.

"I'm here," Mohawk announced, standing in the doorway as his roommate turned to him and grinned toothlessly.

Cobra Tara Singh had aged terribly. Gone was the sinewy but ripped frame of an amateur wrestling stand-out, replaced by a wrinkled skinny Indian man with hunched shoulders and gnarled hands. Cobra's black hair was now fully white, his beard scraggly and down to his hairy chest. He had no muscle definition at all now, wore dentures, and often rocked a tank top and loose kurta pants at home. Cobra mostly wore his turban full-time, embracing his faith more now, and every Sunday, he would mosey over to the Sikh temple a few blocks away. Despite being more pious, he was still an annoying son of a bitch.

"You eat now," Cobra said cheerily in that sing-song voice that made Mohawk's skin crawl at times. "I make aloo gobi. Just for you."

This was a potato and cauliflower medley that Mohawk actually enjoyed but he had no appetite at the moment.

"No, thanks," Mohawk said.

"Okay, okay," Cobra said, taking a swig of beer. "I save aloo gobi for you, eh?"

"Fine."

Despite living in North America for decades, Cobra's English was still rough. He could communicate well enough so it was fine, although Mohawk had to admit that he thought Cobra was faking it at times so he didn't have to do stuff, like deal with a plumber or be on the phone with the cable company.

So how did Mohawk Jones and Cobra Tara Singh end up roomies?

Mostly out of pity.

After that match in 1998, Mohawk and Cobra did wrestle each other a few times more, almost exclusively in Japan, since the money was too good to pass up. They kept things professional, neither taking any shots on the other in the ring, but the animosity between them continued.

Then the bookings to wrestle matches slowed down considerably for both men. They were getting older and couldn't do as much in the ring so promoters didn't want them for shows anymore, even to profit off their long and storied rivalry. This meant that Mohawk and Cobra barely saw each other and Mohawk moved on with his life, trying his hand at golf and even a few acting gigs for shitty low-budget action movies where he played the lead's grumpy, gun-toting dad.

Mohawk had learned that Cobra had retired sometime in the mid-2000s and had amassed a lot of money over his career. He had a huge mansion, owned a fleet of sports cars, wore expensive suits and jewelry, and lived with his loyal wife Kavita in a gated community where celebrities and athletes resided. The man was the envy of many and an example of how the wrestling world didn't need to eat you up and spit you out like it had done with other performers.

However, Cobra Tara Singh's downfall didn't come because of professional wrestling but rather his own appetites and vices. He had lived the party life on the road like no other and it was hard for a beast like him to be domesticated. Cobra had enjoyed his share of drugs and one-night stands and tried to live that life as an older man, traveling around for signings and personal appearances while always on the prowl for a pretty young girl to wine, dine and bed. Eventually, it caught up with him when a vengeful woman named Wanda in Atlanta didn't take their break-up very well. She texted Kavita explicit photos and videos of the various sexual trysts she had with Cobra and Kavita tore into her husband, taking him for everything in a nasty divorce.

As a result, Cobra was broken, his only real income coming from his personal appearances and that was meager. Mohawk had found the poor guy cobbling together the money for a meal at a fast food restaurant after a convention signing and took him in, none of them ever talking about the past. Mohawk couldn't turn his back on the man who had helped him become a wrestling superstar although Cobra still irritated the shit out of him.

What Cobra hadn't realized was that Kavita was more than just his wife…she had taken care of him since they were arranged to be married in their early twenties. Without Kavita, Cobra fell to pieces and now, unfortunately, it was as if Mohawk was his new wife. It was his job to make sure Cobra took his various pills (heart, cholesterol, etc.), make his personal appearances (their agent often booked the two of them together for a nice fee) and various appointments (doctor, physical therapy or chiropractor).

And was Cobra Tara Singh ever thankful for all of Mohawk's help?

Of course fucking not.

"Hey idiot!" Cobra barked, stirring Mohawk out of his thoughts. "I get TV tonight!"

"Alright," Mohawk said tiredly. He knew how passionate Cobra could get about his nightly game shows.

"And go take out the garbage from the upstairs bathroom! It is full!"

Mohawk frowned.

"Do it yourself," he said.

Cobra gave a pitiful, woe-is-me, look.

"It is heavy and I am old," he whimpered. "So many stairs…"

Mohawk grunted. Cobra was full of shit but he just wanted to get away from the guy. Mohawk knew if he stuck around much longer, he would probably end up punching Cobra in the face. It had happened before. A bunch of times, actually. Although Cobra could still dish it as well as take it, more often being the instigator of their brawls. It was a miracle neither of them had become hospitalized yet.

"I'll go empty the trash," Mohawk said, turning to leave. "But next time you cook, turn on the damn fan! Or open a window! It reeks in here!"

"Yes, yes," Cobra said, waving him away. "I will turn on fan and open all the windows. I promise. Bye bye."

This dismissal prompted a fresh surge of anger to go through Mohawk but he was able to control himself. He stomped up the stairs to the bathroom and saw the little trash can by the toilet. It was full of tissues, a toothpaste box, some empty denture cream tube...nothing too disgusting. He lifted the bag out of the bin and tied it up. Mohawk's eyes then went to the toilet roll and he gritted his teeth.

Instead of putting a new roll of toilet paper in, Cobra just rested it on top of the little cylinder dispenser.

That lazy motherfucker...

"Cobra!" Mohawk roared at the top of his lungs.

"Yes, Mohawk Jones?" Cobra said warmly from downstairs. "How can I help you, sir?"

Mohawk wanted to scream and scream and scream.

"Put the toilet paper on the thing next time!" he yelled.

"Thing? What thing?" Cobra asked. "What is this thing you are talking about?"

"Goddammit!"

It was like talking to a fucking child!

Mohawk shook his head, put the toilet paper on the roll and went to his bedroom, slamming the door. He was furious over something trivial, and Mohawk knew this, but it had been a long day so far and he needed to rest. He lay down on his bed and tried to calm himself, resisting the urge to go downstairs and deliver his powerslam to the old asshole in the kitchen. Even from his bedroom, which was on the other side of the house, he could still hear Cobra joyously singing to himself.

Then Mohawk remembered that Cobra's bedroom was on the bottom floor of the townhouse, which had its own bathroom. So why the fuck was he using the upstairs one?

More rage filled Mohawk Jones but he was too tired to go back to the kitchen and have it out. Every time one of these "incidents" happened, Mohawk wanted to toss Cobra out on his butt...but he couldn't.

The guy needs me, he thought, putting his hands behind his head. *He doesn't have anyone else.*

Thankfully, Cobra didn't kick up much noise for the rest of the afternoon and Mohawk was able to get a short nap in. He didn't dream or even move around much in his sleep, waking up in the same position he was in when he had gotten into bed. Mohawk sat up and felt his back stiffen a little. He stretched it out, as well as his shoulders, and then went downstairs.

On his way to the kitchen, Mohawk could see that the door to Cobra's bedroom was closed as well, the man most likely taking a nap himself. Mohawk was hungry and wanted some of the aloo gobi Cobra had whipped up. When he got to the kitchen, he saw that it was an utter mess, like it always was after Cobra had done some cooking. Mohawk sighed but didn't want to make a big deal about it. He cleaned the dishes and cookware, wiped down the countertops, and opened the kitchen window so the place could air out a little.

Mohawk didn't like that he had to do these things, grumbling as he opened the refrigerator...but then sighed again when he saw that Cobra had set up a plate for him, with a generous amount of aloo gobi, plain yogurt to cool off the spice, and some fluffy naan bread to eat the food with.

"Shit," Mohawk said, carrying the plate to the microwave and heating everything up. He then took his meal outside to the backyard garden and sat down at the small patio table. Like always, Cobra's food was delicious and after what Mohawk had experienced at the community center earlier, it was much-needed. He still felt bad after what had transpired but for the moment, he was okay with himself.

Not long after, the kitchen's glass door opened and a somewhat tentative Cobra stepped out. He wasn't wearing his turban, the frayed topknot of his remaining hair sitting on his head. The first time Mohawk had seen Cobra wear his hair like this surprised him but now he knew how Sikh men wore their hair under their turbans.

Mohawk stopped eating, waiting for Cobra to speak. The man stared hard at Mohawk."Food is good?" Cobra asked quietly.

"It's great," Mohawk replied.

"Okay."

Cobra sat down on the chair across from Mohawk, not saying anything else as Mohawk finished his aloo gobi. Cobra had even reduced the spiciness of his recipe so Mohawk could handle it.

The two sat quietly together, enjoying the warm afternoon sun. The townhouse's backyard wasn't big but was enough to move around in, the back open as it led to a small forest. Mohawk had been meaning to build a fence like some of the neighbors had done so no critters would find their way into the yard but, like other things, he just never got around to it. Besides, a few rabbits and deer wandering in weren't a big deal.

"Mohawk?" Cobra said, trying to get his attention.

"Yeah?" Mohawk asked.

"I want to say something to you."

"Go ahead."

Mohawk watched as Cobra Tara Singh sat up straight, a frown on his face.

"Mohawk," Cobra began, measuring his words. "I want to say...I hate you."

Mohawk couldn't help but smile, taking a sip of lemonade he had brought out with his meal.

"I hate living here with you," Cobra continued. "I miss my mansion and all my cars. And..."

"And your wife?" Mohawk offered.

"No, I do not miss her. I miss my money more."

"Sorry to hear that."

Cobra hissed angrily at this, which reminded Mohawk of the man's professional wrestling persona.

"Well, if it makes you feel better," Mohawk said. "I hate you, too."

"Good," Cobra said in reply. "But I will always hate you more."

"That's okay with me."

CHAPTER 6

Not all older men have to wake up several times a night to go pee. Unfortunately, Mohawk wasn't one of those guys but he didn't mind it so much. He wasn't sleeping well anyway tonight. After he had his aloo gobi earlier in the day, he watched television with Cobra, neither of them saying anything to each other as they cycled through a few hours of game shows. Mohawk had no idea why Cobra found game shows so exciting. Still, it was better than him watching those various judge shows on TV. Those really fired Cobra up, to the point that sometimes he would throw something at the screen if he disagreed with a verdict. One time, Judge Josephine had ruled in favor of an unruly plaintiff and Cobra got so mad, he actually punched the wall, putting his hand right through it. Mohawk then had to take Cobra to the hospital because the old fool broke two knuckles.

When eight o'clock rolled around, it was time for Tuesday Night Massacre, the hottest wrestling show on cable. Even though Mohawk had no interest in today's wrestling scene, Cobra watched it religiously, sometimes hoping that Tom Victory, the late Stan Victory's son who now ran his company, would give him a call to appear on the show. Maybe as a manager of some strapping young buck or a color commentator. Mohawk didn't have the heart to tell Cobra that he had no hope in hell of getting a spot like that.

"You should pay attention, brother," Cobra said as the flashy opening credits of Tuesday Night Massacre blew across the TV, accompanied by hip hop music and screeching electric guitars. "When we make our comebacks, these are the motherfuckers we will take to schooling!"

Mohawk shook his head. *This dumb bastard thinks he can still go in the ring.*

Cobra continued on, getting amped-up and waving his bony fists in the air.

"You and me," he said, his voice rising. "Tag team...one last run for the old cowboys!"

"We were never cowboys," Mohawk said tiredly. "That wasn't our gimmick."

"Figure of the speech!"

Cobra rambled on and Mohawk tried his best to ignore him. He watched the first couple of matches and couldn't help but admire some of the kids he saw. They didn't really work the crowd as well as they did back in his and Cobra's day but the wrestlers were definitely much more athletic. There were gymnast-type moves woven with martial arts, death-defying stunts, and submission holds that Mohawk had never even seen before. Mohawk knew that many of the older wrestlers spat on today's style but that was coming from a place of envy. He knew this because he himself was very jealous as he watched two wrestlers exchange German suplexes, backflip somersaults and flying karate kicks in a display that was so crisp, his mouth dropped open.

I wonder if I could have kept up with guys like this in my prime, he thought. Mohawk then smiled. *Of course I could...*

"Feh!" Cobra spat in disgust. "That is not the real wrestling! It is dancing!"

"I dunno," Mohawk said. "Looks pretty good to me."

"Feh! In my day, if someone did a flip in the ring on you, you would punch them and choke them out!"

Mohawk chuckled, because it was probably true, but today's wrestling world was different. He had heard that the kids were smarter with their money and took better care of their bodies. Less steroids, more recovery time, getting out of the game while they were still relatively healthy...Mohawk was glad for this. He had gone to too many funerals of fellow wrestlers in the prime of their lives because of drug use and the other bad shit associated with living on the road.

Mohawk also noticed something: there were no Native wrestlers on the show. He wasn't that surprised but then he remembered his experience earlier in the day with James' teens at the community center.

Are there no Indian wrestlers today...because of me? he wondered. *Because I was such an embarrassment and a joke?*

This sentiment overwhelmed Mohawk and coupled with his envy of today's wrestling stars getting to do what they wanted while he was stuck in his townhouse with his gassy roommate, it was too much for him to handle. He stood up to leave the room.

"Eh?" Cobra asked. "Where you going?"

"Fuck off," Mohawk said, far too harshly. Cobra didn't seem to mind, though. He just shrugged and went back to Tuesday Night Massacre.

Mohawk made his way outside to take a walk. It was late summer and the sun was setting. Most of the neighbors had taken their children inside for the night so he was able to stroll without anyone bothering him. It was a peaceful evening but Mohawk didn't feel at peace.

I should be more, he thought glumly. *Who cares about world championships and headlining Madison Square Garden if people, your own people, think you're a fucking joke?*

So Mohawk walked for a long time, through the neighborhood, through the park...he might have walked all the way back to the city if he hadn't spotted a skunk scurrying near him as he followed the gravel path that went through the trees of a nearby forest. Not wanting to tempt fate, Mohawk took this as a sign that he should head back home.

When he got there, the townhouse was dark but the TV in the living room was still on. Mohawk could see that Cobra had once again fallen asleep while watching. Mohawk stood above his roommate and stared down at him. He had to study Cobra for a few seconds to make sure that the old buzzard was still breathing. Mohawk could check for a pulse but didn't want to touch the guy.

Soon after, Cobra coughed and Mohawk couldn't help but feel disappointment, which he immediately felt guilty about. He considered helping Cobra up and putting him in his bed but wasn't sure if he had the strength or if Cobra might end up fighting him for doing so. Mohawk had warned Cobra countless times to not sleep on the couch because it would mess up his back so whatever discomfort the man would feel tomorrow would be justly deserved. Then again, the guy Cobra would bitch and moan to was going to be Mohawk. It was a lose-lose situation.

Mohawk decided to leave Cobra where he was. He did his best to straighten his roommate a little, stretching his legs out and rolling him onto his back instead of his side. Mohawk also put a small pillow under Cobra's head and a thin blanket over him. Throughout this, Cobra didn't stir at all and Mohawk wished he himself could sleep as soundly. The one saving grace about bunking with Cobra Tara Singh was that the man never snored, although he did complain that Mohawk did, even though Mohawk knew for a damn fact that Cobra couldn't hear him from his bedroom upstairs.

Mohawk went to bed, flossing and brushing first. Unlike Cobra, he still had his teeth intact although he was due for a dental check-up. Mohawk then crashed, feeling exhausted after a long day of confusing and frustrating emotions. However, he tossed and turned and now found himself sitting upright after a visit to the toilet. Mohawk was wide awake so he threw on a pair of sweats and headed downstairs.

After checking on Cobra and seeing that he was sleeping soundly and still on the couch (one of Mohawk's fears was that he would roll off and smack his head on the coffee table...it had happened before), Mohawk made his way to the basement. His plan was to maybe ride the exercise bike down there for a short time, just to work up a sweat that would hopefully help him sleep. However, five minutes on the bike at a leisurely pace resulted in Mohawk's body stiffening up and he hopped off it, cursing his old age.

There was another couch in the basement and the bottom level of the townhouse was fully furnished. Mohawk was planning to make it into some kind of game room but now it was just a quiet place with wrestling memorabilia of his, and Cobra's, careers. Posters of them in their youths were on the walls as well as a glass display of the world titles they had won over the years. Cobra had begged Mohawk to go to Kavita to get back his championship belts and although Cobra's ex-wife had no love for Mohawk, believing that he should have told her of Cobra's philandering, Kavita agreed to give Mohawk many of Cobra's various wrestling mementos. In her words, she had no use for that "bakwaas", which Cobra had translated as "rubbish" to Mohawk.

The basement had a fireplace, which had been used only once or twice by Mohawk, but above it was a mantle with framed photographs and newspaper articles as well as many of Mohawk and Cobra's different action figures. Mohawk took one of his and one of Cobra's toys and sat down with them on the couch. They were from the eighties and were heavy, about six inches tall and made of a rubbery plastic. The figures were stiff and didn't have any joints, just Mohawk and Cobra in wrestling poses. Mohawk's toy was in a flexed biceps state and he wore his feathered headdress while Cobra's doll had a more sinister look, as well as a snake attachment draped around his shoulders. Mohawk smiled at this since never once did Cobra come down to the ring with a snake. The guy was scared of them and refused when Stan Victory tried to convince him to carry a python around.

Mohawk wondered if kids ever had fun playing with these things. They seemed kind of boring to him since you couldn't do any wrestling moves with them. He glanced up at the mantle and saw there were more figures of himself and Cobra, more advanced than the ones he was holding. *Maybe I should have brought these and the title belts to the Indian kids today,* Mohawk thought. *That might have won them over...*

Mohawk returned the action figures to the mantle and moved his way to the glass case with the world titles. He opened it, which he kept unlocked since he didn't want to scrounge around for a key, and lifted up the championship belt that he had won from Cobra. It still looked great to Mohawk and he did a good job maintaining it, polishing the gold plates a couple of times a year or sending it to a belt-maker to re-do the fraying leather strap. Mohawk knew he was being a "mark", a term which meant he was taking wrestling too seriously, but goddammit, winning the title that night on pay-per-view was the best night of his life. And despite those Indian kids making him think he was a joke or a stereotype or whatever, Mohawk would do anything to go back and re-live those wonderful moments.

Tears pricked from Mohawk's eyes and he wiped them fast.

"Stupid, dumb, useless old man," he said softly to himself.

Mohawk put the title belt back in its display case and headed back upstairs, switching off the light, slowly making his way through the darkness of the house, and getting back in bed. He lay down but didn't close his eyes to sleep, feeling a familiar twinge in his groin.

"Fuck," Mohawk grumbled, heading back to the bathroom across the hall.

CHAPTER 7

Mohawk's mood over the next few days didn't improve much. He could barely sleep at night, tossing and turning for hours, and during the day, he was extremely crabby. This was unfortunate for Cobra, who took the brunt of Mohawk's irritability.

"You are being the asshole!" Cobra shouted when Mohawk complained loudly about some crumbs left on the living room carpet from some barfi. Barfi was an Indian sweet treat that Cobra wasn't supposed to eat due to him being on the precipice of diabetes, which Mohawk had laid into him about as well.

"No one's a bigger asshole than you!" Mohawk fired back, before heading to his bedroom and slamming the door.

Mohawk had thought that the disaster at the community center wouldn't have had as lasting an impact on him as it did but he couldn't shake it from his mind. He pondered going online and seeing if there was more information about him and his legacy but decided against it. Even though he had access to his neighbor's WiFi, Mohawk was hopeless when it came to technology. Besides, even if he was an internet expert or whatever, if he found bad news about himself, it might cause him to spiral even more.

A few hours after the barfi fight, Mohawk felt guilty and went to Cobra to apologize. Cobra was still in the living room, watching some old

Bollywood movie. This was Cobra's happy place although Mohawk never understood what he liked about these movies. They were colorful, musical and full of beautiful Indian ladies dancing around but also very long and, to Mohawk, very cheesy.

Regardless, Mohawk wanted to make amends so the best time to do so was during Bollywood Time, where Cobra was usually wide-eyed and grinning like an enthralled child as he watched.

"Hey," Mohawk said gently, standing right by Cobra, who sat on the couch. Cobra didn't acknowledge Mohawk's arrival but he pressed on anyway. "I just want to say that I'm sorry. About the barf thing."

"Barf-EE," Cobra corrected, eyes still on the television. Mohawk glanced at the TV as well and saw a gorgeous Indian girl wearing a bright green sari as she sang and twirled around in a dreamy meadow.

"Barfi," Mohawk nodded. "Sorry."

At this, Cobra surprised Mohawk by pausing the movie and turning to him. He then pointed to the chair opposite him, gesturing for Mohawk to sit. Mohawk did so and Cobra stared hard at him.

"What the fuck is your problem, brother?" Cobra asked harshly. Mohawk's reflexive response would have been to tell Cobra to fuck off but he felt too tired to do so.

"I don't know," Mohawk said with a shrug. "Just feeling off, I guess."

Cobra continued to eye Mohawk and then shook his head.

"Something is the wrong," Cobra said, his arms folded. "Tell me. I am your roomie."

Cobra Tara Singh was not someone that Mohawk usually confided in but the truth was, there really wasn't anyone else he could talk to. He had no family and no real close friends. All he had was the crusty ex-wrestler he lived with. Needless to say, this added to Mohawk's depression a little.

"Well," he began. "You know how I went and talked to those Indian kids the other day…"

"Feh!" Cobra said in annoyance. "They are not Indian!" He added proudly. "I am Indian!"

"Sure, okay."

"I do not know why they call themselves Indian! They have never been to India!"

"It's just a long-standing term. We use words like indigenous now."

"I should go to that community center and tell them...no more calling yourselves Indian!"

"For fuck's sake, Cobra...will you shut the fuck up?!"

Cobra frowned at Mohawk, who was now seething. Mohawk took a deep breath and fought his urge to storm off.

"Okay, I am sorry," Cobra said before Mohawk could speak. "I carried away."

"Yeah," Mohawk said. He licked his lips, gathering his thoughts. "Anyway, I went to that center and talked to some teenagers..."

"Teenagers!" Cobra flared again. "They are the worst! I do not like them! The ones at the shopping mall! They laugh at me!"

"Cobra! Fuck!"

Cobra held his hands up in apology.

"Sorry, sorry," he mumbled. "You keep talking..."

Mohawk took yet another deep breath.

"I talked to the kids," Mohawk said. "And I showed them a video of some of my old matches."

"Was I on the videotape?" Cobra asked.

"Yeah."

"Very good."

Cobra smiled and gestured for Mohawk to continue.

"But they didn't really react the way I was hoping," Mohawk said quietly.

"No?" Cobra said. "What did they do?"

"They...kinda mocked me. Like I was a joke."

"A joke? You were the wrestling world champion!"

"Exactly!"

Mohawk waited, watching as Cobra processed what he was telling him.

"These boys and girls," Cobra said slowly. "They laughed at you?"

"Yeah," Mohawk replied.

"Why?"

Mohawk wanted to answer this in a simple way so Cobra could understand. The man was far from stupid, and probably more intelligent than Mohawk in many things, but his English comprehension hadn't improved much in the decades he had spent in North America.

"They acted like my whole gimmick was making fun of Natives," Mohawk said.

He waited as Cobra nodded at this. The man seemed affected by Mohawk's words.

"I know," Cobra finally said. "I know what that is like."

"You do?" Mohawk asked.

"Yes. They say the same about me. I am making fun of the Indian people because I am heel with turban and do bad things in the ring."

Mohawk brightened. He was connecting with Cobra on a deeper level as they both had suffered through the same thing. Mohawk waited for Cobra to speak further.

"Feh!" Cobra said, waving his hand dismissively. "I do not care."

"Huh?" Mohawk said.

"It does not matter. I made money and made good life for my wife and my family back in Punjab. I send money for schooling of my relatives and medicine for my sick aunties and uncles and gave to my gurdwara temple." Cobra smiled. "I come to this country with nothing and became a world champion!"

Mohawk shook his head in disbelief.

"So it doesn't matter at all that you were a stereotype?" he asked.

"What is this word?" Cobra asked back.

Mohawk didn't really know how to explain so he just shook his head again.

"Never mind," he sighed.

"I miss my money," Cobra said, sighing himself.

The two sat in silence for a few seconds and Cobra, thinking the conversation was over, reached for the TV remote to un-pause his movie. Mohawk also figured their chat, which didn't really make him feel better at all, was over.

Then the phone rang.

"I'll get it," Mohawk said, heading to the kitchen. Cobra had seemingly forgot him, instantly immersed in Bollywood song and dance again.

The phone, which was the only one in the townhouse aside from Mohawk's flip cellphone, which he barely used, was supposed to be mounted on the wall. It had fallen off one day and neither Mohawk nor Cobra cared enough to put it back. They just let it hang out on the kitchen counter now.

"Yeah?" Mohawk said, speaking into the phone. "Mohawk Jones here..."

"Mo!" a jovial voice shouted through the receiver.

Mohawk winced. He hated being called "Mo".

"It's Chris, Mo!" the voice continued, heavily laden with a Boston accent. "It's your manager/agent, bro! Got a gig for ya!"

"Oh?" Mohawk said tentatively. He was interested in doing something to get his mind off his troubles but lately, Chris Sullivan, a thirty-five-year-old hustler who represented all sorts of retired wrestlers on the circuit, hadn't really come through for him. Chris had managed/agented him for the past fifteen years in terms of personal appearances and signings, even booking Mohawk in some actual wrestling matches where he didn't have to do much but nowadays, he only got him shitty gigs. Birthday parties for middle-aged pro wrestling fans who still lived with their parents or the opening of some burger franchise location where he was ignored in favor of a mascot or a clown were jobs that Mohawk could do without.

"You know it, bro!" Chris said. "A wrestling convention! Right by your neck of the woods! Short flight! There's an indie show that night, too!"

Mohawk winced. Conventions were fine, when they were full of comic book or sci-fi geeks. However, a *wrestling* convention meant that Mohawk would have to spend time with other wrestlers, some of his old road buddies or today's stars. It wasn't always a fun time.

"I sense some hesitation, bro," Chris said.

"No, it's not that," Mohawk lied. "I...just have a sore throat."

"Sore throat? You got the COVID?"

"No, I'm good."

"Get some lozenges. Or ginger tea, bro."

"Sure. I'll try those."

Mohawk gathered himself, getting himself focused.

"What do I have to do?" he asked.

"Just the normal stuff," Chris replied easily. "Take some photos, sign some 'graphs. The same fee you always charge. Plus, I'm angling for room, travel and per diem, too. Seems like a lot of old-timers will be there so you're both in demand."

Mohawk's eyes widened in alarm.

"Both?" he asked. "You mean…"

"Yup!" Chris replied. "The promoters want Cobra there, too. Same deal. We'll even put you near each other so you can take rivalry pics together for the patrons. It'll clean up, bro!"

Mohawk stifled a groan. Cobra was always a hit at conventions but he usually went overboard, drinking and partying way too much, with Mohawk usually the one to clean up his messes.

"I'm not sure about Cobra," Mohawk said into the phone, glancing up to see if his roommate could hear him. The Bollywood movie still blared from the living room and Mohawk could hear Cobra singing along a little.

"What's there to be sure about?" Chris said. He then became serious. "Sorry, Mo…this is a package deal. You and Cobra together, bro. It's the way it's gotta be."

Fuck, Mohawk thought.

"Alright," he said to Chris. "Set it up. When is the convention?"

"Yeah, bro!" Chris shouted jubilantly. "The convention's next weekend. I'll shoot you over the details after my Uber shift is done."

"Great."

"See ya, Mo! Great to hear from you!"

"Yeah."

Mohawk hung up and sighed, feeling even older than before. He stumbled his way over to Cobra and gestured for him to turn off his movie.

"What?" Cobra asked. "Who was phoning?"

"Chris," Mohawk replied. "We're going to a convention next weekend. Do some signings."

Cobra's eyes lit up at this and Mohawk knew why. Aside from the partying, conventions made old wrestlers like Cobra Tara Singh feel alive again, being around adoring fans who worshipped the ground they walked on.

"Shabaash!" Cobra yelled, saying the Hindi word for "Bravo!". He tried to jump to his feet to celebrate but was too rickety to do so. Mohawk stood nearby to catch the man if he fell but thankfully, Cobra remained upright.

Cobra then even tried to do some Indian dance to celebrate. Mohawk couldn't help but smile a little at this. The old fuck always had a song in his heart.

"We are going to wrestling!" Cobra cheered, trying to beckon Mohawk into his dance.

"Careful," Mohawk said, eyeing the proximity between Cobra's bony body and the coffee table.

"No time to be careful! We are going to see the fans and the boys!"

"That's right."

Cobra frowned at Mohawk.

"You are not excited?" he asked.

Mohawk shrugged.

"You are too serious, man," Cobra said. He then put his hands up, dancing a Punjabi-style he told Mohawk was called "Bhangra". "Balle balle! Chak de fateh!"

Cobra kept on dancing around the living room and Mohawk let him do so for a few minutes until he got tired of watching out for the guy.

"Okay, okay," he said, guiding Cobra back to the couch. "That's enough dancing for now."

Cobra was breathing heavy and sweat dripped from his forehead. He grinned so wide Mohawk thought his dentures were going to fall out of his mouth.

"So much fun!" Cobra said, cracking his knuckles in nervous energy. "Will there be matches? Maybe I will be booked to wrestle!"

Mohawk certainly hoped the convention organizers weren't morons who would do such a thing but wrestling promoters had always done shady shit. They weren't above booking an old wrestling star to stumble around the ring and potentially injure themselves. Even so, Mohawk liked seeing Cobra happy so he didn't want to piss on his hopes.

"Who knows?" Mohawk said, forcing up a smile. "I'm sure we'll have a good time."

"I cannot wait!" Cobra said. "I wonder what I should wear…"

"Not your wrestling gear."

"No? Why?"

"No one wants to see your saggy ass in tights, Cobra."

CHAPTER 8

To make their short flight to the Longdrift Comic Convention, both Mohawk and Cobra had to be up at the crack of dawn. Usually, when they had an event to attend together, Mohawk was the one who had to drag Cobra out of bed but he was stunned to find that Cobra was already raring to go when Mohawk made his way downstairs, waiting impatiently at the kitchen table.

"Finally!" Cobra frowned, his rolling suitcase by his feet as he ate a bowl of soggy Cheerios. "You are finally awake!"

Mohawk was still half-asleep, dressed in a hooded sweatshirt and jeans and carrying a gym-bag with the few things he needed for the weekend. He then noticed what Cobra was wearing: golden baggy pants, golden curled-toe shoes and a golden turban with ruby jewels on it.

Motherfucker, Mohawk thought, rubbing his eyes and not wanting to deal with this kind of shit so early in the morning. *He's wearing his wrestling gear...*

"Go change," Mohawk said flatly, pouring himself some orange juice from the refrigerator.

"Why?" Cobra asked.

"Because I'm not being seen with you at the airport with you wearing that shit!"

Cobra became indignant.

"How come?" he said, pumping out his chest. "I want fans to see me! They will know that I am Cobra Tara Singh and I am back!"

The quarrel between the two roommates became heated quickly and they almost came to blows. Eventually, Mohawk won out, promising Cobra that he would take him to the movie theater next week when a new Bollywood movie, with a title that Mohawk couldn't pronounce, came out. Satisfied, Cobra strutted to his room to change, reveling in his victory.

"Hurry the fuck up!" Mohawk said irritably. He wondered if he should eat something before they got on the plane. Cobra was already getting on his nerves and he would be easier to deal with if Mohawk had some food in his belly. He didn't have time to cook something so he ate a protein bar he found in the pantry. It tasted awful and was probably full of sugar but Mohawk needed something to give him a boost for the day ahead.

"I am ready now!" Cobra sang happily, sashaying into the room. He had changed into a burgundy Indian kurta with a matching turban and white sneakers, which still irked Mohawk a little. Cobra would definitely stand out in a crowd at the airport and all Mohawk wanted to do was hop on the plane and get to their hotel with minimum fuss.

"Alright," Mohawk said, grabbing his bag. "Let's get going."

The forty-minute cab ride to the airport was uneventful and Mohawk had to fight to not fall asleep again. Cobra didn't have that problem. The guy was snoozing as soon as they had hit the freeway ramp. Luckily, it wasn't hard to get Cobra going when they arrived at their terminal. He was on a natural high since he always did well at wrestling conventions, being one of the wrestling world's greatest bad guys. Cobra loved the attention of the fans and being a snarling villain to them, all in good fun.

Going through all the airport stuff went smoothly although Cobra insisted on getting some double chocolate donuts from a franchise you could only find in an airport. Mohawk didn't want to get into the long early morning line but Cobra's whining broke his resistance.

Christ, he thought, watching Cobra chomp down on the donuts and get some chocolate debris in his beard and mustache. *It's like taking care of a little kid.*

One piss break and a short wait later, Mohawk led Cobra onto their plane where they got settled in business class. The flight was only two hours and most times, Mohawk and Cobra would hop in a car with other old wrestlers and drive all the way to the convention. Having the promoters pay for the flight was a nice change of pace and made Mohawk feel good about himself for once.

"No drinking," Mohawk warned Cobra, who was looking around for a flight attendant.

"Just a little drop..." Cobra begged.

"No drinking."

The firmness in Mohawk's tone was enough to quiet Cobra down, who still pouted for most of the flight. Mohawk knew that despite the donuts, Cobra was upset that no one had recognized him at the airport and it got worse when they landed and there were no fans waiting for them. There was Ronnie, though, a long-haired convention volunteer in his forties and wrestling super-fan tasked with picking Mohawk and Cobra up and driving them to their hotel.

"So glad to meet you, Mr. Jones, Mr. Singh," Ronnie said respectfully as he put their belongings in the trunk of his Ford Focus. Ronnie was keeping his cool although Mohawk could see the man was bubbling over with excitement. Cobra was aware of this and promptly got into character. Mohawk winced, hoping that Cobra wouldn't go too far.

"You go too slow!" he barked at Ronnie from the back seat as they pulled out of the airport lot.

"Sorry, Mr. Singh!" Ronnie said happily, loving every minute of this. "There's a lot of traffic lights!"

"I do not care about traffic lights! You get me to my hotel! And after you bring me food, drink...and women!"

Mohawk turned from the passenger seat to give Cobra a look not to put it on too thick. For all he knew, Ronnie really would try to procure prostitutes for Cobra, who would definitely enjoy it. However, Mohawk, having to share a room with Cobra, would not.

Cobra's eyes twinkled from Mohawk's admonishment and he kept it up during the entire car ride.

"You need a haircut!" he shouted at Ronnie. "It is too long!"

"I promise I'll go to the barber next week," Ronnie said.

"You do it tomorrow! Or I will break you!"

"Yes sir!"

Then came this exchange:

"You have wife?" Cobra asked.

"No," Ronnie replied. "I'm single."

"I see why! You are weak and ugly! Like all Americans!"

Mohawk gritted his teeth but to his relief, Ronnie was grinning like an idiot.

"I should probably hit the gym more, Mr. Singh," he said.

"Yes! Then you will not look like geek!"

Mohawk almost burst out in laughter at this. For all his many, many, many faults, Cobra Tara Singh still had the gift of gab.

The hotel the promoters were putting Mohawk and Cobra in was modest, which was fine with Mohawk although Cobra, more used to expensive tastes, stewed a little about it. After Ronnie had dropped them off, getting a selfie and a longwinded "bit" from Cobra where he refused to tip him since he was a peasant (Mohawk did so on their behalf since he was a "good guy"), the two shambled into the elevator to get to their sixth-floor room.

"Why we share?" Cobra grumbled. "I am Cobra Tara Singh! I am superstar!"

"At least it's paid for," Mohawk said.

"So? I am superstar!"

"Stop yelling at me."

The room was decent, two double-beds with a big TV. Mohawk took the bed closest to the window and looked outside. The view was typically boring, the parking lot and some fast-food restaurants in a nearby plaza. Mohawk could see the convention center where the show was going to be held wasn't too far away.

He turned and saw that Cobra was sitting on the bed, bouncing up and down a little on the mattress.

"This will do," Cobra said, nodding his head in satisfaction.

"No," Mohawk said firmly.

Cobra stopped bouncing and scowled.

"No, what?" he asked.

"No," Mohawk said again. "You're not partying in here. This is my room, too."

Now Cobra was on his feet, gesticulating wildly.

"We are on vacation!" he shouted.

Mohawk shook his head.

"This isn't a vacation," he said calmly. "We're working."

"But I want the women!" Cobra whined. "Two or three!"

Mohawk's head started to throb. He really didn't want to have this conversation.

"Not in a room that I'm in," he said, lying down on the bed. "You want to whore around, go get your own room." Mohawk knew that this would shut Cobra up since he didn't have the money to do that as well as pay for his companionship or whatever drugs he needed to get hard and ready for action.

"Go take a nap for a bit," he continued. "The convention people said we should be there at around three. Ronnie said he'd come and get us."

Mohawk closed his eyes but could still hear Cobra's rage.

"You never let me have any fun!" Cobra roared.

An hour or so later, Mohawk and Cobra got ready for the convention. They barely spoke to each other as they dressed, Mohawk wearing a retro Mohawk Jones t-shirt some online retailer had recently whipped up for him with black jeans and cowboy boots. Cobra was wearing the get-up he had back at the townhouse, combing his long white beard in front of the bathroom mirror and curling the ends of his mustache so it made him look more diabolical.

"Ready?" Mohawk asked.

"Fuck you," Cobra said, not even glancing Mohawk's way.

Mohawk fought the urge to fire back at Cobra, waiting a few minutes longer as Cobra finished up. He was glad the man wasn't going barechested as that would be a sad sight for everyone. Instead, Cobra wore a golden tank-top to match his gear as well as a golden cape to complete the ensemble. Mohawk couldn't help but be impressed. The man knew how to dress for the occasion.

They went down the elevator and met the smiling Ronnie in the lobby. The man seemed eager for more banter but Cobra wasn't in the mood.

"Let's go, asshole!" he barked at Ronnie, who grinned even wider. Mohawk hung back a little and saw some wrestlers he recognized hanging around. Some nodded at him or waved pleasantly while sitting on chairs with their phones.

Cobra and Ronnie had stepped outside and Mohawk saw through the glass door entrance that Cobra was berating Ronnie, who kept on smiling. Mohawk felt he better intervene or else Cobra was going to slap the shit out of the guy.

"Okay, okay," Mohawk said, racing outside and getting in-between Cobra and Ronnie. "Let's get to where we need to go."

Cobra grunted and got inside Ronnie's car. Mohawk turned and saw that Ronnie was staring at him with starry eyes.

"This is an amazing day for me," Ronnie said, his voice quivering. "Cobra Tara Singh almost slapped me...I wish you didn't stop him."

"Huh?" Mohawk said.

"It would be a badge of honor, man."

"Do you want me to call him out here so he can slap you?"

"Would you? Please?"

Mohawk didn't do this because knowing his luck, Cobra would slap Ronnie so hard, Ronnie would sue them both for everything they had. Or maybe Cobra would break his hand after connecting and then Mohawk would have to spend months taking care of the old whiny fuck as he healed up.

Mohawk wasn't sure which situation was worse.

"Let's just go," he said to Ronnie, patting the guy on the shoulder. Ronnie nodded and didn't bring up the subject again during the car ride so Mohawk tried to make his day by chatting him up. Cobra continued to seethe in the backseat and Mohawk took a small amount of glee at having thrown a monkey wrench in the man's evening's plans.

"These kids today are pretty good," Mohawk said, playing things up. "But they weren't as great as Bernard The Behemoth!"

"Wow!" Ronnie said. "You wrestled Bernard? I didn't know that!"

Mohawk smiled, remembering his match in England where the near five-hundred-pound Bernard, one of the all-time greats, let him bodyslam him. Mohawk lost the match but slamming Bernard in front of his rabid European fans was no small thing.

"One of the best men I knew in wrestling," Mohawk said.

"A good, good man," Cobra chimed in. Mohawk knew that Cobra and Bernard had gotten close when they had a feud in the northeast territories for a few months.

Ronnie kept on chattering on and Cobra was more willing to engage with him like a regular human being while Mohawk's mind wandered. He thought of Bernard, dying at age fifty due to his weight issues and barely able to move due to the punishment he had taken over the years in the wrestling ring, his knees and back completely shot and basically bedridden until he succumbed to a massive heart attack.

Such a brutal business, Mohawk thought bitterly. *Maybe I would have been better off if I became a plumber or worked in construction or something.*

Once they stepped into the convention center, Mohawk put these melancholic thoughts aside because he and Cobra were greeted by raucous applause from the fans lining up to go into the main hall. Mohawk couldn't help but smile at how happy the people were to see him. He waved back and gave some high-fives but stopped short of autographs or selfies as Chris had told him, almost sternly, not to give anything away for free.

Mohawk glanced over at Cobra, who was also lapping up the attention. They had decided to have some distance between them, with Mohawk going inside the convention center first so they could still play up the idea that their decades-long feud was still heated. *Hmph,* Mohawk thought. *Imagine if they knew we lived together.*

Mohawk saw that Cobra was hissing angrily at some delighted fans and called over to him.

"Leave those good people alone, Cobra!" Mohawk said in his most heroic voice.

Cobra responded by hissing at Mohawk and being led away to the main hall by Ronnie as the people cheered for him.

"That guy's still a jerk," Mohawk said easily to some of the fans that stood nearby and had witnessed the whole thing.

The fans were middle-aged, mostly dads with little kids of their own, and grinned at being in Mohawk's presence. Mohawk liked this as it was nice to be among people who appreciated him.

"See you inside," Mohawk said as he walked into the main hall. There were tables set up all throughout the room for wrestlers to do give autographs and pose for photos. Mohawk could see some of the guys he worked with back in the day, "Leisure Lad" Lenny O'Byrne, Johnny Dreamboy, The Iron Guardian, Izzie Santiago...all of them were old and worn-out like Mohawk but had big smiles on their faces. Mohawk waved or nodded to them, hoping he would have some time to catch up with the boys later.

There were many other wrestlers around who Mohawk recognized as newer stars but didn't know personally. Some wore their flashy tights and uniforms but none of them looked as tough as Mohawk and his contemporaries did back in the day. Mohawk didn't begrudge them this. As he grew older, he had realized being a professional wrestler was more about performance than legitimate fight credentials.

Mohawk sat at his table with a few black sharpies and a thick stack of photos of him in his prime, posing with his headdress and red tights, to sign. A convention official called out that the patrons would be filing in within the next five minutes and asked if the wrestlers could head to their "stations". Mohawk took a long look at his photo. He didn't like seeing the headdress as it made him feel uncomfortable now but he couldn't deny how great he looked many years ago. He had a thick frame with big arms yet his abs looked fantastically chiseled, too. It was probably the best shape he was ever in.

Mohawk looked up to see Cobra sitting at a table across the room from him, sitting almost like a king on his throne, his back straight and a sneer on his face. Mohawk caught Cobra's attention and he could see the rage in his roommate's eyes. Mohawk hoped that it was just anger from earlier in their hotel room and not Cobra looking to set up for a storyline later when the people were milling around. The last thing Mohawk wanted was to get physical today, even if it was all a show for the fans.

The main doors opened and the attendees flooded in, hurriedly lining up to meet their favorite wrestling stars. Both Mohawk and Cobra had a healthy amount of fans wanting to chat with them and Mohawk saw that Cobra, despite being a bad guy, was brusque but polite to everyone he met. He was especially good with the little kids, asking them to "do a mean face" like he could. This resulted in giggles and Mohawk liked seeing Cobra have a good time.

Mohawk's fans were more interested in asking how he was doing and some specific wrestling questions and Mohawk answered dutifully:

"What was the biggest moment of your career?"

"When I won the world title."

"What are you up to nowadays?"

"Just enjoying retirement."

"Which wrestler do you wish you could have wrestled?"

"The Undertaker."

On and on it went but Mohawk still enjoyed himself. He had thought his line would shrink considerably as the day went on but it stayed steady and kept him busy. Of course, neither he nor Cobra had the line that Betty Buxom, a beautifully curvy wrestling valet from the eighties, had. She was an older gal now but a little plastic surgery and her popular Buxom Fit exercise routine had kept her looking good. Betty's line extended out of the room and it made sense. Many of the men in line to meet Betty probably had their first masturbatory experience with her in mind.

That being said, Mohawk hoped that Betty didn't find her way to him when the convention was over. They had gone out for about a year in '87 and it didn't end well, mostly because he cheated on her with a Denny's waitress. Despite her bombshell looks, Betty was a tough woman and Mohawk's jaw still ached when he remembered how hard she socked him when she found out about the waitress.

"Mr. Mohawk?" a nervous voice said, stirring Mohawk out of his thoughts. He turned to see a large bearded fan in his late thirties with three chubby little boys, clearly his sons, clinging to his corduroy pants. The man extended his hand. "It's really great to meet you. You were my favorite wrestler growing up."

"And I'm not now?" Mohawk said teasingly.

"Oh! You're definitely still my favorite!"

"Good! Nice to meet you..."

"Mike."

Mohawk smiled and shook Mike's hand. He then looked to the boys.

"And these are...?" he asked.

"My kids," Mike said proudly. "Stevie, Jeffy and Blake."

Mohawk nodded at the boys, who remained shy of him. They had to range from about six to nine years old.

"They love wrestling as much as I do," Mike continued. "And they love watching your old matches with me."

"Well, that does my heart good!" Mohawk said with a grin. He leaned down and held out his hand to the boys. "Give ol' Mohawk a high-five!"

This seemed to work and the excited kids slapped hands with Mohawk. He was aware he was giving off a grandfatherly vibe and he playfully shook his hand in pain from the high-fives.

"You boys have some power!" he said, winking at them. "I think we might have some future wrestling champions here!"

"I want to be a wrestler!" one of the boys blurted out.

"Good! But you promise me you'll finish college first. School is important and you should always do your homework, okay?"

Laughter all around at this from Mike and the others waiting in line. Mohawk was loving being the center of attention. It felt good.

"The boys also prepared something for you, Mr. Mohawk," Mike said.

"Oh yeah?" Mohawk asked.

Mike nodded at the boys and they got into formation as Mohawk sat back in his chair. His body wasn't hurting so much today but he was thankful to take a seat.

"Go for it, guys!" Mike said.

Mohawk watched as the boys each took a deep breath...and started whooping and dancing around, Native American-style. They went all around Mohawk's table and many attendees whipped out their phones to film the show as they pranced about in front of Mohawk.

"They're doing your war dance!" Mike exclaimed proudly.

The kids stopped and waited for Mohawk's reaction. He was so furious at the display, which he probably wouldn't have been offended by a couple of weeks ago, he wanted to knock over the table and storm out. Or at least grab Mike by the throat and throw him against a wall.

Of course, he didn't do that. That wasn't Mohawk Jones' way.

"Amazing," he said with gritted teeth, giving the boys more high-fives and thanking Mike for the demonstration. He then signed autographs and posed for photos with Mike and his sons before they headed off.

Mohawk took a few minutes to compose himself, his mind racing back to the time he spent at the community center when the Indian kids made fun of his dance. And now these little white boys were doing the same. It made Mohawk feel like throwing up.

He wanted to leave right away but he still had a lot of fans waiting to meet him. So he grinned and bore it although much of his enthusiasm was now gone. Mohawk signed, posed, and shook hands as best he could, mustering up smiles that hurt to make.

Finally, a couple of hours later, there were only a few fans left although Cobra's line still looked quite robust. Mohawk hoped he wouldn't have to stick around and wait for Cobra to finish before he could go back to his hotel room.

"H-hi h-hello," a girl's voice said shakily. Mohawk looked up and saw a young woman in her late teens, a bit plump but with a somewhat athletic frame dressed in an Adidas track suit, staring down at him. She had tanned skin like a surfer's and long brown hair in a single ponytail. Mohawk was surprised to see such a young fan of his who wasn't accompanied by a parent.

"Hello," he said amiably, grabbing a photo and readying to sign it. "Who should I make this out to?"

"Emily," the girl replied.

"Nice to meet you, Emily."

Mohawk signed and handed the eight-by-ten to Emily. She studied it for a few seconds and appeared unsure of herself.

"Thanks," she mumbled.

"No problem," Mohawk said. "Do you want a picture?"

Emily stared blankly at Mohawk for what seemed to be a full minute and it made him feel uncomfortable. Finally, Emily shook her head, turned, and walked off.

Mohawk watched the young woman leave, expecting her to get in line to meet another wrestler. Instead, she just walked out of the room. Mohawk then shrugged, thinking she was probably a non-fan, getting the photo for her parent or grandparent.

He finished up his line and stood up after the last attendee, stretching his back and thanking the handlers who had worked to keep everything going smoothly during the signing session. Mohawk looked across the room and saw that Cobra was still going, making fight poses with fans during their photos or insulting them when they asked for it.

"You are a nasty woman!" Cobra roared at a chortling lady who was with her husband or boyfriend. "And I am Cobra Tara Singh! I will allow you to leave your man to live with me in my palace in Punjab!"

The lady and her partner chuckled heartily at this and Mohawk rolled his eyes at Cobra's antics before ducking out to the restroom.

CHAPTER 9

After relieving himself, Mohawk ended up at a small snack station the convention people had set up for the wrestlers. The coffee was decent and there was a spread of donuts and other treats that Mohawk had to regretfully turn away from. His doctor had been telling him to watch his sugar levels so he sipped some java and chatted with Siniestro, a popular current star and masked wrestler from Mexico. Siniestro was actually born and raised in Texas and Mohawk had wrestled Siniestro's father and uncles when he went south of the border back in the day.

"My papa always liked you," Siniestro said with great respect. "He told me that Mohawk Jones was a real pro."

Mohawk beamed at this.

"Your dad was the real pro," he said. "I learned a lot from that man. How's he doing?"

"Living the grandfather life in El Paso," Siniestro said, chuckling a little. "He misses the ring but they all do when they retire."

Not me, Mohawk thought.

He and Siniestro talked some more before the younger man had to take a call on his cellphone. They shook hands as Siniestro departed and Mohawk sipped his coffee, enjoying a moment of quiet. This was short-lived, though.

"Mohawk fucking Jones!" a familiar voice called out and Mohawk winced, knowing immediately who it was. He turned and saw the grinning Buddy Blaze heading his way.

"Hi Buddy," Mohawk said, hoping this encounter would be a quick one.

Mohawk didn't hate Buddy but he never enjoyed spending time with the guy. Buddy looked to be in decent shape although the hair on top was definitely thinner and he had a slight gut. He still dressed well, at least for a pro wrestler, wearing a dark blue sport coat, khakis and brown cowboy boots. A few silver rings were worn on Buddy's fingers with a thick silver necklace to match. The man's facial hair was impeccable, the beard groomed and the goatee cut at perfect ninety-degree angles. Buddy's teeth were astonishingly white, too.

"Mohawk Jones," Buddy repeated, vigorously shaking Mohawk's hand. "I haven't seen you in forever. You're looking…good."

"Thanks," Mohawk said. "Enjoying everything today?"

"Kinda, sorta!"

Buddy laughed as if this was some big joke but Mohawk just nodded. Again, Buddy wasn't a bad guy in that he had never screwed Mohawk over in the past, like others had, but Mohawk still didn't trust him. Buddy just had that aura about him.

"What are you up to nowadays?" Mohawk asked, not really caring.

"Working for Stan's boy at Tuesday Night Massacre," Buddy replied with great pride. "I'm Tom Victory's second-in-command."

Mohawk was impressed. Tom Victory owned and operated the Universal Grappling Federation, or UGF, the top wrestling company in the world. Their big show, Tuesday Night Massacre, was not only the most viewed wrestling show on the planet but the most popular TV program in all of cable.

"Nice," Mohawk said, looking around, hoping someone might pull him away from Buddy before he went full-on with the boasting. Unfortunately, they were the only two at the snack station.

"Yep, I do a bit of everything for my man Tom," Buddy bragged, checking out his manicured nails. "I scout and sign talent, help with the booking, keep the boys in line when they need it...you know how it is..."

"Uh huh."

"Maybe I'll take over running the show some day, if Tom just wants to handle the corporate stuff."

"That's great."

Buddy smiled and put his arm around Mohawk's shoulders. Mohawk wanted to buck him off but fought off the urge to do so.

"Listen," Buddy said, leaning in. Mohawk could smell a lot of mint on the guy, which meant he was trying to cover up the scent of whisky or some other spirit. "How about I put in a good word with Tom? Bring you into the UGF fold? Tom likes having the old guys around. I could maybe get you a job as an agent for the matches or on the booking committee. The travel sucks but the money's fabulous."

Mohawk shrugged, mostly to get Buddy's arm off him. Buddy didn't seem to notice as he kept on smiling.

"I like being retired," Mohawk said. "Don't miss the road at all."

"Except for these shows, right?" Buddy said. "You going to the matches tonight?"

"Matches?"

"Oh yeah. Promoters are putting on a show for the people. Thought you would have heard about it."

Mohawk frowned, starting to feel unsettled.

"What do you mean?" he asked.

"I mean, you know Cobra's wrestling tonight, yeah?" Buddy replied.

"What?"

And with that, Mohawk was off and running. He tore down the hallway and almost bumped into Betty Buxom, who looked him up and down.

"Hey, Mohawk," she said, almost seductively. "Always nice bumping into you. Real nice."

Mohawk frowned, knowing Betty was trying to get a rise out of him. He didn't have time for this.

"Gotta go," he mumbled, jogging away. Before Mohawk turned his head, he could see Betty's smile turn into a scowl and he winced a little. What he just did was going to cost him but Mohawk had a more pressing matter at hand: saving Cobra Tara Singh's life.

Thankfully, and to Mohawk's great relief, Cobra wasn't coming out of retirement to wrestle at the convention show later that evening. He wanted to but the promoters realized that they would probably be liable if he keeled over and died during the match. So cooler heads prevailed and Cobra was instead tapped to be the "Special Guest Referee" of the match between Siniestro and another young wrestler named Walker Gaston.

Even so, Cobra seemed pissed about not getting the chance to lock up with someone and as they sat together in a small room at the convention center earmarked as the locker room, he began taking it out on Mohawk.

"This is your fault," Cobra snarled as he wrapped his wrists with white athletic tape, a common practice for wrestlers before they went out to perform. It was believed this was to help stabilize your hands and forearms but also with gripping your opponent or the ring ropes. Or as an aesthetic thing, making your forearms and biceps look bigger.

"I didn't do anything," Mohawk said, folding his arms across his chest. He had been preparing himself to intervene and get Cobra's match cancelled but it had already been done so by the time he stormed over to the promoters.

"I don't believe you."

"I don't fucking care. And why are you taping your wrists anyway?"

Cobra shrugged and kept on taping. Mohawk sighed.

"Do you really think you could have had a real match today?" he asked. "Seriously?"

Cobra smiled, almost childlike.

"I can do anything," he said with more than a hint of confidence. "You know that thing...when things are going good and you feel strong, eh?"

"Adrenaline?" Mohawk offered.

"Yes! The adreenaleen. When that is going, you can do anything!"

Mohawk huffed at this and told Cobra that he would be nearby if anything went awry during the match. He would get Cobra out of there if he needed to. Of course, Cobra waved this away, rolling his eyes and telling Mohawk to stop nagging him.

Mohawk sat with some other wrestlers during the show, which was the first live wrestling he had watched in years. Before the pandemic, he would catch the odd local show here and there, maybe do a signing or a seminar for trainees, or even go backstage when a bigger company came by to say hello to some old friends. It was fun watching the action as a spectator on this night and Mohawk was impressed with some of the wrestlers' ring work. They went a bit fast for his liking but the fans were into it and that's all that really mattered.

Mohawk saw Buddy Blaze watching the matches from the backstage curtain, just out of sight of the audience. To his credit, Buddy seemed to be paying close attention to what was going on in the ring and Mohawk could see he took his job as a talent scout seriously. It made sense, though. If Buddy discovered the professional wrestling world's next big star, his reputation would sparkle even more.

Soon it was time for the main event and Siniestro and Walker Gaston made their way to the ring to considerable cheering and applause. However, when Cobra was announced as special guest referee, the place erupted and even Cobra, dressed in his wrestling finery but with a black and white zebra ref shirt, looked surprised by the ovation.

"They know who the real star of the main event is," Mohawk said out loud, mostly to himself, but under the din of the crowd.

However, that was pretty much the highlight of the match.

Cobra was a terrible referee. He could barely move around the ring, was getting in the way of the wrestlers' sequences, and struggled to get down to the mat to count pinfalls. Mohawk could see the frustration on Siniestro's and Walker Gaston's faces and it was almost contagious, spreading to the three hundred or so fans in attendance.

"Please don't boo," Mohawk whispered, hoping for the best but expecting the worst. He knew if the crowd turned on the match, and on Cobra, his roommate would not react well.

And then, right on cue, the boos started raining down, accompanied by "Cobra sucks! Cobra sucks!"

This stopped the entire match with the confused Cobra standing in the middle of the ring and Siniestro and Walker Gaston standing in opposite corners with bemused looks, wanting to see how this played out.

Mohawk felt like he should do something but he couldn't seem to move.

Now Cobra's instincts were kicking in. He glared at the fans and gestured to the ring announcer to pass him the microphone. The ring announcer nervously shook his head and this angered Cobra even more.

"You people are the garbage!" Cobra screamed, so loud that he didn't need a mic. "I am legend! You will respect!"

More boos and Cobra answered this by throwing up middle fingers to the people.

"You are all nothing!" Cobra shouted, his face red and eyes wild. "I am Cobra Tara Singh!"

He hissed and Mohawk could tell he was genuinely furious. This wasn't an act.

"You better get in there," Izzie Santiago said. He was standing beside Mohawk. "Before he does something even more stupid."

Mohawk nodded and got moving. He made his way through the crowd, saying "excuse me" a bunch along the way till he got to ringside. Once there, Mohawk saw a familiar face, the young woman who he had signed for earlier. Her eyes met with Mohawk's and she looked as worried as he did.

"What's wrong with him?" Emily asked Mohawk as he contemplated hopping the guardrail, which would be a mistake at his age.

Mohawk didn't answer and Emily followed his eyes. She then pointed to the end of the guardrail, where there was a small opening.

"Over there," she said.

"Thanks," Mohawk said in reply, hurrying over and making his way out of the crowd. He could see that many fans were recording what was happening on their phones and whatever transpired tonight was definitely going to be on the internet when it was over.

Mohawk slid into the ring and some fans began cheering, recognizing him immediately. He went over to Cobra but kept his distance.

"Cobra," he whispered, using a technique that many wrestlers could do, speaking audibly with minimal lip movement so the crowd couldn't pick up on the communication in the ring. "Let's go. Show's over."

"No!" Cobra fired back. "I hate these people!"

"I know. But this is enough."

"No!"

Mohawk reached for Cobra, who glared at him and violently slapped his hand away. The crowd "ooh"-ed at this, many believing that something big was about to happen.

Mohawk realized that he and Cobra were now facing off in the ring. It seemed like they were about to fight and being two legends of the pro wrestling game, this looked to be a genuine moment. Mohawk knew he had to de-escalate things and do it fast.

"Kid," he said to Siniestro. "Help me out here."

Siniestro nodded and came over as did Walker Gaston. They tried to calm Cobra down.

"Mr. Singh," Siniestro said kindly. "Come on now..."

"Don't you touch me!" Cobra raged. He then shoved Siniestro away and did the same to Walker Gaston. The crowd murmured, some shouting that they wanted to see a fight, and both Siniestro and Walker Gaston looked to Mohawk for help.

Mohawk's mind raced...and then he took a deep breath.

He hated what he was about to do but they were wrestlers. They all knew the game.

"Jump him," Mohawk whispered to Siniestro. Siniestro looked at Mohawk like he was bat-shit crazy but the older man nodded again in an insistent way. "Do it."

Without hesitation, Siniestro began hitting Cobra with forearms to the neck and back. These were soft shots that didn't hurt Cobra at all but Cobra, sensing what Mohawk's scheme was, began selling the shots like he was, well, getting shot. Walker Gaston picked up on the cue and joined in with some more "punches", both younger man beating Cobra down to his knees.

This got the reaction from the crowd that Mohawk was hoping for. They began to boo Siniestro and Walker Gaston as despite Cobra's actions, he was still an old man and a legend, and didn't deserve to be treated this way.

Now it was Mohawk's turn. He leaped into the fray, attacking Siniestro and Walker Gaston with his trademark punches and chops and the fans erupted. They were all on their feet and cheering their fucking hearts out as Mohawk was doing something unfathomable.

He was saving his most hated foe. In wrestling lore, this was huge!

Now Cobra was back on his feet and giving Siniestro and Walker Gaston some weak-looking punches which both men treated like knock-out blows.

The crowd was going bananas as Mohawk Jones and Cobra Tara Singh cleared the ring of Siniestro and Walker Gaston, sending both wrestlers stumbling back to the locker room, humbled and in pain.

Then came the biggest moment of all. Mohawk and Cobra, now fully in their wrestling characters, were left in the ring, staring at each other with wide-eyes, shocked at what had just happened. The fans clapped for them and chanted their names and both men soaked it in, acting confused as to what they should do next.

Finally, Cobra Tara Singh, the hated heel and consummate bad guy, offered his hand, as if saying, "I'm sorry for the past. Thank you for saving me, my friend."

However, could Mohawk Jones trust this man? What if it was all just a trick?

Mohawk looked to the fans. What should he do?

The crowd clapped, wanting him to take Cobra's hand. So he did, the two cementing things with a manly handshake, their enmity now gone and mutual respect winning out.

And the audience nearly blew the roof off the place with their never-ending cheering.

What a moment.

Mohawk felt a delirium of emotions as he stood in the ring, flexing and posing with Cobra for the fans. He spotted Emily in the crowd, who was so happy and cheering so loud while wiping tears from her eyes. Mohawk even saw Buddy Blaze, out from behind the curtain and giving him a megawatt smile.

What a fucking moment.

When it was over and Mohawk and Cobra were backstage again, they were both in rough shape. Neither had expected to be doing anything so physical tonight and they hadn't prepared for it. Mohawk was sore and would be feeling it tomorrow but Cobra was in worse shape. The man could barely move and Siniestro, after he and Walker Gaston thanked the older men for the experience tonight, helped Cobra unwrap his wrists.

Buddy Blaze and Betty Buxom came by to congratulate Mohawk and Cobra. This time Mohawk was more receptive to Betty's flirting but once she saw she had his attention, she giggled and walked away from him in mid-sentence, knowing that she had Mohawk's number once again. This didn't bother Mohawk, though. He knew he deserved it for blowing Betty off earlier.

"Excellent work out there!" Buddy said jubilantly, clapping Mohawk on the back.

The promoters of the convention were also in the room but kept their distance. They were grinning it up, knowing that the show's main event would be talked about online and in the professional wrestling circle and this made them feel like big deals. Ronnie stood nearby, patiently waiting by the doorway to take Mohawk and Cobra back to their hotel room but Cobra was taking his sweet time, excitedly gabbing away with the other wrestlers.

"I still have it!" Cobra declared and the others cheered for him. He then added, "Let's go to the bar!"

More cheers and Mohawk watched as everyone headed out to leave together. He had a fun time tonight but also came to a stark realization.

Cobra Tara Singh was no good for him. And he needed to get the guy out of his house as soon as possible.

CHAPTER 10

It wasn't easy for Mohawk to get in touch with Cobra's ex-wife Kavita. He had her phone number, which he had gotten out of Cobra's battered address book, but she had hung up on him twice. Mohawk couldn't blame the woman...she had dedicated years of her life and her love to a louse of a man who made it a sport to cheat. Sure, she got Cobra's money in the divorce but it wasn't like she could build a time machine and get the prime of her life back.

On the third call, Mohawk got lucky. He must have caught Kavita at a moment of weakness and the two actually had a pleasant conversation. Kavita apologized for her rudeness in hanging up on Mohawk before and she was aware that her ex-husband was living with him although she didn't ask about Cobra. From this, Mohawk assumed that Kavita couldn't care less about Cobra Tara Singh and he knew this made his mission to get her to take him back even more difficult.

"It's good to talk to you again, Kavita," Mohawk had said, meaning it.

Kavita then invited Mohawk to her home for brunch the next Sunday.

"Can I bring...Cob...I mean, Tara...?" he asked tentatively. And to Mohawk's shock, Kavita said yes.

So now the two were riding in a car that Kavita had arranged to pick them up, driving across the city to Fairbury, a small and exclusive township/gated community. When Mohawk had told Cobra that Kavita had asked for them to visit with her, the man was so excited, he jumped off the couch like it was the top rope. Mohawk had smiled at this. The old man was still apparently in love with Kavita. This was a good sign.

Mohawk sat in the back of Kavita's luxurious BMW with Cobra, a sunglassed and silent driver sitting in the front. Mohawk glanced at Cobra, dressed in nice slacks and a cardigan, his beard groomed and a well-creased black turban on the man's head. He could even smell a hint of cologne on Cobra.

Cobra stared thoughtfully out the window and then turned to Mohawk. He seemed nervous.

"I am not sure this is good idea," he said quietly. "Are you sure this is what Kavita is wanting? For me to come?"

"That's what she said to me," Mohawk replied.

Cobra nodded but still appeared unsure. He took a deep breath.

"It has been so long," he continued. "I have made many mistakes, Mohawk."

"We've all made mistakes," Mohawk said. "You just gotta keep living and making up for them."

"I will. I will make it up to Kavita."

"Good."

Mohawk clasped Cobra on the shoulder and spent the next twenty minutes of the car ride giving Cobra a pep talk, hoping that the idiot would keep his cool. Finally, as they neared their destination, the driver spoke up, glancing back at his passengers.

"We'll be in Fairbury in five minutes, gentlemen," he said respectfully.

At this, Cobra began to panic. He coughed, pulled at his collar, and shook his head repeatedly.

"This," he said. "This is no good...I do not want to do this..."

"Stop it," Mohawk snapped. They had gone this far and couldn't pull out now, not when Mohawk was so close to being free of this motherfucker. "This is going to be a great day. For all of us." He leaned in closer to Cobra. "Time to be a man, man."

The driver maneuvered the BMW through the elegant black gate of the Fairbury community. Mohawk hadn't been here before but had definitely heard about it. A beautiful lakefront village, Fairbury was home to celebrities, professional athletes and corporate executives, all living in picturesque mansions with sprawling, professionally manicured lawns and gardens. There was also a golf course and recreational center and Mohawk was suitably impressed by everything he was seeing.

"Ahhhhhh," Cobra sighed happily. "I am home."

Cobra hadn't lived in Fairbury in over a decade but Mohawk resisted saying so. They then pulled into the long smoothly-paved black driveway of one the grandest estates in Fairbury, a magnificent multi-storied home that shone like an exquisite pearl. The grass surrounding the house was the greenest Mohawk had ever seen and everywhere he looked were floral arrangements, mostly of white and red roses.

Mohawk had been to a lot of rich people's houses in his day but nothing like this. He had to fight back a flash of anger towards Cobra. This is what the man gave up to tumble around with some bar floozy?

As the driver, who was named Michael, held the car door open for them and Mohawk helped Cobra out of the BMW, the two took in everything around them. The air smelled fragrant from the roses and he noticed that Cobra was very much at peace. He also saw that the man's eyes were darting around, searching for something.

"What are you looking for?" Mohawk asked.

"The dog," Cobra replied. "His name is Amar..." He called out. "Amar! Daddy is home!"

Mohawk winced and glanced at Michael. He could tell Kavita's driver was thinking what he was thinking: the old man's dog was long dead.

"Cobra," Mohawk said gently. "Let's go inside."

"Yes, gentlemen," Michael said, gesturing to follow him. "Right this way."

"I will take it from here, Michael," a woman's voice said, a tone full of poise and confidence. "Thank you."

Mohawk turned and saw Kavita standing in the front doorway of the mansion. When Mohawk had first met her, she was in her early twenties and he thought she was pretty, albeit a bit reserved and mousy. However, now Kavita was a beautiful and sophisticated East Indian woman, dressed in black flats, gray pin-striped slacks and a light blue blouse with a flower-patterned scarf around her neck. Kavita's wrists had gold bracelets and her dark and silver hair was professionally coiffed. She radiated warmth, wealth and success and both Mohawk and Cobra were drawn to her.

"My darling," Cobra said, trying too hard to be charming. "You are the lovely."

He went to Kavita, who deftly side-stepped her ex-husband and smiled at Mohawk.

"Mohawk Jones," she said warmly, with just a tiny hint of an East Indian accent. "So wonderful to see you again."

Kavita hugged Mohawk and he kept his eyes on the disappointed Cobra. He hoped that Cobra would keep calm after Kavita had basically spurned him in her introduction.

"Great to see you, too," Mohawk said. He glanced around. "This place is incredible. Thanks so much for inviting *us*." Mohawk emphasized the "us" part since Kavita still had not looked Cobra's way once since they had arrived. However, Kavita didn't seem to notice Mohawk's emphasis.

"I am proud of it myself," Kavita said. "I have taken a keen interest in architecture and landscaping over the years."

Now Kavita looked over at the hapless Cobra, standing timidly by the side.

"Tara," she said coldly. "Good of you to come."

Cobra nodded as a response and Kavita turned towards the house again.

"Let's brunch," she said, stepping inside. Mohawk and Cobra followed with Michael behind them. Mohawk wanted to take Cobra aside to tell him to stop being a sad-sack. Yes, Kavita wasn't too nice to him right off the bat but that was to be expected, no?

The interior of Kavita's home was as incredible as the exterior. Expensive art mixed with different South Asian antiques, imported rugs, designer furniture, and high-end electronic appliances all professionally styled with splashes of vibrant color, an oil painting here or a Corinthian leather recliner there, that fit perfectly with everything. Mohawk wasn't much for fancy surroundings but everything around him took his breath away.

"Incredible," he whispered, which Kavita seemed to have heard. She glanced back at Mohawk and shrugged.

"I have a good decorator," she said bashfully.

"I'll say."

A flush of a toilet and the shuffling of footsteps caught the group's attention. They spotted an ancient Indian woman, dressed in a cream-colored salwar with a headscarf, slowly making her way towards them. The woman had to be in her late eighties, possibly her nineties, but still moved quite nimbly. She also had a very deep, very scornful frown on her heavily-wrinkled face.

"Mama-Ji!" Kavita said in anguish. "Why are you downstairs? You know Michael or me should be the one helping you...did you take the elevator?"

Elevator? Mohawk thought. *This place has an elevator, too?*

Kavita conversed with her mother in rapid-fire Punjabi and Mohawk stood respectfully as they went back and forth with each other. Kavita's mother gave Mohawk a cursory glance and then focused the entirety of her attention on Cobra.

Mohawk had never seen such an expression of pure, unadulterated hatred on a woman's face before as Kavita's mother glared at the cowed Cobra. It shook him to the core.

"Mama-Ji," Cobra croaked out, leaning forward to touch Kavita's mother's feet, a sign of respect for elders. Mama-Ji stepped back, though, out of range.

"Maaderchod!" Mama-Ji spat back at Cobra before Kavita stepped in between them. Mohawk had recognized the word her mother had used, which meant "motherfucker". Mama-Ji probably would have slapped the shit out of Cobra if Kavita hadn't gotten in the way.

"Michael," Kavita said gently. "Please help my mother to her room for her afternoon rest and then come to the kitchen to assist with the meal prep."

"Yes, madam," Michael said. He offered his arm to Mama-Ji, who took it, but her angry eyes never left Cobra.

"Let's go sit," Kavita suggested. She glided away, clearly having enjoyed her mother's exchange with her ex-husband, and Cobra shakily followed. Mohawk was right behind, just in case the man fell over as he would be right there to catch him.

The trio walked through different corridors, lavish sitting rooms and a well-stocked library until they reached the very spacious and bright-lit kitchen. Kavita gestured to a wide sliding glass door.

"It's a lovely day," she said. "Let's eat outside."

Without waiting for Mohawk and Cobra's acquiescence, Kavita led them to an expansive back patio overlooking the lake. Forest and mountains under a blue, cloudless sky sat beyond the water. The view was breathtaking.

"Sit, please," Kavita said, taking a seat herself at a medium-sized dining table with cushioned chairs. Mohawk and Cobra did so and it took a few seconds for Mohawk to gather himself after everything he had seen of Kavita's home. He knew Cobra had a prosperous career but this was something else.

"So how have you been keeping busy, Mohawk?" Kavita asked casually, again not looking directly at Cobra. Michael had appeared again, pouring each of them a glass of sparkling water.

"Just enjoying retirement," Mohawk replied with a smile.

"No more wrestling?"

Mohawk laughed.

"I'm way out of shape for that," he said. "I do make appearances... actually, we both do."

Mohawk gestured to the sullen Cobra but Kavita didn't look his way.

This was not going well. Mohawk had hoped that maybe he could help rekindle the love once shared between Cobra and Kavita but this woman obviously still hated her ex.

No, she fucking despised the guy.

"What have you been up to?" Mohawk asked, trying to keep things going.

"Mostly investing," Kavita replied. "After I divorced, I went back to school…business, economics, real estate, that sort of thing…took the money I had and made more." She smiled, almost devilishly. "A lot more."

Mohawk was impressed and he could tell that Cobra was as well. He wasn't just staring down at the ground now, he was intently watching his ex-wife.

Michael showed up here and there, bring out food. Some salads, omelets, sandwiches, decadent-looking desserts…a nice spread and Mohawk enjoyed it immensely. The conversation was sputtering, though. There really wasn't much to talk about and Cobra wasn't helping much, either. Mohawk had all but given up on his ploy to dump the old bastard back on his ex-wife.

"Philanthropy is a big passion of mine," Kavita said with enthusiasm. "I have a few charitable foundations and believe in being generous with my money."

"My money," Cobra said bitterly.

Oh shit, Mohawk thought. He glanced over at Michael, dutifully standing nearby in case someone needed anything. No longer wearing sunglasses, Michael's dark eyes had widened ever so slightly at Cobra's words and he and Mohawk exchanged glances. They were on the same wavelength.

If Cobra Tara Singh had wanted Kavita Singh's attention, he definitely had it now. Mohawk expected her reaction, or at least her demeanor, to be similar to her mother's but Kavita kept her cool although now she was staring daggers at the man she once loved.

"Your money, eh?" she scoffed. "The money you wasted on your women and your drugs?"

Mohawk had never heard of Cobra using hard drugs before but it wasn't surprising. The eighties and nineties were a wild time for pro wrestlers. He had smoked and snorted his share of stuff.

"I make the money!" Cobra shouted back. "Every day, I wrestled and I hurt for the money and now I hurt all the time, every day, and I have no money…and no wife!"

Kavita stayed quiet and Mohawk knew that she was just waiting for Cobra to finish. The man shook his head in dismay.

"I make mistakes," Cobra said, continuing in a more level tone. "Many, many mistakes. But I never stop my love for my wife."

He looked away in embarrassment for Mohawk knew the man wasn't accustomed to speaking this way. Mohawk watched Kavita closely. Whatever happened next was going to be huge.

"Do you miss me?" she asked simply. "Or do you miss..." she waved her hand around the house and their surroundings. "...all of this?"

At this, Cobra hesitated and Mohawk felt like strangling him. It was an easy slam dunk and the fool botched it by not declaring that his passion for his ex-wife, the love of his life, was never-ending.

Instead, Cobra didn't have an answer and Kavita, looking imperious, was undoubtedly victorious.

"That is what I thought," she sighed, leaning back and holding up a glass, which Michael promptly refilled with a sparkling cider. She sipped lightly and Mohawk could see that the woman was carefully choosing her next words.

"I am glad," Kavita said, looking directly at Cobra. "I am glad I never had children with you. I am the one who took care of you when you were hurt after all the body slams. When your whores came to the house asking for things, I paid them and made them go away. I clean your costumes, stitch your cuts, negotiate your contracts...you said it is your money..." She scoffed. "It is all mine and you will get nothing. Ever. So I will spend it how I please and give to hospitals and schools and refugees and poor children and you will never say one word to me about it."

Kavita paused.

"Do you hear me?" she asked.

"I hear," Cobra replied, almost immediately. The man was defeated and he knew it. Mohawk felt defeated, too. Brunch was nice but he had completely failed in what he had set out to do today.

Kavita stood up, staring down at the seemingly tiny Cobra Tara Singh.

"Now get out of my house," she said. "Michael will drive you back home."

Mohawk knew that Cobra would never lash out at his wife but was glad that Michael, who he could now see was actually far more intimidating than he first appeared to be, a man who was slightly smaller than an NFL linebacker, was strolling over to the browbeaten remains of Kavita's ex-husband to help him out of his chair. The two headed back into the house to get to the BMW parked out front and Mohawk was about to join them when Kavita touched him on the shoulder.

"Wait," she said firmly. "You stay."

The two stood on the patio, looking out to the water together. It was cooler closer to the lake, a slight breeze in the air, but Kavita showed no sign of any discomfort.

"I am getting married again," she said finally and the announcement surprised Mohawk.

"Congrats," he said, meaning it. Kavita was a good person and she deserved happiness.

"Thank you," she said. "He is a Sikh doctor at one of the hospitals that I am on the board of. A good man with two grown children." Kavita smiled. "I never had babies but they call me 'Ma'...this is very nice."

Kavita was becoming a little emotional. Mohawk stepped closer to her, unsure what to do, but she waved him away.

"I like them very much," Kavita continued. "They have welcomed me into their family. And I love their father. Much more than I ever loved...him."

"I get it," Mohawk said. "I'm glad for you."

"The wedding is in a few months. I would like you to come."

"I'm honored. Thanks for the invitation."

"But leave him at home."

"I will."

Kavita nodded and Mohawk could see that she was become very tired. For all her grace and maturity, this brunch had taken a lot out of Kavita and she was drained, starting to unclench ever so slightly.

"I hate the wrestling," Kavita said. "It has taken so much from me. I never watch it on the television." She laughed. "My mummy loves it, though. Every Tuesday she watches with Michael. I go out of the house at that time."

Mohawk laughed as well. Kavita then turned to face him, hands on her hips.

"I know why you came here," she said. "You came to try to bring him back to live with me."

Mohawk's jaw dropped. He hadn't anticipated Kavita being so savvy.

"I...no...that's not...true," he stammered unconvincingly, which made Kavita chuckle some more.

"I knew it right when you called," she said. "There was no other reason to get in touch with me." Kavita's eyes narrowed. "You hate him as much as I do."

At this, Mohawk shook his head. Yes, he hated Cobra Tara Singh but no one could hate him as much as Kavita Singh.

"He's...not easy to live with," Mohawk said helplessly. "Every day, it's something new with the guy. He acts like a little kid, he's a mess of a person, and some days it takes everything I have not to murder the guy in his sleep."

"I understand," Kavita said. "I once tried to stab him. He had brought a whore to our bedroom...he thought I was out shopping. I found them and grabbed my biggest kitchen knife..."

She stopped herself and smiled at the memory. Mohawk probably should have been scared at that moment with Kavita showing a dangerous side of her but if anything, he felt a bond with her. He got where she was coming from. Mohawk had once or twice eyed his own biggest knife in the kitchen and daydreamed of stabbing Cobra with it.

The guy just inspired thoughts of murder. He was that loathsome.

"I just can't deal with him much longer, Kavita," Mohawk said, feeling deflated. "I don't know what to do."

Kavita clucked at this, which Mohawk took her understanding his plight. He watched as Cobra's ex-wife headed back to the table, taking a clean flute glass and filling it with champagne.

"First, you must take this," she said. "Please."

Kavita gave the glass to Mohawk and then took one for herself.

"I do not drink very much," Kavita said, eyeing the glass in her hand. "Sometimes I have red wine but that is what my boyfriend says I should do…" She giggled. "My boyfriend…so silly for me to say that. I am an old lady."

Kavita raised the champagne flute to Mohawk, as if toasting him.

"To you, Mohawk Jones," she said with gravitas. "I salute you."

"Salute me? For what?" Mohawk asked incredulously.

"For taking care of a maaderchod like Cobra Tara Singh."

She drank the champagne in one gulp as Mohawk sipped at it. It didn't taste good to him but it was probably not the champagne's fault.

"Do you need money? I can help you if you need some…to help with taking care of him," Kavita offered. "It is no problem at all. Whatever you need."

"I'm fine for money, thanks. You're not the only one who can handle a bank account," Mohawk said with a rueful smile. He then countered Kavita's offer. "I'd rather you take the money so we can set him up somewhere."

To this, Kavita shook her head.

"No, I will not do that," she said firmly. "That is too good a life for Tara. I will not pay for him to live the luxury life. No. I am sorry." Kavita stared hard at Mohawk. "He needs to be with someone like you. You are the only one who can take care of him."

"I don't want to," Mohawk said petulantly.

Kavita took the champagne flute from Mohawk, placing her own and his flute on the oak railing of the patio. She then tenderly took Mohawk's hand in both of hers and looked deeply into his eyes.

"Tough shit," she said.

CHAPTER 11

Both Mohawk and Cobra were in dark moods on the car ride back, so much so that even Michael seemed slightly concerned for them as he drove Kavita's BMW.

"Everything alright back there, gentlemen?" he asked politely.

"We're fine," Mohawk said with Cobra adding a grunt for his reply. The drive continued in silence as Mohawk ruminated over spending the rest of his life being Cobra Tara Singh's caretaker, or at least until one, or both, of them were committed to a nursing home.

Knowing my luck, Mohawk thought with a grimace. *We'll be roomies there, too.*

As Michael drove the car to the outskirts of the city, not too far away from the townhouse, Mohawk got an idea. He tapped Michael on the shoulder.

"Yes sir?" the driver said.

"Can you pull over, please?" Mohawk asked.

Michael dutifully steered the BMW to the side of the road as Mohawk unbuckled his seat-belt. He gestured for Cobra to do the same.

"Let's go," he said.

"Sir, wait," Michael said, startled by what was going on. "My instructions were to drop both you and Mr. Singh off at home."

"That's okay," Mohawk said. "You can drop us off here. We're going to walk home."

"We will walk?" Cobra said in surprise.

"Yeah."

Michael protested some more and Cobra did as well, citing how walking for too long caused his ankles to swell. Mohawk was adamant, though.

"If Kavita gets angry at you, just say I threatened your life," Mohawk told Michael.

This caused Michael to burst out in laughter and he warmly shook Mohawk's hand before driving off.

Cobra stared coldly at Mohawk.

"I don't want to walk," he grumbled.

"Tough shit," Mohawk said in reply, the same words that Kavita had uttered, which had felt like cold daggers in his stomach.

The two men walked through what appeared to be an industrial area of the city, a neighborhood full of warehouses, factories and gravel roads. Trucks roared by Mohawk and Cobra as the two shuffled along a cracked sidewalk, causing dust to kick up and both men to cough from it.

"This is the stupid," Cobra sputtered, waving his thin fingers through the dust. He then looked around. "Are we lost?"

"No," Mohawk replied. He had been through this part of town before, back when he was a jogger. They were only twenty minutes or so from the townhouse if they went at a leisurely pace.

They continued to walk a few more yards when they arrived at a group of construction workers, a burly collection of young men who were on some kind of break. Some of the workers nodded at Mohawk, showing respect for an elder.

"Have a good day, sir," one of them said to Mohawk, getting out of the way so he could pass.

"Thanks," Mohawk said appreciatively. However, Cobra eyed the construction workers with distrust and after the brunch he had just experienced, Mohawk could tell the old bastard was spoiling for a fight.

"Out of my way!" Cobra said grumpily, attempting to shove a fellow twice his size way from him. The worker was bearded, well-muscled, and very tattooed and although Cobra could have taken him apart back in the day, the man could dismantle Cobra with hardly any effort.

"Easy, Cobra," Mohawk whispered. The last thing he wanted was a skirmish on their way back home. His plan had been that maybe the walk would help Cobra get out of his doldrums after being humiliated by his ex-wife.

"No!" Cobra shouted. He then whirled around and pointed a finger in the bearded worker's face. "Asshole!"

"Hey, fuck you, old man!" the bearded worker fired back. Some of his co-workers were on their feet now, trying to get him to curb his temper.

"Fuck you!" Cobra yelled. He curled up his fists. "I am going to...fuck you!"

The construction workers froze at this.

"Say what?" the bearded worker said, his brow furrowed in confusion.

"You heard me!" Cobra said, shaking with rage. "I will fuck you!"

"He means he wants to fuck you up," Mohawk sighed, completely embarrassed.

At this, the construction workers laughed and turned away from Cobra, who looked ready to pounce. Mohawk caught him in mid leap and dragged him off.

"Stop!" Mohawk said, shoving the seething Cobra along the sidewalk as the construction workers finished up their break and headed back to work.

"Why you stop me?" he screamed. "I want to break that man!"

Cobra tried to get around Mohawk again but Mohawk corralled him again.

"That guy would have broken *you*," Mohawk said. "Let's keep walking."

"Why?" Cobra said. "Walking is stupid."

"You need the steps."

Mohawk sighed again as they strolled out of the industrial zone and ended up at the park near their home.

"I want to confess something to you," Mohawk said carefully. "I brought you to Kavita because I was hoping she would take you back."

Cobra nodded at this.

"I was hoping same," he said. Cobra then added, much more sorrowfully, "But there is no chance, eh?"

"No chance," Mohawk replied.

Now Cobra sighed. He was becoming emotional and looked away from Mohawk. All around them, young couples and families were enjoying the day together.

"I really miss my money," Cobra sniffled, wiping his eyes. He then turned to Mohawk, adding in a grateful tone. "You are my best friend."

Mohawk winced, hoping that he wouldn't have to say the same thing back to Cobra.

"I do not treat you nice," Cobra continued. "That will change. I will be good to you now, I promise."

"Alright," Mohawk said.

"It is true. I am telling truth. I will be good."

"Sure."

Cobra frowned, getting in front of Mohawk and stopping them on the path they were walking upon. He put his hands on Mohawk's shoulders, forcing him to stare into his earnest face.

"From now on, you and me are tag team," Cobra said.

Mohawk smiled.

"We would have been a great tag team way back when," he said.

"Yes," Cobra agreed. "The very best."

They continued on, joking and laughing together. Cobra talked about a match he had with their old wrestling friend Kenya and how he had accidentally broken Kenya's nose with a head-butt. Cobra was so afraid of what Kenya would do to him when they got backstage but instead, Kenya snapped his nose back into place himself and then took Cobra out for Chinese food, never speaking of his nose once even though he was definitely in some discomfort.

"A true hero," Cobra said sadly.

"I loved that man," Mohawk said. He made a mental note to check in with Kenya's widow. She lived somewhere in Seattle and Mohawk hoped Kenya's family was doing well.

As they neared their home and Cobra told another story about Kenya, this time how both of them wrestled at the Tokyo Dome and Kenya had no patience for a German wrestler who tried to suplex him without consent. He laughed as he talked about how Kenya just landed right on the German, crushing him, as Mohawk looked ahead and saw someone sitting on the front stoop of their townhouse. It was a young woman and Mohawk recognized her from the wrestling convention they had just attended.

"Hello," he said as the young woman nervously stared up at him once they stopped in front of her.

"Hi," the woman said, standing up, folding her arms around herself and looking down. "I'm Emily."

"I remember you."

"You...you do?"

"Yeah. From the convention. You cheered for me when I ran in to save this guy."

He gestured to Cobra, who didn't seem to have heard him. Cobra was confused, not wanting to be left out of what was going on here.

"Who is this?" he asked.

"It's Emily," Mohawk replied. He smiled at the young woman. "What are you doing here?"

"I came to see you," she said softly.

"Why?"

"Because I'm your kid."

CHAPTER 12

"It's true," Emily said, stepping forward to the confused Mohawk, who instinctively moved back a few paces. This seemed to hurt the young woman's feelings. "I'm really sorry to tell you this way…I wanted to do it at the convention but it didn't seem right…in front of all those people…"

"How did you find me? How did you find where I live?" Mohawk asked, accusingly. For his part, Cobra remained silent, although he did have a fascinated expression on his face.

"I asked around," Emily replied. "Did some research…talked to that Chris guy? I think he's your manager?"

"He used to be my manager," Mohawk said. "He's definitely fired now."

Emily stared blankly at Mohawk, his stomach aching and his ears burning. He returned Emily's gaze with a harsh one of his own.

It hadn't been the first time where someone claimed to be his kid. It hadn't happened for a while, though. Mostly some woman who claimed that while he was on the road, they had slept together and she got pregnant, often greeting him with a baby or a toddler at a hotel after a show. These accusations usually came to nothing when it was determined it wasn't his child…although Mohawk knew that there was a distinct possibility that he had sons or daughters out there. He did his share of fooling around in his day.

However, Mohawk was in no mood to entertain the idea that he had an adult daughter at this moment. Just looking at this young woman was making him upset, especially the fact that she wore a light blue denim jacket, just like he liked to do when he was on the road.

"I'm not sure what I'm supposed to say," Mohawk said. "You want some money or something?"

"No!" Emily said angrily. "I'm not here for that. I...I really am your daughter. My name's Emily, if you didn't hear me the first time."

"I heard you."

At this, Emily's demeanor changed dramatically. She put on a big smile on her freckled face, her eyes full of happiness.

"Dude," she said giddily. "You have no idea how long I've waited to say I'm your daughter. Like, soooo long!"

She giggled and Mohawk watched in surprise as she moved over to Cobra.

"I'm Emily," she said, offering him her hand.

"Cobra Tara Singh," Cobra said with great dignity, his shoulders square as he gave Emily a firm shake.

"I know! I've seen a lot of your matches! You're Mohawk Jones' biggest rival! I think you're great!"

Cobra looked over at Mohawk, clearly enjoying the compliment.

"I like her," Cobra said.

"Sweet!" Emily said. "I like being liked!"

She and Cobra laughed together and Mohawk felt like he was in some surreal fantasy. What the fuck was going on here?

"Okay," he said, facing Emily with hands on hips. "What do we do now? What do you want?"

"Mohawk, do not be rude," Cobra said.

"You stay out of this. This doesn't concern you."

Cobra was greatly offended, his chest puffed up as if he was ready to throw down.

"You do not speak to me like that," he said.

"Cobra, go inside," Mohawk said sternly. "Now."

He tossed Cobra the keys to the house and the old man caught them. Mohawk knew that when he wanted Cobra to do what he wanted, the best course of action was to be firm. Cobra could be bullied sometimes and Mohawk hoped that this was one of those times.

"Okay," Cobra said, taking a deep breath. He then bowed his head slightly at Emily. "It was very nice to meet you, Miss Emily."

"You, too, Cobra Singh," Emily said, bowing as well.

The two smiled at each other as Mohawk rolled his eyes. His roommate and this strange girl had become friends.

Not for long, Mohawk thought. *I'm gonna get her out of here fast.*

Cobra fiddled with the front lock for a few excruciating seconds and then disappeared inside the townhouse. Now it was just Mohawk and Emily.

"I know you have a lot of questions," Emily said.

"I do," Mohawk said.

"I'll answer anything. I promise you, I'm not here to scam you, man."

"Uh huh."

Mohawk was ready with his first question when the young mom, his neighbor with a small child, walked by, once again pushing her stroller. She smiled at Mohawk and was surprised to see Emily.

"Hello!" the young mom said, stopping on the sidewalk in front of Mohawk's house.

"Hi," Mohawk said curtly, wishing the woman would be on her way quickly.

"Hope you've had a great day. Who is this?"

Damn it! Mohawk thought. *Mind your own business, lady!*

"I'm his daughter!" Emily said brightly as Mohawk groaned inwardly. He saw the surprise on the young mom's face as Emily skipped over to the stroller. "Aww! Your kid is soooo cute! I'm Emily, by the way!"

"Uh, hi, Emily," the young mom said, glancing over at Mohawk, who couldn't do anything but shrug. "I haven't see you before. Are you visiting?"

"I am!"

"That's wonderful. Well, we better be on our way…"

"Okay!"

Mohawk could tell that the young mom sensed this was an awkward situation so she hurried off. Emily turned back to Mohawk, who regarded her coldly.

"I think you should go," he said.

"What?" Emily said, baffled. "You said you had questions for me. Here I am…shoot'em at me!"

"Alright, fine. Who is your mother?"

Emily looked away.

"She's dead now," Emily said quietly. "But her name was Linda. She said she met you in Philly. That's where I grew up."

Mohawk definitely knew a Linda from Philly.

"How come you didn't come find me before?" he asked.

"I didn't know who you were," Emily said. "My mom and step-dad raised me. They both died in the last couple of years and my mom told me just last year before she went."

"How did she die?"

"Cancer. In her pancreas."

"I'm sorry."

"Thanks."

Mohawk wished he felt real sympathy for this girl who had recently lost her mom but he couldn't muster any.

"I just…I just wanted to talk to you and get to know you," Emily said. "I'm not mad at you for not being there for me. I had a nice childhood without you. But you're my real dad and I'm your daughter."

This was the third or fourth time the "daughter" part had been said and it irritated Mohawk.

"You're not my daughter," he said. He then turned away without waiting for Emily's reaction and went inside the townhouse. Cobra was waiting for him.

"Well?" he asked eagerly. "What is the happening?"

"Shut up," Mohawk said. He went to the living room window, hiding behind the curtain and peering out. Emily was staring at the ground.

"She's just standing there," Mohawk said.

He watched as Emily sat down on the steps, facing out to the neighborhood and looking to be in deep thought.

"Now she's sitting on the steps," Mohawk said.

"You cannot just leave her there, Mohawk," Cobra said.

"Should we call the cops? Get her tossed for trespassing?"

Mohawk heard a furious growl, which startled him. He turned to Cobra, who was seething.

"You are the asshole!" he shouted before heading to the front door and stepping outside himself.

Mohawk watched as Cobra sat down beside Emily. From his spot at the window, he could see, and hear, everything. He wasn't that far away from the two of them.

"Do not mind Mohawk Jones, Miss Emily," Cobra said kindly. "He can be an old fool."

Emily sighed a little.

"I don't blame him for being pissed," she said. "I should have called first. Maybe that would have helped."

"Maybe," Cobra said. Mohawk then heard him change the subject. "So...you like the wrestling, eh?"

"Yes!"

"Who is your favorite?"

Mohawk watched Emily ponder this, desperately hoping she wouldn't say that he was her favorite professional wrestler.

"Mikey Storm," Emily told Cobra. She then grinned. "The Main Event Heartthrob!"

"Mikey Storm?" Cobra said, playfully grimacing. "That skinny boy?"

"He's so good! He does the best moves and has the best matches! Did you ever meet him?"

Cobra laughed.

"Meet him?" he said. "I help train that skinny boy!"

"Really?" Emily squealed.

Mohawk shook his head in dismay, watching Cobra and Emily bond over wrestling, joking around together.

"This is a fucking nightmare," he whispered to himself. Mohawk saw Cobra lean in and hoped the old pervert wasn't going to try and hit on Emily. Then he would have to intervene.

"Are you sure you want to be here?" Mohawk heard Cobra ask.

"I'm sure," Emily said. "This hasn't been as bad as it could be. At least my dad didn't scream at me and slam the door in my face."

Mohawk winced, feeling like a jerk. *Yeah, I didn't do that*, he thought. *But I did consider calling the cops on you.*

"I'm really not here to take his cash," Emily said. "My mom and step-dad took care of me. I'm good."

"You are just a girl," Cobra said. "How old are you?

"Nineteen."

"Nineteen...what about school? College?"

Emily shook her head.

"I tried for a bit," she said. "To be a nurse or a teacher or something. It wasn't for me."

"What do you want to do?" Cobra asked.

At this, Emily didn't answer. Instead, she turned and stared at Mohawk in the window. Cobra did the same.

"Fuck," Mohawk said to himself. He then took a deep breath and headed outside. Without a word, he sat down beside Emily, Cobra on the other side of the young woman.

"I don't know what to make of all of this," Mohawk began. "But the least I can do is invite you in for supper while we figure this out."

"I'd really like that," Emily said, eyes twinkling.

"And she should stay the night as our guest!" Cobra suggested, which Mohawk really wished he hadn't done.

"No, no, I can't," Emily said hastily. "I'll just find a motel or Airbnb it."

"Feh!" Cobra said. He then took Emily by the hand and led her inside the townhouse.

Mohawk stayed out on the front steps for a few minutes and with a wheeze, go to his feet. He then reached for the doorknob.

"Fucking hell," Mohawk muttered, feeling older than ever.

CHAPTER 13

Although Cobra wanted to handle dinner, Mohawk didn't feel like subjecting Emily to his unpredictable cooking. Instead, they ordered pizza, which Cobra was delighted by since he and Mohawk rarely got delivery.

The wait for the pizza was thirty minutes and it was spent in awkward silence. Mohawk was too nervous to speak to Emily about anything and he could sense that she was just as uncomfortable. Cobra wasn't any help as a buffer since his attention was taken by an episode of Family Feud. So the three of them just watched the show together in silence, other than Cobra's guffawing at Steve Harvey's antics as host.

When the pizza finally arrived and the three of them sat down together at the kitchen table, the atmosphere improved. Pizza seems to have that effect on people although Mohawk did worry that Cobra, with his wonky digestive system, was having one too many slices.

The whole house smelled like pepperoni now, which was nice.

As the meal ended, a medium and a half pizza later, Mohawk stared ahead at Emily. It was time to get down to business.

"You're nineteen," Mohawk said.

"Yes," Emily smiled. "Thanks for the pizza."

"You're welcome. So…I was still wrestling around the country. And I was still, um, active. It's possible that your mom and me, uh…"

"So it is true?" Cobra said. He then yelled happily at Emily. "Welcome to the family!"

"Cobra!" Mohawk snapped at his roommate. His focus went back to the young woman seated opposite him. "Let's just say it's possible. What do you want from me?"

Emily looked a little uneasy.

"I guess I want to know you," she said simply. "You're, like, a really interesting guy. You were a big wrestler...I just want to hear your story and stuff...because it would be my story, too." Emily looked at Cobra. "Yours, too. You're kinda my uncle, right?"

Mohawk couldn't help but be touched by this. He glanced at Cobra, who he could tell was similarly moved.

"Yes," Cobra said, his voice cracking. "I suppose I am...if it is true...and you are...his..."

"Do you have a photo of your mom?" Mohawk broke in abruptly.

"I do," Emily said. She dug into her pocket and pulled out an old polaroid. Emily stared at it for a second, looking reluctant, and then handed it to Mohawk. "You can keep that if you want."

Mohawk took the polaroid and was stunned by what he saw in it. It was a young him, dressed in a red Gold's Gym tank top to show off his biceps, and he recognized the woman beside him, hugging him around the waist, immediately. Tall, slim, dark brown hair...he hadn't thought of this woman in years but he definitely knew her.

Linda.

"Excuse me for a second," Mohawk croaked, rushing out of the kitchen.

"Can I have another slice of pizza?" Cobra called out after him.

"I don't care!"

Mohawk went upstairs to his bedroom and closed the door. He had trouble breathing and rubbed his temples as he sat down on the bed.

"Holy Christ," Mohawk said out loud. It could definitely be true. It's really actually possible.

I have a daughter.

And her name is Emily.

Tears came to Mohawk's eyes. He felt an overwhelming sadness.

I could have been there for her, he thought. *I missed out on everything.*

I have a daughter!

She's mine!

My kid!

Mohawk rubbed his eyes and took some deep breaths. He couldn't help but think of things like paternity tests but also remembered he still had the polaroid in his hand. He stared at Linda in the photo, then himself, and then brought up Emily's face in his mind.

The kid does look like both of us, Mohawk thought. *She has my eyes. And my nose, too.*

Holy shit!

Mohawk wanted to run back downstairs and give Emily the biggest hug ever...but that didn't seem right. She was a friendly and kind young woman yet she could still hate him as an absent parent.

Mohawk cleared his throat and stood up. It was better if they took things slow although his heart was overflowing with...love?

Is it possible to love someone so quickly after meeting them for the first time, when they're a part of you?

"Damn," Mohawk said, smiling a little. "What a fucking day."

He took a minute or two to compose himself and went to the bathroom. Mohawk washed his face and put back the grim expression he had been wearing since Emily dropped her bombshell. When he arrived in the kitchen, Cobra was waiting, watching him intently. For her part, Emily was clearing the table.

"You don't have to do that," Mohawk said.

"I don't mind! It's totally cool!" Emily said in her fluttery voice that now made Mohawk's heart sing. He watched as she deposited the dishes in the sink and piled up the cardboard pizza boxes.

"Let's take her to the basement," Cobra suggested to Mohawk. "And show her our things."

"Okay," Mohawk said, still fighting back his emotions and hoping his voice sounded normal. He held out the polaroid for Emily but she shook her head at him.

"That's for you, remember?" she said.

"Right," Mohawk said. He then looked Emily in the eyes. "I do remember...her."

Emily got Mohawk's meaning immediately. They stared at each other for a few seconds.

"Let's go!" Cobra said, once again interjecting himself into the moment. "Down to basement!"

Mohawk nodded and stepped back, allowing his daughter to walk past him and follow his excited roommate down to the lower level of the townhouse.

As they made their way downstairs, Mohawk felt excited to show Emily his memorabilia.

"You're going to love this," he said, trying not to sound too enthusiastic.

"Hope it's something cool," Emily said, before adding with a grin. "And hope this thing isn't some kind of freaky torture sex dungeon."

Both Mohawk and Cobra froze at this.

"Excuse me?" Cobra said, stopping halfway down the staircase to stare blankly at Emily.

"Sorry," she said, looking awkward. "Stupid joke."

Cobra glanced over at Mohawk, who shrugged. They hadn't really been around young people that much in recent years.

Once they got to the basement, Emily's eyes lit up as she looked around.

"Whoa," she said, making her way to the mantle and looking at the old action figures of Mohawk and Cobra. "This stuff is seriously vintage!"

She reached out to grab a Mohawk figure but stopped herself, looking at Mohawk for permission.

"Go ahead," he said. "I've got a box of them in a closet down here."

Emily tentatively picked up the action figure, weighing it in her hand.

"This thing is heavy," she said. "Super cool, though." She smiled at Mohawk. "This is you!"

"It is," Mohawk said.

"You're so lucky! You have a toy of you!"

"I have one, too!" Cobra said, not wanting to be left out. He handed Emily his matching action figure and she held them both up, as if they were facing off.

"So rad," Emily said. "So many little kids were playing with dolls of you guys. That's super rad."

Mohawk didn't know what to say to this because it didn't seem like a big deal to him. Emily handed the action figures back and he replaced them on the mantle. She then moved to the posters on the walls of him and Cobra in action.

"Wow," she said. "How did you get these?"

"My friend," Cobra said with pride. "He was the best wrestling photographer. His name was Roy Janvier."

"Ray," Mohawk corrected. "Ray Janvier."

"Roy, Ray...whatever."

Cobra stood beside Emily, both admiring a blown-up photo of him coming off the top rope with a double axe-handle move onto a stumbling opponent. The man's face was unseen, only his bare back showing with tousled hair and normal black wrestling trunks.

"Do you remember who this is?" Cobra asked Mohawk. "It is not you."

"Definitely not me," Mohawk said. He took a closer look himself. "I think it might be Ed Roscoe? Or maybe Miguel Martinez?"

"It's Sam Johnson," Emily said confidently.

"How do you know that?"

"I just do."

Mohawk and Cobra exchanged a glance and stepped closer to the poster, studying it.

"I think she is right," Cobra said.

"Yeah," Mohawk agreed. "He's got the boots that Sam used to wear. The ones with the weird patterns. Like bowling shoes."

Both he and Cobra turned back to Emily, who was now leaning on the back of the basement couch.

"How did you know that?" Mohawk asked again.

"I know about wrestling," Emily said nonchalantly.

Mohawk took this in and then made his way to the Lucite trophy display case. If Emily claimed to be as big a fan of professional wrestling as she hinted at, she would love this.

"Look at this," he said, reaching in and pulling out his world heavyweight championship belt.

"Be careful!" Cobra said. "That is my belt!"

"It's my belt, too."

"It was mine first."

"Until I beat you for it."

This was the checkmate on the mini-bickerfest and Cobra quieted down, although he didn't look too upset about losing the squabble. Like Mohawk, he appeared very interested in seeing Emily's reaction to the belt.

Emily's eyes were as wide as they could get as Mohawk held out the world title. He offered it to her.

"Go ahead," he said encouragingly. "Touch it…you can even hold it, if you want."

Emily reached for the title belt but as her fingertips were poised to caress the gold and silver plating, she pulled back her hand.

"No, I can't," she said, looking to the floor and shaking her head.

This confused Mohawk.

"Why not?" he asked. "It's sturdy…you won't break it."

"I really shouldn't," Emily replied. She then added, "Can we go back upstairs? Please?"

She gave Mohawk a pleading look and he nodded.

"Sure, let's go," he said.

"Thanks," Emily said quietly.

She headed for the stairs and went upstairs without waiting for Mohawk and Cobra.

"That was the weird," Cobra said.

"Yeah," Mohawk said, placing the championship belt back in the case.

When they made their way upstairs, Emily was waiting by the door. She wasn't upset but was taking this as her cue to leave.

"This has been…amazing," she said happily, smiling at both Mohawk and Cobra. "Thanks so much for today. I'll never forget it. But I better be going."

"Why go?" Cobra asked. "Stay for night."

"I can't," Emily replied. "You've both done way more than I expected."

She turned to Mohawk, waiting for him to add something.

"I think you should stay," he said. "We'd love to have you."

"Really?" Emily said softly.

"Really."

Mohawk wasn't sure if he should embrace the girl so he didn't make a move to do so. It didn't seem like the right moment for something like that and Emily wasn't going for a hug, either. Instead, they all sat in the living room and chatted about wrestling.

This girl sure likes Mikey Storm, the amused Mohawk thought, listening to Emily rattle off a list of her favorite wrestling matches.

Both Mohawk and Cobra had never really stayed up till eleven in a very long time but Mohawk could see his roommate was fading. Cobra sleepily said good night to Emily, again gallantly bowing his head before he shuffled off to his bedroom. Mohawk was very tired himself and offered his bedroom to Emily for the night since they had no spare rooms in the townhouse. He himself would sleep on the pull-out in the living room.

"No way," she said. "That's your room, man."

Instead, Emily requested that she sleep on the couch in the basement. Mohawk protested this, especially in the light of her reaction when he had shown her his title belt, but Emily was adamant. Mohawk was too worn-out to argue so after getting Emily a thick blanket and a couple of pillows from the linen closet, he made up the basement couch for her.

"Thanks again," Emily said, nestling down to sleep.

"No problem," Mohawk said.

The two locked eyes for a second but Mohawk then turned away, heading towards the stairs.

"See you in the morning," he said.

"You, too," Emily said in return.

A few minutes later, Mohawk was in bed himself, a whirlwind of emotions going through him.

What a fucking day. Damn...

However, as he closed his eyes to rest, one thought persisted through everything and kept him awake for a long time.

Linda.

CHAPTER 14

The year is 1987 and Mohawk Jones' world title run is not going well. Ticket sales are steady but not as spectacular as Stan Victory had hoped. Worst of all, Mohawk's big title defense on pay-per-view against Buddy Blaze does poor business and there's rumblings that the heavyweight champ might be booked to lose his title soon.

Personally, Mohawk is struggling big-time. The pressure of being the top guy in the company is more difficult than he thought. Not only does he have to travel all over the United States, defending the title non-stop from coast to coast almost every day with no downtime, Mohawk also has to make the media rounds, going on morning talk shows and doing all sorts of meet-and-greets and charity functions. He barely has time to hit the gym, his stellar physique getting noticeably softer.

Mohawk's not enjoying being world champion and to compensate, he's drinking a lot more, fucking random women a lot more, and even snorting a line or two to keep him going a lot more. Mohawk's in-ring work is getting sloppy, too. He almost drops Kenya on his head during a powerslam attempt in Sacramento and concusses another wrestler with a full-on shoulder tackle that smashed the guy in the face. It's getting to be too much for Mohawk and when Stan Victory takes him aside and tells him that Rex Darkhold, a new "evil" bad guy who is over seven feet tall, is going to beat him for the title in Montreal, Mohawk is almost relieved.

Mohawk lost the match to Rex, who hugged him and burst into tears backstage after, and had no idea what to do next. He desperately wanted time off but Stan said he needs him for a loop in Europe, going to Ireland, England, France and Spain. Mohawk knew this tour would not be good for him as international excursions were usually wild party times for the wrestlers. So with a heavy heart, he asked Stan for his release. This resulted in a heated argument where Stan screamed that he was a "pussy" who had invested a ton into, but Mohawk stayed firm. Eventually, when things calmed down, the two shook hands like gentlemen, and Stan floated the idea of Mohawk returning when he "got his head on straight".

Soon after, Mohawk returned to his parents' home for some rest, relaxation and most importantly, recuperation. He had an apartment in New York since Stan's operations were located on Long Island and he wanted to be near headquarters, but didn't want to deal with the noise of the city. So Mohawk planned on spending time with Ted and Barbara, who were elated to have their son back. Plus, it was a place where he didn't have to be Mohawk Jones anymore...he could just be Morris.

"When are you going to marry and give me a grandkid or three?" Barbara would playfully ask, poking her son in the stomach.

"Mom, when I find the right lady, I'll give you a whole mess of grandkids," Mohawk replied, kissing his mother on the cheek.

Ted Jones was also glad to have his son back home, mostly because they had a large garage to clean out and Mohawk's physical strength was an asset to move the heavy stuff. Mohawk did this without complaint since he was lucky to have a dad like Ted. Many of the kids he grew up with had harsh fathers, angry men who disciplined violently via a belt or their fists but Ted never raised a finger to his son. Maybe it was because Mohawk was adopted and Ted, who couldn't have a biological child with Barbara, saw him as a blessing in his life. Why would he want to hurt a blessing?

These few weeks with his parents were just the tonic Mohawk needed to get his life in order. He got clean, his muscles returned as his dad put him to work, and he just felt good about himself. Mohawk even went on a few dates with women he reconnected with from high school. Nothing serious but it was nice to be a normal person again, doing normal things.

Maybe it's time to finish up, Mohawk had thought a few times in regards to his wrestling career. He was still relatively healthy and had a decent nest egg he had accrued over the last decade. It should have been more but the party lifestyle on the road was not a cheap one. Still, Mohawk could definitely see himself laying down roots somewhere and living a peaceful existence. It wasn't a bad idea at all.

And then Mr. Sanada died.

The news hit Mohawk hard, like if one of his parents had passed away. Mr. Sanada, a heavy smoker, had been dealing with lung cancer and Mohawk cursed him (immediately regretting it afterward) for not telling him he was sick. After chatting with his wife Christine, a woman from Nebraska who Mr. Sanada had met during a vacation in Hawaii and was married to for nearly forty years, Mohawk discovered that the cancer came swiftly for his mentor.

"He didn't want anyone to know," Christine told Mohawk at the funeral, which was in Scottsdale, Arizona, where she and her husband had settled with their family. "Especially you. He was always so proud of you, Morris. You were his pride and joy in wrestling. The world champion he trained."

Mohawk wept openly at this and hugged Christine tight. The funeral was attended by some pro wrestling personalities like Kenya and Stan Victory but Mohawk paid them some basic courtesy, kept his distance, and just grieved quietly by himself. Cobra Tara Singh was also there but the two avoided each other, still having heat from the match where Mohawk beat Cobra for the world title.

When Mohawk looked at his deceased trainer in his open casket, he was pleased to see the man looked as sturdy in death as he did in life.

"Goodbye, sensei," Mohawk said softly, bowing to Mr. Sanada as he did so.

A few weeks later, Mohawk headed to Japan for a tour.

He felt he needed to, to pay respect to Mr. Sanada by wrestling in the man's native country. Mr. Sanada had become an American citizen many years before but he always kept strong ties to Japan, which had probably the most respected wrestling culture on the planet. Professional wrestling was treated as honorable there and the Japanese wrestlers and fans were regarded as the best in the world. Needless to say, when Mohawk arrived in Tokyo, he knew he had to bring his "A" game or else he would be shit on immediately.

In hindsight, Mohawk believed he should have had some warm-up matches before flying over to Japan since he hadn't wrestled much since leaving Stan Victory's employ. He wasn't in "wrestling shape" and his first opponent, a hot-tempered young martial artist-turned-wrestler named Hideo Kobayashi, didn't take it easy on him. Most Japanese wrestlers were respectful of "gaijin", or foreign, veteran wrestlers but Kobayashi wasn't one of them. He saw his match as an opportunity to make a name for himself against a former world champion and he tore into Mohawk from the onset.

The bell rang and Kobayashi went on the offensive. He fired hard kicks and chops at Mohawk, nailing him in the abdomen and chest. The Japanese fans were usually quiet and respectful during matches, almost eerily so, but Mohawk could hear their gasps with every blow Kobayashi hit him with.

"Slow the fuck down!" Mohawk said to Kobayashi, shoving him into the corner. Kobayashi had avoided him backstage so Mohawk didn't even meet him before the match. Kobayashi didn't speak English, either, although the universal language of pro wrestling while two performers were in the ring was enough for them to communicate.

Unfortunately, Kobayashi wasn't up for listening to whatever Mohawk had to say. He kept on kicking at Mohawk, working his legs, and Mohawk was definitely feeling the shots.

This fucker is trying to cripple me, he thought, whipping Kobayashi into the ropes and hitting him with a solid shoulder tackle. Mohawk was definitely stronger but Kobayashi was a trained fighter. If things broke down into a real brawl, Mohawk wasn't sure he could take the kid.

Even so, he wasn't going to let Kobayashi continue to unload on him. It was time to fight back. Mohawk didn't have the lightning-fast kicks that Kobayashi had in his arsenal but he did have some stiff forearms and he reared back, nailing Kobayashi a few times in the jaw before walloping him with a brutal clothesline. This knocked Kobayashi to the mat and his eyes rolled back in his head. Mohawk had rung his bell and didn't feel great about it since he was always taught to protect your opponent and not hurt them…but at least Kobayashi now knew that the American he was in the ring with was no pushover.

There would be no war dances in this match. This was a fucking fight.

The fans clapped vigorously for Mohawk, showing their appreciation for his "fighting spirit". The rest of the match went very well as Kobayashi became more cooperative and worked a much safer style. By the end of the twenty-five-minute bout, the spectators were on their feet as the end result was a double count-out. No one had won but the match was so hot that Tanaka-san, the head booker of the Japanese company Mohawk was working for, clapped excitedly for him in the locker room.

"Very good!" Tanaka-san shouted with a thumbs-up. Mohawk, bruised, sweaty and wearing a towel around his waist, bowed back and gave a thumbs-up himself. He was the only foreigner on the tour but the other Japanese wrestlers gave him respect for his match and even Kobayashi did so, bowing and mumbling an apology for his rudeness. Mohawk accepted this and the two shook hands.

The rest of the tour was a whirlwind, ten dates in fourteen days, and for Mohawk, the matches were just as brutal as the first one with Kobayashi. These Japanese wrestlers were no joke…they wrestled almost every match like it was their last and it wasn't easy for Mohawk to keep up with them. He did his best and Tanaka-san seemed pleased so Mohawk must have been doing something right.

Tanaka-san paired Mohawk with a young trainee named Shiro, an affable kid who was skinny but tall for a Japanese man. Shiro showed Mohawk around Tokyo, hitting some bars and other hotspots. Mohawk drank to excess many times during this, often to quell the growing loneliness in him as a non-Japanese speaker in the country and to deal with his aching body. He was also offered the companionship of many Japanese girls but mostly turned it down. Mohawk was in such pain that he couldn't really perform sexually. And it was the last thing he wanted. Deep down, all Mohawk really wanted was to go back to his hotel room and sleep.

The Japanese tour ended with a rematch at the famed Tokyo Dome with Kobayashi. It wasn't the main event of the show but that was fine with Mohawk. He also learned from Shiro that Kobayashi was being primed for a major title run, which is why he really laid in his strikes on Mohawk. The kid had a lot of eyes on him and couldn't afford any missteps. Mohawk understood and during their match, he gave Kobayashi a ton of offense and sold his ass off for him. At the end, Kobayashi hit him with a sensational spinning kick off the ropes followed by a top rope flip, the prettiest moonsault Mohawk had ever seen when he watched the match back later on, and pinned Mohawk for the one, two, three. The fans roared in approval and Kobayashi bowed deeply to Mohawk afterward in the middle of the ring, a sign of incredible respect. The match was runner-up for best of the year in Japan and made Mohawk somewhat of a wrestling legend in the country.

His big moment now over, Kobayashi left the ring immediately, allowing Mohawk to wave goodbye to the audience. He received a stirring ovation and enjoyed it greatly but also learned a very bitter truth at the same time.

Mohawk Jones was not done with professional wrestling yet.

On the long flight back to the States, Mohawk considered his future. He wanted to wrestle full-time again but not for Stan Victory. The money would be good with Stan and maybe Mohawk might even get another world title run, this time being better equipped to handle it. However, the schedule would be awful and possibly destructive. So returning to the Victory fold was out.

Mohawk considered wrestling in Mexico and Puerto Rico. They were definitely interesting territories where a lot of fun could be had. However, the money wasn't much and the fans could be troublesome. Mohawk had learned of how some wrestlers had been robbed, beaten up, and even stabbed after the shows. Maybe if he was younger, Mohawk would entertain this kind of thing but he was too much of a veteran now to do so.

The southern states were always solid for professional wrestling but Mohawk didn't want to deal with the politics. Most of these companies were run by the sons of promoters and these guys were brats who were only interested in getting themselves over as stars. Plus, the shows were boring with plodding in-ring styles so even though Mohawk liked the southern fans, he didn't like most southern professional wrestling.

There was one territory that was on fire, which was in Philadelphia. Philly always had a more hard-hitting style and even though working on Japan was painful, Mohawk appreciated the intensity of it. He felt rejuvenated and wanted to show off his new lease on pro wrestling in Philly's main company, which was the MWA, or the Maximum Wrestling Alliance. The MWA was mostly made of wrestlers who couldn't make it in Stan Victory's company but were carving out their own niche. Some of the storylines were a bit risqué, with lots of sex and violence that Mohawk was uncomfortable with, but the actual matches and atmosphere were amazing. As soon as he arrived back at his New York apartment, Mohawk called up the MWA promoter Clay Hopping.

"Clay Hopping here," the man said, sounding out of breath.

"Hey Clay," Mohawk said. "This is Mohawk Jones."

"Yeah, right."

Clay almost hung up but Mohawk spoke up again.

"Not kidding you, Clay," he said. "It really is me."

"Holy shit," Clay said excitedly. "Mohawk fucking Jones!"

Mohawk smiled. Clay Hopping was known as one of the brightest minds in professional wrestling but also a huge fan of the history of the sport.

"Yeah, I'm wondering if you've got a spot for me," Mohawk said tentatively.

"You're joking, right?" Clay said. "You want to come work for me? For MWA?"

"I like what you're doing. Can you book me for a few matches?"

"I can do better than that, Mr. Jones. You're in my next main event."

A month later, Mohawk drove himself down to Philly and found himself matched up with Sammy Santana, one of MWA's brash young stars. Sammy was known as a new breed of "high-flyer", a wrestler with mainly top rope moves. Many old-timers didn't like this kind of wrestling but Mohawk thought it looked incredible and was easy to work with. All he had to do was be there to catch Sammy when he did his thing. One thing Mohawk prided himself on was that he still had impeccable timing and footwork in the ring and that would mesh well with a kid like Sammy, who would make Mohawk's power moves appear devastating.

The MWA arena was a small building that housed about a thousand fans but they were very vocal and they knew their wrestling. When Mohawk stepped through that curtain for the main event, just like Clay had promised, he got a rousing reaction but he knew had to wrestle hard tonight. These fans were hardcore and they wouldn't be polite if he just wrestled like a cartoon character.

Like with that first match with Kobayashi in Japan, there would be no war dances on this night, just a straight-up, down the middle wrestling match. Mohawk brought his best, as did Sammy, and by the end of the match, which Mohawk won with his trademark powerslam, the fans gave both a standing ovation.

However, to Mohawk, this was just another match. Nevertheless, it was nice to work for MWA and he had a good time for the seven months he was exclusive to the company. Clay had protected Mohawk well by booking him strong, paid him on time (not always the case with some of the smaller promoters) and even booked him to face the MWA champion Rugs MacIntosh. Mohawk lost that match but was happy to give Rugs' career a boost since the kid was so respectful both in and out of the ring.

Even so, MWA was just a footnote in Mohawk Jones' storied wrestling career. To him, spending so much time in Philly was more notable for the brief love affair he had there.

Linda.

Mohawk met her at a coffee shop after the matches one night. After his tour of Japan and months of wrestling in MWA, Mohawk's gloominess over failing in his world title run was returning to him. He thought he would have gotten over it after escaping the wrestling business and spending some time at his childhood home but being back in the thick of things resulted in it all rushing back to him. Plus, Mr. Sanada's death was still weighing heavy on his heart. He was happy the man had been proud of him but wished he had the opportunity to honor him somehow, maybe just a dinner at a nice restaurant to tell him that he had changed his life with his wisdom and instruction.

The coffee shop was just around the corner from the hotel Clay had put him in and Mohawk brooded over a piece of pecan pie. It was past midnight and he was the only one sitting in the place, except for a harried-looking woman who was nervously sipping from a mug as she read, wrote on and jostled a bunch of papers on her table, which was just a few feet from Mohawk.

The noise the lady was making was starting to annoy Mohawk and he glanced over at the woman several times, hoping she would look up, see his scowl, and knock it off. She never did so Mohawk cleared his throat and coughed a few times. This didn't work, either.

All Mohawk wanted was some peace and quiet. So he got up to leave the shop to return to his hotel room, hoping that the younger wrestlers staying on his floor weren't being so rowdy and loud now. He knew that after a wrestling show, most performers were still amped-up, which resulted in massive partying. Mohawk himself was an off-hours legend in his prime, sometimes not even sleeping the whole night before having to catch an early flight or hitting the road at six in the morning to get to the next show.

"Sorry," the woman said to Mohawk, not looking up from her work. "I know I'm kicking up a ton of ruckus. I just gotta finish grading these damn exams." She smiled at Mohawk. The woman wasn't conventionally pretty but had an intelligent look about her, soft brown hair with a sharp nose and striking gray eyes. She was probably in her late twenties and Mohawk felt warmed by her immediately.

"It's okay," he said, awkwardly smiling back. He then glanced at the paper piles on the woman's table. "Looks like you've got a lot there." Mohawk looked at the nearly empty coffee cup. "Let me get them to refill that."

"No, you don't have to do that," the woman said.

"Don't worry about it."

Mohawk gestured to the waitress, who grouchily shuffled over and filled the mug. The woman took a grateful draught and grinned.

"Thanks," she said to Mohawk. "I'm Linda."

"I'm Moha, uh, Morris," Mohawk said. It felt odd introducing himself with his real name.

Mohawk left right after this, paying the waitress and telling her to bring some pecan pie to Linda after he had exited. He had a match the next day to rest up for but couldn't get the woman from the coffee shop out of his head when he went to bed or even during his rematch with Sammy Santana in front of twelve hundred fans.

Linda.

Mohawk couldn't help himself and returned to the coffee shop the next three nights. Linda didn't show up and Mohawk even walked around the neighborhood a few times, hoping for a glimpse of her. Maybe she lived nearby?

On the fourth evening, Mohawk ordered a slice of the pecan pie, which admittedly wasn't very good, and finally, he saw Linda again. She spotted Mohawk immediately and hurried over to his table.

"Hi!" she said, sitting down without an invitation. "I'm glad I got to see you again. Thanks for the pie!" Linda appeared giddy. "Sorry, I'm a bit hyped...I finished grading those tests and now I'm free!" She then frowned. "Uh, what was your name again?"

"Morris," Mohawk said, which came out more easily this time. "And you're Linda."

"I am!"

Linda was a graduate student at a local college that Mohawk had never heard of. She was finishing up a degree and explained her scholastic focus, something about psychology, which bewildered Mohawk. He didn't care, though. He just wanted to get to know this woman better.

So he did.

They went from the coffee shop to a nearby bar for a drink and then got cheesesteaks at a local dive right after. Mohawk wasn't too interested in Linda's school life but he loved hearing her just go on and on. She was clearly a chatterbox and enjoyed that he was a good listener.

Not once did Mohawk mention that he was a professional wrestler and Linda didn't seem to know that he was a celebrity. He was thankful that during this spontaneous date, they hadn't bumped into any wrestling fans. When Linda did ask him what he did for a living, he shrugged and just said, "salesman". This seemed to satisfy her enough.

What surprised Mohawk is that he didn't feel any desire to get Linda in bed that night. He definitely found her attractive but he also enjoyed just being with her. She seemed to feel the same, nuzzling against him as they walked together through the Philly streets, which were mostly deserted. Normally, this might be a somewhat risky proposition but Mohawk was a big dude. No one was going to fuck with him and Linda appeared to recognize this.

"You're huge," she said with a laugh as they turned a corner. "Did you play football?"

"Yeah," Mohawk said. "In high school. Defensive line."

"I knew it!"

She giggled, making some joke about how she never even went to her high school's football games, preferring to spend time in a library. Mohawk wondered if he would have even known of Linda's existence if they went to high school together. Probably not.

"I want to see you again," Mohawk blurted out suddenly.

"Sure, how about tomorrow night?" Linda said. "Meet you at Mel's? Same time as tonight? I'm a night owl...hope you are, too."

Mel's was the name of the coffee shop. Mohawk nodded eagerly to the suggestion and Linda then left him with a kiss on the cheek, heading to her bus that was just arriving at its stop. Mohawk wanted to go after Linda, pick her up in his arms, kiss her passionately, and carry her off to his hotel. Instead, he waved goodbye and she blew a kiss at him before hopping on the bus.

The next couple of nights had some tough matches for Mohawk. He was distracted by thoughts of Linda and his wrestling performances, at least in his estimation, were subpar. Luckily, the MWA audience and Clay Hopping didn't seem to care. The tickets were sold and the fans were surprisingly happy just to see a former world champion do his thing. Mohawk was coasting on his reputation, which is something he never wanted to do, but at this point of his life, he didn't mind too much.

Spending time with Linda was the only thing he wanted right now.

They went to some nice restaurants and even a night club, sleeping together on their third date, which is also when Mohawk revealed to Linda that he was a professional wrestler. At first, she looked stunned, and then she burst out in laughter, which hurt Mohawk's feelings, until she kissed him and begged to be taken to his next match. This would be the trilogy match against Sammy Santana, which Mohawk was thankful for, since Sammy would definitely make him look good. During the match, Mohawk looked for Linda in the crowd, making sure she had a great view of the action. Not ringside, since that was where MWA's rowdiest fans were, but just off to the side. Before the show, Mohawk had taken Linda backstage to introduce her to the other wrestlers and he beamed at how she, a complete wrestling novice, was respectful to everyone. As a result, Rugs MacIntosh, the gentleman that he was, asked his wife Tanya to keep Linda company when the show was on.

In the heat of the match, Sammy accidentally caught Mohawk with a kick to the right temple, which causes a temporary bout of vision blurriness so he couldn't truly see if Linda was enjoying his match. It cleared up when he got backstage and Tanya had brought Linda over to meet him in the corridor near the men's locker room. To his dismay, Linda wasn't that impressed with the wrestling and more concerned about his well-being, particularly the ugly bruise on his head where the apologetic Sammy had nailed him. However, when they got back at his hotel room and Linda iced his injury as he lay his head in her lap, she became excited.

"I really liked how you picked him up and threw him around so easily!" Linda exclaimed.

This caused Mohawk to laugh and he explained some of the intricacies of wrestling such as how Sammy purposely made himself "go up", becoming lighter so it was easier for him to carry him for his moves. Also how punches were made to look like they were thrown hard but there was an art to them, such as how fists were held loose, which wouldn't hurt when they connected. With the kick that Sammy had thrown, it was an honest mistake, which happened every now and then.

Linda seemed to enjoy getting a peek behind the professional wrestling curtain and after they made love, Mohawk wondered if the heat he was feeling in his heart as he watched Linda sleep was genuine.

Unfortunately, this ended up being the highlight of Mohawk's romantic connection with Linda. The wrestling world is cruel when it came to personal relationships and after Mohawk's run with MWA, he was off to Germany for a month to wrestle some of Europe's best while Linda was in Vermont to spend time with family. They drifted apart soon after and truth be told, Mohawk hadn't thought of Linda very much in the years that had passed.

They did re-connect briefly in the early 2000s when Linda came to a small show Mohawk had done in Philly, went on a couple dates, and then went their separate ways for good. So it was completely possible that Linda had become pregnant during these trysts, the product of which was now sleeping in his basement. They hadn't used protection that last night they were together and Linda was too proud a woman to try to track down the globetrotting professional wrestler that had knocked her up.

So now what do I do? Mohawk thought, lying in his bed and completely wide awake.

CHAPTER 15

The next morning, Mohawk awoke with the same old aches in his back, shoulders and hips. However, his right knee was also screaming and he winced, knowing that sooner or later, he would have to get the joint replaced. Going through a surgery with a difficult rehab and recovery was not something Mohawk was looking forward to and he hoped the pain would go away, like it would have in his younger days, but it probably wasn't going to happen.

"I don't heal up like I used to," he said out loud for some reason before limping his way to the bathroom. He urinated and then brushed his teeth before washing his face. Mohawk then went back to his bedroom and stretched as best as he could. He groaned and moaned with each exercise, trying his best to touch his toes from a standing position but his lower back was too tight and his stomach too big to really bend over.

Mohawk sighed. He knew that all his physical problems were because of his wrestling days. Too many hard landings on the canvas, which was just planks of wood with a very thin "cushion" over it. Mohawk had once heard a fellow wrestler describe "bumping" in a ring like landing on a pool table, both hard surfaces with little to no give. Years of flying dropkicks and taking backdrops had added up and now Mohawk was paying for it.

At least he had tried to keep up with his physical fitness as best he could. Cobra hadn't exercised in years and was in far worse shape. The man didn't seem to care, though.

Mohawk changed into a gray sweatshirt with navy blue sweatpants and a pair of white socks. It wasn't easy to pull the socks on but it was worth the discomfort. Mohawk didn't like trudging around the house barefoot. His feet got cold.

He went downstairs to the kitchen and saw that Emily was already there, sitting at a table and eating cereal. Mohawk smiled upon seeing her. It felt good to have her in his home. Everything seemed a little brighter in the place now.

Emily had her hair pulled back, scrolling through her phone. She was dressed in pajama bottoms with a hoodie and like her old man, white socks, although Emily's footwear had yellow stars on them. She heard Mohawk coming and smiled at him.

"Good morning," she said cheerily.

"Morning," Mohawk said back.

He eyed her cereal, which was Honey Nut Cheerios, and winced.

"Don't eat that," Mohawk said.

"How come?" Emily asked.

"Did you get it from the pantry? Isn't it stale?"

Emily shrugged.

"It's not so bad," she said. She then became apologetic. "Sorry. I wanted to make you something to surprise you but…I'm not much of a cook."

"That's alright," Mohawk said. "I'm not much of a breakfast guy. Give me a minute and I'll join you."

He went to the pantry and pulled out the Weetabix. This was a breakfast "biscuit" from England and Cobra suggested they get it from the supermarket. Cobra really enjoyed Weetabix, a fiber-based cereal full of grains, oats and that kind of stuff. You plop the biscuit into a bowl, pour some milk on it and there's your breakfast. Not much in terms of flavor but Mohawk didn't mind it.

He took his Weetabix and sat at the table with Emily. Right away, she put her phone away, which impressed Mohawk.

Kid's got manners, he thought, taking his first spoonful of his soggy Weetabix.

"How'd you sleep?" Mohawk asked.

"Pretty good," Emily replied, yawning.

"Not too cold down there?"

"Nah. I was fine. It was a bit weird, though…"

"Oh?"

Emily leaned back, taking a spoonful of Cheerios. Mohawk waited. He could tell she had something on her mind that she wanted to share but was being careful about it.

"I could see all the stuff you did in your life," Emily finally said. "In your career. You've done so much and you've seen so much in the world…you went to Japan!" She became sullen. "Feels like I haven't done anything in my life yet."

Mohawk wasn't used to doling out fatherly advice but here was a prime opportunity to show if he could.

"You got time," Mohawk said, trying his best to sound comforting. "You're still real young." He smiled. "You have any plans? For your future?"

"Kinda," Emily said.

"Yeah? Tell me."

"I can't."

Mohawk had forgotten his Weetabix, which was getting mushier by the second.

"Why can't you tell me?" he asked.

Mohawk watched as Emily lifted her bowl and slurped the milk. She didn't see that Mohawk was staring hard at her.

A buzz came from Emily's phone and she read the text message.

"Huh," she said. "The Flyers just fired their coach."

"You're a hockey fan?" Mohawk asked.

"A little. They look like they'll be pretty shitty for a while. Not happy they traded Giroux away. He was my favorite. But they're rebuilding so it'll be okay. Maybe they'll get some stud draft pick in the next year."

Mohawk didn't know much about the NHL (he was a football guy himself) but he made a mental note to try to learn about the Philadelphia Flyers when he had a chance. Just as something to bond with Emily about. Maybe they could go watch a game together.

"Dad?" Emily said tentatively.

And there it was. She dropped the D-word. Mohawk's eyes widened but he kept his cool.

Then he smiled. Mohawk liked the way "Dad" sounded coming from Emily and yeah, he was this girl's father. Mohawk knew it and was happy about it.

"Yeah?" he asked.

"I want...to be a wrestler," Emily said. She didn't quite blurt this out but it sure felt like she did.

"What?"

"And I want you to train me."

"What?"

Mohawk saw the frown creep across Emily's face.

"Really hoped you'd be more excited," she said.

Now it was Mohawk's turn to frown.

"How the hell did you expect me to react?" he said, his voice rising. "You show up here, out of nowhere, me not knowing that you even existed, and now you want me to train you to be a wrestler? Are you out of your damn mind?"

Mohawk knew he had stepped over the line with his words. It was the kind of thing that might alienate Emily from him when he just got her in his life.

Fortunately, Emily nodded.

"You're right," she said. "It's unfair for me to drop all of this on you." She smiled. "Too much, too soon."

"Yeah! Way too much!" Mohawk said, and they both laughed.

Emily leaned back in her chair, looking thoughtful.

"You know why I didn't want to touch your championship belt yesterday?" she asked. "Because I haven't earned it. The only belt I wanna touch is the one I win myself."

"You do know that wrestling's worked, right?" Mohawk asked. It was a silly question to pose to Emily but Mohawk had come across his share of fans who believed everything about professional wrestling was a "shoot", or real.

Emily rolled her eyes.

"Yes, Dad," she said, with a hint of annoyance. "I know wrestling's fake."

"Not fake," Mohawk said. "The bumps hurt. A lot."

Emily said nothing, a cue that she wanted her dad to continue.

"Wrestling fucking hurts, Emily," Mohawk said, with full seriousness. He hadn't meant to curse but it felt necessary to do so. "It's a brutal business on your body. And it's scummy, too. There's a lot of people in wrestling who are looking to screw you over, both for your money and because it's fun for them."

"There's people like that in every business," Emily countered.

"Yeah, there is."

Mohawk sighed.

"I don't want my kid to be involved with wrestling," he said. "I wasn't there to protect you when you were younger…but I can protect you now."

Emily flushed at this.

"So you're saying…no?" she said brokenly.

Mohawk sighed again.

"Dad, can you stop doing that?" Emily said.

"What?" Mohawk asked.

"Those deep breaths every time you're about to say something. It's hella annoying."

"Sorry."

Mohawk fought back another sigh as Emily stared hard at him. It wasn't easy avoiding her fierce eyes, her gaze almost overpowering him and causing his armpits to feel a little sweaty.

"Let me think about this," he said quickly, trying to cut the tension. "I have to...really think..."

"You are eating my Weetabix!"

Both Mohawk and Emily turned to see a scowling Cobra Tara Singh, standing in the doorway of the kitchen.

"There's more Weetabix in the damn box," Mohawk said testily, although he was glad that Cobra was here now. Hopefully he would distract Emily for a short time while he figured out a way to dissuade her from professional wrestling.

"What is goings on here?" Cobra said, obviously aware something was amiss.

"My dad's pissing me off, Uncle Cobra," Emily said, her eyes not moving from Mohawk's face.

Cobra beamed hearing Emily's words.

"Uncle Cobra," he repeated happily. "I like very much."

Emily tore her glare away from her father to smile at Cobra.

"I want to be a wrestler," she said. Emily then pointed at Mohawk. "He won't let me."

"What?!" Cobra said.

He threw the Weetabix box across the room, over the heads of the others. Some wheat debris flew into the air, falling upon the table and the tiled floor.

"Now hold on a minute," Mohawk said, holding up his hands.

"You shush!" Cobra roared. Now he was the one pointing, his wrinkly brown finger extended towards Emily. "This beautiful young girl wants to become a wrestler...and you say no?!"

"Yeah, I say no!" Mohawk said, feeling defensive. "You know how messed up the industry is! I don't want her in it!"

Cobra promptly took a seat right beside Mohawk, his hands on the man's shoulder's.

"We will train!" he cried. "She...um...what...is..."

"Emily," Emily said, reminding Cobra.

"Yes! Emily! She will become a champion! And very rich!"

Cobra hopped back on his feet, almost dancing.

"Lady wrestling!" he said. "It is very good now! Emily will be legend!"

"Hell yeah!" Emily shouted, jumping up. "I wanna be a legend! And a champion! And rich, too!"

"We will all be rich!"

Emily and Cobra high-fived and Mohawk stared blankly at them.

"You two are insane," he said tiredly. "I can't let you do this."

Emily knelt down beside Mohawk. He felt his daughter's small hands against his cheeks as she maneuvered him to look deeply into her eyes.

"Dad," she said softly. "This is my dream. You gotta help me."

"I can't," Mohawk said. "I have to protect you."

"Then protect me. Teach me everything you know. So I can avoid all the stuff you're worrying about. That way I'll be safe and won't make any mistakes."

"I will teach, too!" Cobra said, rubbing his hands eagerly.

Mohawk stayed quiet, his mind processing everything.

She's gonna do this, with or without you, he thought. Mohawk saw the level of determination within his daughter. She came all the way to meet the father she never knew to chase her dream.

That takes balls. And at least if she learns through me, I can make sure no one takes advantage of her.

Even so, Mohawk didn't want Emily to win that easily. She had a long road ahead of her and the first lesson he had to teach her was that she couldn't persuade her old man every time she desired something. Mohawk didn't want his daughter to have that kind of power over him.

"I'm gonna take a walk," he said, standing up. "I'll be back."

"When will that be?" Emily asked.

"When I'm back."

Mohawk strode to the front door, his head up and shoulders square, put on his comfortable, arch-supporting Skechers, and left the townhouse without another word. Once outside, Mohawk went straight to the park and sat on a bench. There was a chill in the air but everything was nice and quiet, a few bundled-up joggers and cyclists on the pathways but overall, the park was deserted.

The perfect atmosphere for Mohawk to consider what his daughter was asking of him.

Beyond the physical toll professional wrestling can take on a body, Mohawk thought of the sordid side of the industry. Drug and alcohol abuse was the big one that worried him. He had seen so many wrestlers lose their way, or their lives, to addiction and outside of some fans, no one gave a shit. There was no medical insurance or pension plan in wrestling. You have to take care of yourself.

At the same time, Mohawk had noticed that the business had been getting better, at least compared to his heyday. Wrestlers were in better shape due to exercise, nutrition, and rest, while finding alternate streams of revenue, like social media endorsements and merchandise, so they didn't have to rely on a promoter, who would most likely fuck them over. The money was alright, not as good as it should be in the big companies, although some independent shows were paying top dollar for talent.

We could do it the right way, Mohawk thought, his hands behind his head as he stared at an unused basketball court near him. *Make sure she doesn't make the same mistakes me and Cobra made.*

Then Mohawk felt a sharp pain in his shoulder due to his arms being up and stretched backwards. Even sitting like this was taxing on his body. He grimaced.

I don't want her to be hurting like I do. It's not worth it.

Mohawk had made up his mind. He loved Emily...wow, he really did...but because of this, he couldn't watch her throw her life away for wrestling. He would do his best to persuade her to change her mind and chase another, safer, dream.

I gave my life to wrestling and all I am is a sad and angry old man.

"Hello!" a cheery voice said, accompanied by the sound of rubber wheels on the gravel path near Mohawk. He turned and spotted the smiling young mom, pushing the stroller that Mohawk always saw her with, her wide-eyed baby staring all around while seated inside. The child, dressed in a blue and red Superman onesie, locked eyes with Mohawk and he forced up a smile.

"Hi," Mohawk said.

"Can I sit beside you there?" the young mom asked.

"Sure."

Mohawk scooted over and the young mom took a seat. She sighed tiredly, steering the stroller in front of her so she could keep an eye on her baby, who still stared at Mohawk.

"He loves the morning walks," the young mom said. "One of the only things that calms him down."

Mohawk didn't know what to say to this. So he just nodded.

"I don't think we've really been introduced to each other," the young mom said.

"I'm Morris," Mohawk said.

"And my name's…Karen."

The young mom let this linger in the air, clearly expecting some kind of reaction but Mohawk had no idea of the negative present-day connotation of the woman's name.

"Nice to meet you, Karen," he said.

Karen relaxed just as her little boy gurgled in his seat. Both she and Mohawk stared at the child, his mother swiftly wiping some drool from his mouth.

"Is it hard?" Mohawk asked. "Taking care of a baby?"

"What do you mean?" Karen asked in return. "You've never done it? What about that girl at your house? Your daughter?"

"I wasn't around when she was young."

"Oh."

Karen brightened.

"It's the best thing I've ever done," she said proudly. "But it's definitely a lot of work. Not really the physical part of feeding, changing and all that stuff, but more the mental part of it."

"Mental?" Mohawk asked, very much interested.

"Yeah. Like always being aware where they are and what they're doing and that they don't hurt themselves. That's the exhausting part."

Mohawk nodded. No one had really presented parenthood to him in this way.

"I'm lucky, though," Karen continued. "I've got good help from this little guy's dad. He's hands-on although he doesn't like the stroller walks in the park. So we made a deal. He handles the laundry and I do the walks."

She laughed and Mohawk smiled. It was nice talking to a person who seemed genuinely happy with their life.

He looked down at the baby again, who yawned, seemingly fighting the urge to fall asleep, the kid's movements sluggish and his eyelids heavy.

"You ever think about what he's going to be when he's a grown-up?" Mohawk asked.

"All the time," Karen replied. "My husband wants him to be a college professor like he is. He's already trying to get him to read." She chuckled again. "I just want him to be passionate about whatever he decides to do. Oh, and be a good person, too, of course."

"Of course, yeah."

Karen stayed with Mohawk for a few more minutes, chatting about parenting and baby stuff, before heading off to administer her son's next feeding. Mohawk himself stayed in the park, walking a lap around the grounds for exercise, which did help his bad knee, and then made his way home. Emily and Cobra were waiting for him, seated on the front steps.

"Did you make up your mind?" Emily asked, not wasting time. "About me wrestling?"

"I did," Mohawk replied.

He stood before his daughter, staring hard at her. Mohawk didn't bother to glance at Cobra but could tell the man was also waiting anxiously for the verdict.

"I'm going to train you," Mohawk said evenly. He saw Emily's eyes light up, bracing herself to deliver a flying hug, so he put his hand in front to stop her in her tracks. "But we're going to do it my way. The old-school way. At first. And then see where you are and if you've got what it takes."

This did nothing to quell Emily's excitement and she bounded forward, embracing her father tightly.

"Yes yes yes!" she squealed. "Thank you thank you thank you, Dad!"

"It's not gonna be easy," Mohawk warned.

"I know! But I'm crazy serious about this! I really am!"

"You might end up hating me."

"I would never! You're my dad!"

Mohawk sighed, enjoying the hug. Emily was delirious with joy, chattering away, and he couldn't help but imagine his daughter, standing victorious in a wrestling ring, holding up the world title...

Stop, he told himself. *One step at a time.*

Mohawk then felt an extra pair of arms joining into the hug.

"This is a wonderful moment!" Cobra exclaimed. "I cannot wait to join the training!"

"Oh yeah?" Mohawk said.

"Yes! I am the Uncle Cobra! I am very very very excited! Chaalo, let's go!"

CHAPTER 16

Cobra's excitement carried over to the next morning. He was the first one awake in the townhouse, heading over to Mohawk's bedroom at around five-thirty a.m., dressed in a black tracksuit.

"Chaalo, Mohawk!" the old man bellowed from the hallway in front of Mohawk's door. "Time for the training!"

Mohawk groaned. He was already awake, and had been for about twenty minutes, planning the agenda for the day. Even so, hearing a giddy Cobra's raspy voice so early and so loud, was still irritating.

"I'm coming, dammit!" Mohawk shot back. He got off the bed, ready to go in a tracksuit of his own. Mohawk did a quick appraisal of his body, as he did every morning, and found his various aches were raging less than they usually were. Maybe it was the fact that he had something new to look forward to today.

Mohawk opened the door and saw the grinning Cobra, the man's hands on his hips. Cobra was wearing a fresh-looking green turban and it looked like he had combed his white beard, which wasn't so straggly.

"This is a good day," Cobra said happily.

"We'll see," Mohawk responded, keeping his enthusiasm at bay.

It was definitely there, though.

Both men made their way down the stairs. It was still dark in the house as the sun hadn't made its daily ascent yet so they switched on the lights. When they got to the front hallway, they found Emily waiting for them.

"Good morning!" she said, too jubilantly for Mohawk's tastes. They were about to embark on some serious business and he wanted Emily to approach it in such a way. Fortunately, Cobra was on the same wavelength, his big smile gone as he greeted Emily with a simple grunt.

"Morning," Mohawk said gravely. "Ready to get to work?"

"I'm ready!" Emily said, turning towards the door. "I'm guessing we'll get breakfast on the way? Let's get moving then!"

"Wait."

Mohawk watched as Emily turned around. She was wearing blue sweatpants with white sneakers and a basic red tee. Decent work-out clothes.

"Where do you think we're going?" Mohawk asked his daughter.

Emily appeared confused by the question.

"I'm...not sure," she replied. "Maybe some gym with a wrestling ring?"

At this, Cobra burst out laughing.

"Oh no, no, no," he said. "You are not ready."

"I'm not?" Emily said.

"No," Mohawk answered. "You're not."

He looked Emily up and down.

"How tall are you?" he asked.

"Five four," Emily replied.

"How much do you weigh?"

"One thirty-five...okay, maybe one forty."

Mohawk nodded at this, glancing at Cobra.

"Fat," Cobra said.

"Hey!" Emily said. "I'm healthy!"

Mohawk studied his daughter some more.

"You look like you're in decent shape," he said. "Did you do any sports? Growing up? Or in high school?"

Emily bit her lip and looked down.

"Um, not really," she said. "I made the basketball team in junior year but didn't really play much. I try to jog a couple of times a week, too."

"Okay," Mohawk said, not impressed at all. "Have you done any wrestling training? Somewhere else?"

"No."

Mohawk looked at Cobra again, who shook his head. Emily noticed this and became indignant.

"Just because I'm not..." she began.

"Stop," Mohawk said, raising a hand. "It's not a bad thing. We'll just have to start from scratch."

"Yes," Cobra added. "We will train you hard and you will hate us."

"I could never do that," Emily protested.

Both Mohawk and Cobra smiled, almost deviously.

"Alright," Mohawk said. "Let's go to the garage."

The townhouse's garage was a disaster. It was barely ever used, just a dusty, hot and filthy chamber full of grime and cobwebs. Sagging and water-stained brown boxes full of junk, a rusty lawn mower, and broken garden tools sat on the unswept floor. Mohawk couldn't even remember the last time he had actually opened the garage door. However, the garage was surprisingly spacious for a smaller home and a good section of it was cordoned off as an exercise area for Mohawk and Cobra, although it had been quite a while since they had last used it.

"This is where we'll start," Mohawk declared to Emily. He wanted to see if she was going to have some prissy attitude about it but was glad to see that she just nodded, not betraying any sense of disgust or annoyance about the situation.

"Sounds good," she said. "You're the boss."

Mohawk nodded himself and pressed the garage door opener. It squeaked and groaned to life, taking some time to get going due to disuse, but did its job, allowing the morning sun to shine in.

"We have to clean up first," he said.

As Cobra sat on the garage steps watching, Mohawk and Emily took the junk out to the curb and swept the floor. There were some big hairy spiders nesting throughout the garage but Emily handled them with ease, shooing them outside with a dustpan. She never looked squeamish once, which surprised Mohawk, although Cobra shrieked a little at the sight of one arachnid that had crept close to him.

"Maaderchod!" he yelled, trying to squish the spider, which had fled away from him, with his sneaker.

Next, Emily took a soapy rag and a big sponge and scrubbed the gym mats on the floor clean. She wiped them dry with some paper towels as Mohawk pulled off an old sheet in a corner, revealing a rack of ancient-looking dumbbells. Emily grinned upon seeing them.

"Old school," she said, lifting and admiring a ten-pound weight.

"We're going back to basics with you," Mohawk explained. "Start you from the bottom and build you to the top."

"I like the sound of that."

"Good."

Mohawk studied his daughter and could tell that just cleaning the garage had been a tough work-out for her. Still, she seemed keen on continuing, not even asking for some water. Mohawk still asked Cobra to bring them some as Emily had done a good job tidying up and deserved the refreshment. He also didn't want her to pass out before they had actually gotten started.

"That's nice," Emily said as she took a long draught of water. "Thank you, Uncle Cobra."

Cobra grunted again as a response. He pointed at Emily's feet.

"Shoes off," he ordered. "Better for exercise."

Emily dutifully took off her shoes and socks. She stood in the middle of the gym mats, awaiting instruction.

"Let's rock," she said.

Cobra glanced at Mohawk, giving him a signal to begin the day's lesson.

"One of the most important aspects about being a good pro wrestler is cardio," Mohawk began. "It's not always about how big your muscles are, how loud your promo is, or how many cool moves you can do. If you're in good shape, you can hang with anyone in the business."

"Need good cardio," Emily nodded. "Got it."

Just then, a series of buzzes came from Emily's pocket. She pulled out her phone, which annoyed Mohawk.

"Sorry, sorry," Emily said, checking her texts. "It's just a friend from back home..."

"You have no friends!" Cobra barked. "You are a wrestler! Give me!"

Startled, Emily tossed her phone to Cobra, who lifted his hand to throw it against the wall.

"Stop," Mohawk said calmly. "You don't need to do that."

"Yes," Emily pleaded. "Please don't."

Cobra paused in mid-throw and placed Emily's phone in his pocket. He grunted at her, eyes blazing.

"Push-ups!" he shouted. "You do twenty! Now!"

Emily instantly got down on the mat and Mohawk and Cobra watched her closely. She got through the first ten push-ups easily but then started to falter, her arms shaking.

"You fall...twenty more!" Cobra yelled.

Emily stopped at sixteen push-ups, holding herself in the extended plank position. She looked to her father for help but Mohawk coldly stared back at her.

"You heard him," he said. "You fall...twenty more."

Mohawk saw Emily grit her teeth and she kept on going. She finished her set and stood up, waiting for the next instruction.

"Now you do Punjabi squats!" Cobra said. "They are not Hindu squats...they are Punjabi!"

He demonstrated the exercise for Emily, which involved the arms being extended in front and then rotated backward in a circular motion while doing a squat. Emily began a set of twenty but began to wobble when she hit six.

"Too hard?" Cobra taunted. "I did five hundred, every day! I will show!"

"You don't have to do that," Mohawk said, worried about his roommate's well-being.

"You shut up! I show!"

Mohawk put his hands up and stepped back, giving Cobra some room. Cobra did the Punjabi squats with Emily, finishing their set of twenty together.

"More twenty!" Cobra demanded.

Emily didn't argue, which pleased Mohawk. He knew this squat exercise was no joke and she was going to feel the pain later. Cobra again kept up with Emily, which impressed Mohawk even more.

It went on like this for the next two hours. Simple, archaic exercises to test how fit Emily was but also her resolve. The sweat poured off her and onto the mat but Mohawk and Cobra didn't let up on her at all.

Emily didn't complain, either. She kept her mouth shut and kept on going.

"Now you skip the rope!" Cobra said, tossing an old-school jump rope to Emily, the kind that had wooden handles. Emily smiled, wiping her brow.

"Easy," she said, expertly whipping the jump rope over her, her feet moving perfectly with each little hop. Mohawk and Cobra watched her and then stepped away for a quick chat.

"Well?" Mohawk asked. "What do you think?"

Cobra turned his back on the skipping Emily so she couldn't see the glee on his face.

"She is not in shape," he chuckled. "But she has heart. No complaining. She is a fighter and will not stop." Cobra laughed some more. "This is fun!"

Mohawk could tell that Cobra was enjoying torturing his "niece" so he would have to act as a bulwark if the old man took his training too far. They began to discuss the next stage of the day's work-out when Emily abruptly stopped. She then made her way to the door to the inside the house.

"Eh?" Cobra said angrily. "Where you going?"

Emily sighed.

"I gotta go inside for a minute," she said, not looking at either man.

"Why?" Mohawk asked.

"I have to...go change my pad."

Emily then dashed inside and the confused Mohawk could hear her hurried footsteps. He had to think on her words for a few seconds until he finally understood what his daughter was telling them.

"Oh," he said out loud.

"Oh?" Cobra asked. He still had no clue. "Change her what?"

Mohawk, to his utter dismay, then had to explain to Cobra Tara Singh about it being Emily's "time of the month", which instantly made the old man squeamish.

"Oh," Cobra finally said, swallowing hard.

Needless to say, it was hard for Mohawk and Cobra to make eye contact with Emily when she got back to the garage but she smiled, picked up the jump rope, and got back to skipping.

"I got this!" she shouted, amping up her skipping pace.

And so it went for the next four weeks. Early morning rise, hours of exercise, protein-laden meals, watching television with Mohawk and Cobra in the evenings, and going to bed early every night. Emily hardly complained although she did get testy with her trainers at some points. This was natural since her body was sore all the time. Mohawk expected a blow-up eventually.

"No more fucking skipping!" Emily yelled at Cobra, tossing the jump rope aside. He had effectively ruined her love of skipping rope after countless sessions of it. Cobra appeared shaky from the outburst so Mohawk, who had stepped aside to allow the man to oversee his daughter's physical building up, got back involved.

"Let's take a walk," he suggested to Emily, which she eagerly agreed to, needing to cool off and glad for any easy exercise. The two headed out of the townhouse garage, Emily gingerly making her way along the sidewalk.

"You okay?" Mohawk asked.

"Fine," Emily replied, rubbing her left calf. "My leg's just cramping up."

"Yeah, they'll do that."

Emily shot Mohawk a look but he kept on walking. She caught up and they headed down the street to a small plaza, which had a laundromat, convenience store, and Chinese take-out. Father and daughter said nothing to each other and Mohawk led Emily into Jain's Cigar Shop. Jain's son, a skinny Nepalese teen with a poofy hairstyle watching a soccer game on his phone, was manning the cash register.

"Hello," the boy said politely.

Mohawk nodded in return and went to the refrigerator. He bought a blue Gatorade, paid Jain's son, and gave the bottle to Emily.

"Drink," he said.

Emily did as she was told and both continued walking.

"You need to apologize to Cobra," Mohawk said.

"I know," Emily said sullenly.

"He knows what he's doing."

"I get it. I fucked up."

They rounded the corner, arriving back on Mohawk's street.

"Hey," Emily said. "How am *I* doing anyway?"

Mohawk shrugged as a response, which made Emily frown.

"Do you think I'll be able to, you know, actually wrestle soon?" she asked hopefully.

"We'll see," Mohawk replied. "Ready to get back to work?"

Emily finished her Gatorade and licked her lips.

"Yeah," she said.

When they arrived back at the garage, Cobra was waiting for them. He stared hard at Emily but she walked past him, picked up the jump rope, and took her spot on the gym mats again.

"I'm sorry for what I said, Uncle Cobra," she said with great respect. "I love skipping. I love it so much."

Emily then began jumping rope again, her eyes steely and determined. Cobra glanced at Mohawk and nodded, very pleased.

A couple weeks later, the physical change in Emily was apparent. She had slimmed down and muscled-up, and she knew it, too. She was often in the garage before Mohawk and Cobra, warming up and lifting weights, and added her own exercise routines to Cobra's regimen, such as yoga at night to ease her sore body and aid with recovery, or a jog here and there to augment her cardio.

Mohawk and Cobra observed Emily's progress and both were becoming satisfied with her dedication. She was strong, agile, quick, and her stamina was improving every day. Sometimes they even had to pull her away from the garage so she would stop working out and take a break. Overtraining was now a concern.

"She is ready," Cobra declared as he and Mohawk sat together in the backyard. They had sent Emily off to pick up groceries at the local supermarket, just a few blocks away.

Mohawk nodded. Part of him had hoped that maybe Cobra's demanding training might have scared his daughter off of pro wrestling. If anything, it made her hungrier for it. On her off hours, Mohawk noticed that she would study matches on her phone. He saw that Emily still watched as a fan, not getting the intricacies of wrestling yet...but her body was more than prepared to handle real training.

"Are we doing the right thing here?" Mohawk asked.

"Yes!" Cobra replied, without hesitation. "She will be world champion!"

Mohawk rolled his eyes. He had tamped down those wild expectations a short while ago. Now he would be content just for Emily to become a respected pro, someone who knew the craft well and how to take care of their opponents' safety in the ring.

"I'll make the call tomorrow," Mohawk said. Cobra clapped his hands in delight but was warned to keep it quiet so Mohawk himself could tell Emily the news.

After a basic dinner of pasta and a salad, Mohawk, Emily and Cobra sat in the living room together. Emily wanted to go to the local community center to swim some laps but her father and uncle convinced her to give her body a break. Emily didn't put up a fuss about it and relaxed on the couch as Cobra put on a Bollywood movie. To Mohawk's dismay, Emily really liked Indian films, particularly the dancing and an actor named Shah Rukh Khan, a charismatic Bollywood legend, and often pulled up Cobra to dance with her during the long musical sequences.

"C'mon, unc!" she squealed as Shah Rukh broke into a spirited dance with a beautiful Bollywood starlet on the television screen. "Let's do this!"

However, Mohawk interrupted the moment by pressing pause on the remote. Both Emily and Cobra groaned as Mohawk cleared his throat to speak.

"We gotta talk," he said gravely, the tone getting Emily's attention in a hurry. "You've been training for awhile…"

"Yeah…" Emily said, becoming tense.

"And you've done a good job. You're in decent shape now. So Cobra and me…we think it's time you actually do some real wrestling training."

Emily's jaw dropped.

"You really mean it?" she asked.

"Yes," Cobra replied. "It is time like your daddy said."

Emily's hands began to shake…and then she jumped up and down.

"I'm gonna be a wrestler!" she screamed happily. Both Mohawk and Cobra grinned at this as Emily ran around the room, waving her fists in excitement. "I'M GONNA BE A FUCKING WRESTLER!!!"

Emily then grabbed the remote, pressed play, and the living room became filled with upbeat Bollywood music.

"Now we dance!" Emily shouted. She helped Cobra to his feet and they both danced, Bollywood-style. "You, too, Dad!"

Emily attempted to get Mohawk into it but he evaded her reaching for him.

"No," he said. "I don't dance."

"You will! Some day!"

CHAPTER 17

"C'mon, kiddo," Mohawk said impatiently, standing in the front door and ready to go. "This is what you wanted, right?"

"More than anything," Emily said. She kept her hands in the front pocket of her hoodie, looking down at the floor. "I'm just…nervous."

"No nervous!" Cobra called out from outside. He was standing in the driveway, waiting to hit the road as well. "You want the wrestling? Now we wrestle!"

Mohawk nodded, putting a hand on Emily's shoulder.

"He's right," Mohawk said. "Now it's time for the real work to begin."

Emily nodded herself and then smiled. She took a deep breath.

"Okay, let's go," she said.

Mohawk led his daughter outside where his black 1989 Jeep Cherokee stood. It was too big to put in the townhouse garage but Mohawk couldn't bear to part with it. So he left it with his mechanic Mohammed, who had a private storage facility for vehicles. Even though he was an older gentleman, Mohawk's driver's license was still valid and he would take the jeep out for a spin every six months or so. For where they were going today, it seemed appropriate for Mohawk to drive them all.

"Sweet ride, pops," Emily laughed, taking her seat on the passenger's side. Cobra sat in the back, which he preferred, so he could stretch out.

"It is nice car," Cobra agreed. "Not as nice as my Mercedes. Or my Corvette."

"You mean your ex-wife's Mercedes and Corvette," Mohawk reminded his roommate.

Cobra scowled at this...but then chuckled. Ever since Emily arrived and they had started training her, the man was mostly in high spirits. He and Mohawk still squabbled from time to time but for the most part, their relationship hadn't been this strong in years. Maybe all the two old guys needed was a project to work on together.

"Alright, seat-belts on," Mohawk said to his crew.

"I do not want to wear," Cobra complained. "You no make me."

"Damn right I can. I'm not getting a ticket because you won't put a seat-belt on. Strap in. Now."

Cobra grumbled but did as he was told. Mohawk then turned the ignition and the jeep roared to life. He grinned, pleased that Mohammed, an old friend, had maintained the vehicle at no cost.

"Sounds fierce," Emily said, appreciating the jeep's engine. She then added, mischievously, "Can I drive?"

"Not today," Mohawk said. "But maybe next time we go."

"Really? I was just kidding and shit."

"Why not? Okay, let's get moving. Last thing I want is to piss off your new teacher."

He backed out, pausing to wave to Karen, who was pushing along her son in his stroller as always, and the jeep turned a corner to drive out of the neighborhood. Mohawk drove through some intersections, his hands at ten and two on the steering wheel, enjoying the freedom that comes with handling a car.

"You look happy, Dad," Emily said.

"I am. Feels like a good day," Mohawk said.

"Yeah, totally."

From the backseat, Cobra snorted.

"Not a good day for long," he said warningly to Emily. "You are in for day of pain!"

Emily took this in and looked over for Mohawk, probably for some reassurance. Mohawk shrugged.

"He's right," Mohawk said. "It's gonna be a tough one for you."

He saw Emily gulp a little.

"It's alright, though," he continued. "You can handle whatever comes your way today."

"I hope so," Emily said.

"Me and Cobra made sure that your conditioning and strength is where it's supposed to be."

"This is true!" Cobra said proudly.

Emily looked out the window on her side. Mohawk was nearing the freeway leaving the city, driving on the ramp and picking up speed.

"Is the school far from here?" she asked. "Is that what we call it? A school?"

"Not far," Mohawk replied. "What else would we call it?"

"I dunno. A dojo?"

Both Mohawk and Cobra laughed.

"That's what they call wrestling schools in Japan," Mohawk said. "Here, they're just schools."

"A very good experience in the dojos," Cobra chimed in. "The Japanese trainers are the best! Your papa trained with Mr. Sanada!"

This seemed to interest Emily greatly. She turned in her seat to face her father and better converse with her Uncle Cobra.

"Oh yeah?" Emily said.

"Yeah," Mohawk said. "Although I went to Mr. Sanada's school in San Diego, not in Japan. It was dojo-style, though."

"What does that mean? What was it like there?"

Mohawk sighed, the memories flooding back to him.

"It wasn't easy," he said. "Really demanding. You lived a very basic life. Lots of routine, lots of exercise, and lots of serving older wrestlers, who would be our teachers. You learned about respect and had to live at the school for a full year, doing all kinds of chores. We called it the three C's: Cooking, Cleaning and Calisthenics."

"I read about Mr. Sanada," Emily said. "He was a real legend in wrestling and a tough dude. The training sounds hella tough."

"Hmm. But it prepared me well for the business."

Emily turned her head to Cobra.

"Did you train with Mr. Sanada, too?" she asked.

"No," Cobra said, shaking his head. "I was wrestler in Punjab."

"Amateur wrestling," Mohawk added. "Almost Olympic-level."

"Really?" Emily said, very much impressed. "Wow! That's sick, Uncle Cobra! You better teach me some moves!"

Cobra beamed at this.

"We will see. If you have the spirit," he said teasingly.

Mohawk exited the freeway, moving onto an off ramp.

"He trained in Minnesota with a bunch of other amateur stand-outs," he explained for Emily's benefit. "His trainer was a guy named Brian Devereaux. He was a gold medalist at the world championships and won the pro wrestling world title in the fifties. But since Cobra was already so good and athletic, he didn't train as long as I did. He picked up pro wrestling a lot faster than me and was working actual matches in a couple of months."

"I was very good," Cobra said proudly.

Mohawk stopped at a red light and glanced over at Emily. He saw that she had become thoughtful, her eyebrows furrowed.

"What's the matter?" he asked.

"I'm just wondering about my trainer," she replied. "You guys got trained by the best...I hope he's as good as yours was."

"She," Mohawk corrected.

"Huh?"

"Your trainer is a she."

"She" was waiting in an old warehouse in an industrial neighborhood. Mohawk drove his jeep on an ancient and cracked pavement road, passing by storage units, factories, auto shops and truck depots. There weren't many people around, about ten in the morning on a Saturday, but during the week, this area of town was probably bustling with workers in protective gear and boots.

Mohawk knew exactly where he was going, having spent time at Emily's prospective wrestling school some time ago. He was invited to do a seminar for some trainees, giving them some coaching about what to do and not to do in the ring. It was more a glorified meet-and-greet but Mohawk was impressed by the level of respect given to him by the students. This, coupled with the relative proximity to the townhouse, made the school an ideal spot for Emily to start her training.

He pulled into a small parking lot, only about six spots to park in, assuming the one closest to the open garage door. It was dark inside the warehouse but Mohawk could see the outline of a wrestling ring from his seat. The warehouse itself was small and unkempt, the bricks crumbling and paint drastically fading. It wasn't too far removed from crack house status.

"Here we are," Mohawk said, unclicking his seat-belt.

"A dump!" Cobra moaned, looking all around.

"It's a wrestling school. It doesn't have to look pretty."

Mohawk looked over at Emily for her reaction. She was staring ahead at the wrestling ring.

"C'mon, guys!" she cried, leaping out the door of the jeep.

"Emily, slow down!" Mohawk said, hurrying out himself.

He got in front of the giddy Emily as a grunt came from the backseat of the vehicle.

"Someone help me!" Cobra said.

"On my way, Uncle Cobra," Emily said dutifully. She opened the door to the backseat as Cobra was having trouble getting out. Emily offered her hand but Cobra scowled at her.

"Give me arm," he said.

Emily looked momentarily confused but stuck out her arm to Cobra. He grabbed her forearm to steady himself and used this to climb out of the jeep. Cobra then nodded his thanks to Emily and the trio formed up in front of the wrestling school.

"There's no sign," Emily said. She peered into the garage of the warehouse where the ring and a solitary figure waited for them, leaning on the ropes.

"Come on," Mohawk said, making a few steps as the side door of the warehouse opened and Betty Buxom stepped out. She looked glamorous as ever, dressed in blue jeans and a dark green pullover with shiny black heels. Both Emily and Mohawk's jaws dropped upon seeing her.

"Betty," Mohawk said as his ex-lover slinked over to him.

"Wanted to be here," she said smoothly. "To meet your kid."

Betty turned to the stunned Emily and extended her hand. Emily handled it like a delicate flower.

"Emily...so nice to meet you, sugar," Betty said warmly, a southern belle twang to her voice.

"Nice to meet you, too, Betty," Emily whispered quickly. "I watch your wrestling stuff all the time on YouTube!" She then excitedly turned to Mohawk. "Am I gonna be trained by THE Betty Buxom?!"

Both Betty and Mohawk laughed good-naturedly at this.

"No, no, no," Betty said. "I could do some stuff in the ring way back when but I was more a valet and manager. My bumping days are long over, sweetie."

Betty turned her attention to Cobra, who was gaping at her.

"Cobra Tara Singh," she said. "Looking handsome as ever."

Cobra grinned. He and Betty never hooked up in the past but not from a lack of trying on Cobra's part.

"And you," he said gallantly, bowing his head slightly. "More beautiful every time I see you."

Betty giggled and Mohawk was becoming impatient. He wanted to get Emily's in-ring training started, knowing she had a long road ahead of her.

Betty turned away from Cobra to take a closer look at Emily.

"She's definitely in good shape," she said, squeezing Emily's bicep and studying her back and stomach. Betty smiled at Mohawk. "I can tell you and Cobra put her through it."

"Yes," Cobra said proudly. "My niece is in tip-top shape."

Betty raised an eyebrow.

"Niece?" she asked Mohawk.

"It's a thing they're doing," Mohawk replied, shrugging a little.

Betty chuckled.

"I guess we're all family here," she said. Betty went back to eyeing Emily. "I think our head instructor will have fun with this one."

This appeared to confuse Emily.

"If Betty's not my wrestling trainer," Emily said. "Who is?"

"My cousin," Betty replied. "Follow me. I'll introduce you to her."

She walked into the warehouse, beckoning Mohawk, Emily and Cobra along the way. Even though the exterior of the school was less-than-inspiring, the inside was pristine. Exercise machines, weight racks, punching bags, and amateur wrestling mats all surrounded the ring itself, which was of the professional standard twenty foot by twenty foot dimensions with a set of bleachers for spectators to watch.

Mohawk glanced at Emily and saw that she was in awe of everything around her. She also stayed close to Betty, hanging on her every word.

"Our facilities aren't too shabby," Betty said humbly. "I put most of the money into the wrestling and training stuff. Locker rooms and showers are inside the actual building and they're pretty Spartan."

"I don't mind!" Emily said. She nodded at her father. "I'm here to train, not get pampered."

Mohawk nodded back at his daughter, quite pleased as he could see Betty was impressed by Emily's words.

"Tuition can be expensive," Betty said airily. "We're the best school in the state...of course, I'll give you a friends and family discount..."

Emily opened her mouth to speak on this but Mohawk beat her to the punch.

"Not a problem," he said. He jerked a thumb at Cobra. "Me and him got it covered."

Emily became surprised and appeared like she was ready to protest but Mohawk shot her a look to keep quiet. This was not to be discussed.

"It is our gift to you," Cobra explained, smiling at Emily.

Emily mouthed the words "thank you" to both Mohawk and Cobra and Mohawk could see her eyes were watery with gratitude. He felt a little emotional himself. So did Cobra, who put a hand on Mohawk's shoulder.

"Okay!" Betty said, interjecting herself into the moment. "Let's meet your trainer!"

Betty's cousin, and Emily's new trainer, was a retired ex-wrestler named "Wildcat" Becca Stone. She stood in the corner of the ring, the furthest away from the new arrivals, and leaned on the ropes, watching them all like a hawk. Mohawk recognized Becca immediately. He had never met the woman but her reputation preceded her.

"Becca?" Betty said. "Got a fresh one for you here."

She put an arm around Emily, who smiled at Becca as she approached the section of the ring closest to them. Mohawk took a closer look at Becca Stone, a squat but powerful-looking woman in electric purple workout gear, probably in her late forties. Even though she and Betty Buxom were related, Becca wasn't a bombshell like her cousin. She had the hardened look of a former pro, her nose bent slightly, having broken it a few times, and some scars on her shoulders. Becca's demeanor was stern and although she wore some make-up, it did little to soften the lady. Her short frizzy blonde hair added to her severity, too.

"Your cousin is The Wildcat?" Mohawk asked.

"Sure is!" Betty said proudly. "Say hi, Becca."

Becca just nodded, keeping her eyes locked on Emily. Although women's wrestling is popular now, it wasn't during Becca's era. Mohawk knew she mostly plied her trade in Japan and Europe and most likely didn't make much of a living from it. However, Becca was one of the soundest wrestlers of her time, and Mohawk was honored to be in her presence.

"Pleased to meet you," Mohawk said respectfully.

"Yes, me too," Cobra added. He was aware of Becca as well.

Mohawk struggled to keep the pleasure off his face. Becca Stone being in charge of his daughter's wrestling training meant she was in good hands.

"Get in here," Becca said sharply to Emily, which seemed to startled the girl. "Let's see what you've got."

"Yes, ma'am," Emily said, glancing at Mohawk and Cobra, who nodded at her.

"Knock off the ma'am stuff. I'm a coach."

"Yes, coach."

Emily didn't know her away around the ring yet but she had watched enough wrestling to get that you can slide under the bottom rope to the canvas with a little hop. Emily did so and Becca shook her head.

"No," she said. "Wrong right off the bat."

"What do you mean?" Emily asked. Mohawk could tell she was slightly embarrassed. He realized that Becca was going to be a tough taskmaster right away, especially when it came to wrestling etiquette.

"When you come inside the ring, go up the steps," Becca explained. "You're a newbie and you don't know if your character is going to be someone who just slides in."

"Got it," Emily nodded.

"Also, wipe your shoes on the outside canvas before you get into the ring so you don't track anything in."

Becca got out of the ring through the ropes and jumped to the floor, right by Mohawk and Cobra.

"Excuse me," she said, showing some courtesy to two veterans of the ring. "Step back, please."

Mohawk and Cobra did as they were asked, now standing with Betty Buxom, who was watching everything.

Becca turned to Emily, still standing in the ring.

"Look what I do here," she said.

Everyone then watched Becca stroll to the ring steps, jog up them, walk along the side of the ring, wipe her Nikes on the canvas, and step into the ring through the ropes.

"Your turn," she told Emily.

Emily got out of the ring and repeated Becca's routine. Becca then asked her to do it again. And again. And then once more.

"Good," she said to Emily. "That's how you'll get into the ring from now on. You might be wondering why I asked you to do it a few times. It's because that's how we learn. Repetition. Over and over until it becomes second nature."

"That makes sense," Emily said. "Sorry for screwing up."

"Don't say sorry. You didn't know."

Mohawk was becoming increasingly impressed by Becca. He had never seen a trainer work like she did. Most of the trainers he knew, including Mr. Sanada, were crabby bastards, some of whom liked to inflict pain on and humiliate their students. Becca was stern but also fair with a dollop of kindness in there.

Becca walked around Emily, trying to get a sense of her.

"Next session, I want you to wear elbow-pads and knee-pads," she said. "There's going to be some mat burn."

"Okay," Emily said.

"You have any training at all?"

"Not really."

Emily gestured to Mohawk and Cobra, still watching with Betty Buxom.

"They got me in shape for training," she said.

"Hmm," Becca said.

What happened next was so shocking to Mohawk, it took his breath away. Without warning, Becca had scooped up Emily in a body slam-position and dropped her to the mat. Hard.

"Oh my god," Mohawk said, eyes wide.

He knew that the body slam was done with full force and Becca hadn't taken it easy at all. Emily was gasping for air, holding her back and trying to get her bearings.

"Get up!" Becca shouted.

Emily moaned slightly but followed orders, struggling to her feet. And then wham! Becca nailed her with a running clothesline across the upper chest and shoulders, like she was trying to take Emily's head off.

Emily collapsed to the mat and Mohawk couldn't take anymore. He stepped forward to intervene but felt a firm hand squeeze his wrist. Mohawk turned to see a grim-faced Cobra.

"No," he said simply, telling Mohawk not to interfere. Mohawk then glanced at Betty, who had the same expression on her face.

"Becca knows what she's doing," she said quietly.

Helpless, Mohawk turned back to see Becca walking around the prone Emily, stalking her like a predator.

"Get up," she said evenly.

"Yes, coach," Emily replied weakly.

She got to her feet again and Becca measured her for another move. She executed a picture-perfect dropkick, high to the face. However, the move just harmlessly glanced off the surprised Emily, who reflexively fell backward. Becca then scrambled up and offered Emily her hand.

"Whoa," Emily said, completely in awe of The Wildcat. This caused Becca to laugh and she pulled her young student to her feet.

"I didn't mean to beat your ass," Becca explained. "I wanted to demonstrate to you the different aspects of the art of professional wrestling."

"Ah, very good," Cobra said, pleased. He seemed to enjoy the "art" part of it.

"What I'm saying is there's some pain involved with bumps, slams, running the ropes...all that stuff," Becca explained. "But a good pro will be able to protect themselves, protect their opponent, and do moves so well that it'll look killer but not feel killer. Does that make sense?"

"Yeah," Emily said. "I want to be the best pro I can be."

"Good. Glad to hear that."

Becca turned away and faced Mohawk and Cobra.

"Well? Do I have your permission to train your kid?" she asked.

"Yes!" Cobra said emphatically.

Becca grinned and faced Mohawk, awaiting his approval. He looked away from her to Emily. It wasn't fun for him to see his daughter get beat up and it was only going to get worse. Even so, he saw the pleading look on Emily's face and took a deep breath. Mohawk really didn't have much of a choice here.

"You've got my permission," he said, before adding. "And don't take it easy on her."

"I won't," Becca said.

She went back to Emily, standing before her.

"You need water or a break or something before we continue?" Becca asked.

"No," Emily said, so very determined. "Let's get to work."

Becca enjoyed hearing this and Mohawk and Cobra watched the training session continue. Becca started with a basic lecture on conditioning and nutrition, not just for Emily's sake but also for Mohawk and Cobra, to make sure Emily stuck to it. This was fine as it was mostly what they had already instilled into Emily.

Next up was some basic amateur wrestling and lock-up stuff, loosely done so Emily could get a feel for an opponent and the dimensions of the ring. Becca explained she didn't want to do rope drills or bumping (learning how to fall safely) just yet as she wanted Emily to become more comfortable before teaching some more advanced techniques. It was all fascinating for Mohawk to watch and he could tell Cobra was enjoying it immensely, the latter yelling encouragement to his niece, which Becca didn't seem to mind.

"She looks good for a rook," Betty told Mohawk. She had stayed during the entire session and Mohawk was very much aware of her presence, the woman as sexual as ever. "Coffee?"

"Sure," Mohawk said. It wasn't easy for him to pull himself away from the ring but he knew Emily was in good hands. Most importantly, she was focused and taking this seriously although Mohawk could tell that she was enjoying herself, trying her best to hide a small smile from Becca when she did something correctly.

That's my girl, he thought proudly. Mohawk then followed Betty out of the training area, doing his best not to ogle her shapely booty while doing so.

CHAPTER 18

"So!" Betty said as she sat behind her desk in her cramped office. A dented laptop sat on the beat-up desk that Mohawk was seated in front of, his butt planted in a chewed-up computer chair. Large file cabinets surrounded the two and Mohawk wondered if Betty's office was actually an old janitorial closet or a refurbished bathroom.

Betty hadn't been lying when she told them that the wrestling school's money mostly went to the training facilities. The rest of the building was shoddy but Betty didn't seem to care.

Both Mohawk and Betty had plain black ceramic mugs in their hands. The coffee tasted fine but Mohawk was uncomfortable being in closed quarters with Betty. Not just because of her brazenness but her intoxicating perfume also wafted freely throughout the tiny room. A man could get swept away in a situation like this.

"So!" Betty repeated, smiling naughtily at Mohawk. "You've got a kid."

"Yeah," Mohawk was able to croak out.

"You and me...we were supposed to have a kid. Way back when. Remember?"

Mohawk grinned.

"There's still time," he said, in spite of himself.

Betty chuckled at this, which cut the tension considerably.

"Funny," she said. She then appraised him. "You look different, you know."

"What do you mean?" Mohawk asked.

Betty leaned forward on her elbows and Mohawk had to look away so as not to take an inappropriate gaze at her ample bosom.

"Not sure exactly," Betty replied. "Maybe a bit happier?"

"I guess I kinda am," Mohawk admitted. "I feel…I dunno…lighter?"

Betty nodded. They could hear the muted thumping sounds of Becca and Emily working on the ring mat and Betty jutted her chin towards the outside of her office.

"Because of that girl," she said. "She seems like a good egg."

Mohawk felt a swell of pride at this.

"She really is," he said.

Now Betty leaned back in her leather chair, which was a relief to Mohawk.

"You gotta protect her, Mo," Betty said gravely. "You know they're gonna come after her. Hard."

Mohawk knew what Betty was referring to. He and Cobra had a similar discussion the night before.

"Every dickhead promoter is going to want to sign her," Betty continued. "Just because of your name. Once word gets out that the daughter of Mohawk Jones wants into the biz, there's gonna be a lot of money flying around."

"I know," Mohawk said. "She's got me, though. I'll make sure she's alright."

Betty frowned and Mohawk could see she didn't seem convinced by his words.

"The business has changed, Mo," Betty said, steepling her fingers. "The TV deals for wrestling are massive. Even Tom Victory himself comes by every now and then to scout talent…he's the one you gotta watch out for because he'll want Emily as soon as he sees her."

She laughed.

"Mohawk Jones Junior," Betty said. "Tom Victory'll make her a star…and then he'll chew her up and spit her out."

Mohawk shot Betty a displeased look.

"Tom's not so bad," he said. "Him and his dad have always treated me right."

"That's because you were a star yourself," Betty said. "If you were an underneath guy, they'd low-ball you, make you work hurt, screw with your contract...I hear Tom's not much better than his old man. Actually, he might be worse, even though UGF is raking in billions."

Mohawk's eyebrows raised.

"That much money, eh?" he said.

"Yup," Betty replied. "And more to come with the next TV deal. He's got a streaming service, too. Seven ninety-nine a month to watch all the wrestling you can. It makes UGF hundreds of millions a year."

All of this was a surprise to Mohawk. He needed to plug into the pro wrestling industry again and learn what the hell was going on.

"Thanks for the advice," he said, downing the last few drops of his coffee. Mohawk got up to leave but Betty gestured for him to remain seated.

"Don't go yet," she said. "Becca's going to be putting that poor girl through her paces for a while longer. Let's catch up."

Uh oh, Mohawk thought. He really didn't want to have an awkward conversation with Betty about their past.

"I'm not mad at you, you know," she said. "I used to be but not anymore."

"That's...good," Mohawk said.

Betty smiled, seemingly enjoying Mohawk's discomfort.

"I did love your stupid ass," she said, shifting in her seat. "But that was a long time ago."

"Yeah," Mohawk said. "Sorry for how I was back then. Young and stupid."

"Don't be sorry. I've had a good life and I love what I'm doing now with Becca."

"How're your kids?"

Betty grinned as brightly as possible.

"Amazing!" she said delightedly. "My girl works in finance in Boston. My boy's in Hollywood. He's an editor on a big movie franchise."

Betty pulled out her phone, scrolled through it and showed Mohawk a photo of a little girl, maybe around three years old.

"My grandbaby," Betty beamed. "Tara. I'm going out to see her next weekend."

Wow, Mohawk thought. *Betty's got a grandkid. Wonder if I'll be a grandpa someday...*

"She's a cutie," Mohawk said.

"My everything," Betty said proudly.

Mohawk was unsure how to broach something with Betty.

"Sorry about your husband," he said. "Someone told me about his passing a while back."

Betty became quiet for a few seconds, steeling herself.

"Thank you," she said softly. "It was hard for a few years. But I'm alright now."

She gave Mohawk a sad smile and he could tell that despite Betty's sometimes outrageous attitude, she might be feeling lonely underneath it all.

"Look at us," Mohawk said. "Old but still kicking."

"Speak for yourself!" Betty said. "I still got lots to give!"

She stood up and walked over to Mohawk from behind her desk.

"Let's go see how your kid is doing," she suggested, offering her arm.

Mohawk accepted Betty's elbow and their bodies bumped into each other in a clumsy but intimate way, which resulted in Betty giggling a little. She danced her way out of the room but Mohawk hung back a few seconds, as a familiar stirring hit him down below, something that hadn't happened in a long time.

When the startled Mohawk returned to the training area to check on Emily's progress, Betty stood with him as they watched the young woman practice running the ropes. It's a lot harder to do than most fans believe, the ropes strung so tight. Taking them on your back can bruise your body and hurt your kidneys. Emily was learning this the hard way, wincing every time she ran and hitting the ropes right on the lower back. Mohawk grimaced himself, knowing full well the soreness Emily was going to be feeling the next morning.

As Becca took Emily aside to demonstrate how to properly run across the ring, Betty excused herself, telling Mohawk she had some errands to run. She gave him a flirty smile, touched his shoulder, and kissed him on the cheek before she strolled off. Mohawk couldn't help but watch her go. He then sidled up beside Cobra, who was standing outside the ring and studying Emily and Becca closely.

"How's she looking?" Mohawk asked.

"Not good," Cobra said grimly. He then shrugged. "It is to be expected."

"She'll get there, though."

"Yes."

Cobra turned and gave Mohawk a coy look.

"Betty Buxom, eh?" he said slyly. "Well, well, well…"

"Shut up," Mohawk said irritably. He wasn't in the mood to be teased by Cobra. The man would keep it up for weeks.

"She is very sexy, eh?"

"I told you to shut up."

"You will make me?"

Mohawk stared at Cobra's mocking face and then rolled his eyes in annoyance. The men turned their focus back to the ring where they saw that now Becca was going to instruct Emily on how to take a back bump. This was a fundamental skill for a professional wrestler, being able to "fall" on the mat without hurting yourself, and being able to do it continuously so your body became accustomed to the impact.

"Watch me first," Becca told Emily. Mohawk was surprised that Becca was going to demonstrate the back bump herself. Usually instructors would get a younger wrestler with less miles on their body to do so. Mohawk and Cobra watched as Becca hopped up and fell backwards, crashing onto the mat. She then used the momentum to spring back to her feet.

"Very good," Cobra said.

Mohawk agreed. It was a perfect bump, one that had minimal damage. Once again, Mohawk was comforted by the knowledge that Emily was being trained by someone who definitely knew what she was doing.

"The key is to spread the impact as far as you can along your back and rear," Becca explained to Emily, who nodded dutifully. "You try."

Mohawk believed this was a key test for Emily. If she could weather her first back bump, recognize this was part of the pain of being a wrestler and still want to continue on, she had passed her first major test. Many trainees quit after their first training session because they didn't want to endure the bumps.

Emily's first attempt at a back bump was a disaster. She fell backward smoothly but groaned from the impact, getting the wind knocked out of her.

"Wrong," Becca said. "You took it too hard, right on your spine."

"I know," Emily coughed. "I feel it in my spine."

Becca laughed a little.

"C'mon," she said playfully, offering Emily her hand. "You're not that hurt. Just a bit shook up."

Emily took the hand and Becca effortlessly yanked her to her feet. The trainer eyed Emily closely, who was looking withdrawn.

"You ready to try again?" Becca asked.

Emily glanced over at Mohawk and Cobra.

Don't give up, kid, Mohawk thought. *You'll learn...you'll get better.*

Maybe he should have said these things to Emily out loud but Mohawk felt this was a decision for his daughter to make. He couldn't coddle her. Professional wrestling doesn't really allow for that.

"Yeah," Emily said, turning back to Becca. "Let's go again."

"Very good," Cobra said again, pleased at Emily for showing some guts.

The rest of the session only lasted a few more minutes. Emily took some more back bumps before Becca told her that was enough for the day. She then gave Emily a long talk about respect while in her classroom and how she would not tolerate any bullshit.

"People watch wrestling and think it's all a clown show," Becca explained. "But everything in this ring can be dangerous. People can get hurt, paralyzed, or even killed. So take this shit serious."

"I will," Emily said.

"Great. Go take a walk and hit the showers. The locker room is just out that door and to the right."

Becca pointed to a far door at the rear of the gym area and Emily went off. She limped a little and Mohawk could see her body was going to be very bruised up later in the day.

"Gentlemen," Becca said, peering down at Mohawk and Cobra from the ring. "Come join me?"

Mohawk and Cobra made their way into the ring, going up the steps and wiping their feet before stepping inside the ropes. Mohawk absentmindedly tested the mat with his weight. The ring had some give but would still smart when you got slammed into it. Mohawk had worked in some very stiff rings in his day, to the point that when he was an older veteran, he refused to take any bumps out of fear of permanent injury. Becca's ring was fine for a trainee, though.

"I think she'll be okay," Becca said, as if reading Mohawk and Cobra's minds. Asking if Emily was any good was obviously the first question they were going to pose to the woman. "Her body's ready to take on wrestling training. So many newbies that come here have to put in serious gym-time before they can even get in the ring. Your girl, though…she can start right away."

"Great," Mohawk said. He then added, very seriously, "But don't take it easy on her."

"Not my style. She's not just going to be repping you guys out there if she makes it. She'll be repping my school, too."

Mohawk nodded, liking the fact that Becca Stone would be just as invested in Emily's future as they were.

He shook Becca's hand and both saw that Cobra was capering around the ring, bouncing off the ropes and climbing the turnbuckles. Mohawk really hoped he wouldn't attempt to take a back bump.

"Stop that," Mohawk said in exasperation.

"No!" Cobra said. He was now eyeing Becca, facing off with her. "You! Lock-up with me!"

Without hesitation, Becca and Cobra locked up, their arms and hands entwined. They jockeyed for position and Mohawk could tell that even though Cobra was straining with all his might, Becca was just messing around.

They broke their lock-up, ending with a stalemate, and Becca grinned at Cobra.

"Strong lock-up, old man," she said, rubbing her wrists.

Cobra did a double biceps flex.

"I still have it!" he bellowed, his voice echoing throughout the gym.

A short time later, Mohawk was driving Cobra and Emily home. Cobra now sat in the passenger seat as Emily needed to be in the back to recline and rest after an intense workout. She was also very quiet.

"You okay back there?" Mohawk asked, more than a little concerned.

He glanced at Emily through the rearview and Emily caught his eye. She nodded as an answer and then stared out her window, seemingly lost in her thoughts. Cobra opened his mouth to say something but Mohawk shook his head at him to leave Emily alone.

Emily went straight to the basement to rest when they arrived at the townhouse and Cobra brought a sandwich to her. When he got back upstairs, Mohawk was waiting.

"She is not talking," Cobra said, almost sadly.

Mohawk knew he had to take action and make sure his kid was alright.

He went downstairs and found Emily sitting on the couch, watching YouTube on her phone and taking tiny bites out of her sandwich. She was dressed in a t-shirt and shorts and Mohawk noticed some bruises on her forearms and shins from Becca's first training session. Mohawk also saw that Emily, although still living out of a suitcase, had slowly made the basement her own, with folded piles of her clothes, her laptop, and other personal belongings all around the room.

At least she's keeping the place clean, Mohawk thought. *We should get her some shelves and a dresser, though.*

He wasn't sure what Emily was watching but for the first time, it wasn't wrestling-related. It was some kind of comedy prank show. Emily wasn't laughing at it, though.

Without a word, Mohawk sat beside his daughter. She didn't acknowledge him at all, still staring at her phone. He gently pried it from her.

"Dad," she said, reaching for her cell. "Give me that back."

Mohawk held the phone away from Emily and gave her a stern look.

"We need to talk," he said.

"We do?" Emily asked petulantly.

"Yeah. You've been all quiet since we finished with Becca today. Are you okay?"

Emily sighed.

"I'm okay," she replied.

"You don't have to do this if you don't want to," Mohawk said. "I know wrestling hurts. My body is always hurting because of it. It's fine if you want to quit."

Emily shook her head, almost violently.

"Oh, I'm not quitting," she said. "Definitely not quitting."

"Then what's up?" Mohawk pressed.

Emily sighed again. She stood up and limped around, gesturing to the different wrestling memorabilia around her, the action figures, the posters and the wrestling belts.

"I didn't know," Emily began. "That I was so far behind…"

"Far behind? What do you mean?" Mohawk asked.

"It's, like, there's so much to learn…I didn't know…it's like I know nothing. It's kinda scary."

It seemed like Emily had more to say so Mohawk didn't push her. He waited a few seconds for her to continue.

"You and Uncle Cobra," Emily said. "You're, like, legends. You did everything. And I want to be a legend, too. A world champ. But now I don't know if I'll be good enough. I thought wrestling would be…easier."

Mohawk burst into laughter, which seemed to annoy Emily.

"It's not funny, Dad," she said.

"It's fucking hilarious," Mohawk said. "You thought wrestling was easy? It's like the hardest thing there is, kiddo. You've got to keep in great shape, connect with the most demanding fans on the planet, know all sorts of moves and routines, travel the world, live with pain…it's damn hard."

He stared hard at Emily.

"It's definitely not easy," Mohawk reiterated. "But you'll learn. Cobra and me…we had to start where you are. But we'll teach you and Becca will teach you. You'll get where you want to be if you work your ass off and don't give up. I promise."

Emily took all of this in.

"Alright," she said, smiling. "You were really as bad as I am right now?"

"Worse!" Mohawk replied. "My first day, I fell out of the ring running the ropes! Hit my head on the floor and knocked myself out!"

"No way!"

"Yes way! But I kept on going. And I got better. Never fell out of the ring again."

He softened, standing up and putting his hands on his daughter's shoulders. Emily winced.

"Ow," she said. "A bit ouch-y there."

"Sorry," Mohawk said, removing his hands and folding his arms across his chest. "Look, today was just day one. Rest up, come upstairs, and hang out with two old guys. Let's watch a movie and just relax."

"I was thinking about going for a run," Emily said.

"No. You gotta take it easy. No over-training."

"Okay, Dad."

That night, Mohawk, Cobra and Emily watched a movie called "Pitch Perfect", which was Emily's favorite and Mohawk had to admit he enjoyed it a little. The next day, Emily was really beat-up from her session with Becca but took a nap in the afternoon and did some stretching in the evening. The day after, she was back working out in the garage gym. The day after that, she was training with Becca again at her school, Mohawk and Cobra with her, every step of the way.

This is how it went for the next few weeks and months. Emily no longer needed to be told to go work out, when to rest and what to eat, and her improvement in her training sessions was noticeable. It was very slow at first, doing basic exercises like bumps and rolls to simple moves like hip tosses, snap-mare takeovers and even body slams. She also did some amateur mat wrestling (which Cobra happily assisted with) and finally mastered running the ropes. Emily then graduated to working with Becca's other trainees and they practiced drop-down sequences and different reversals.

It was slow going but Emily was getting there. She would sometimes scrape an elbow or sprain an ankle but nothing kept her from missing her training sessions.

Most importantly for Mohawk, Emily always had a smile on, often excited about learning a new move and then practicing it diligently. This enthusiasm would take her far and Mohawk hoped she kept it as long as possible.

CHAPTER 19

There was one key element of professional wrestling that Mohawk could teach Emily better than anyone and that was selling. In his day, Mohawk was one of the best in the game at selling and neither Cobra nor Becca Stone had the expertise that Mohawk had in this regard.

Selling, in wrestling, was displaying to the crowd how moves hurt during the action of a match. If you were attacked, it was the "acting" of how much pain and agony you were in. If a match was long and competitive, it was showing the fans that everything was taking a toll on your body. Selling was a fundamental part of the "story" of professional wrestling and too little, or too much, could hurt the show.

Mohawk had asked Betty if he could borrow the ring for a one-on-one session with Emily to teach her the finer points of selling. Betty agreed, on the condition that he conduct a seminar on selling for the other students sometime in the future. This seemed to be a fair trade for Mohawk.

Emily was excited to be in a private lesson with her dad. She was showing no nervousness in the ring now and appeared quite comfortable, running the ropes and doing some forward rolls to warm up.

"Are you gonna show me your powerslam today?" she asked, sizing him up. "I think I could probably do it on you if you go up light for me."

"No powerslams," Mohawk said, bemused. "We're gonna learn about selling."

Emily didn't protest although she did mention that Becca had taught her some basics about selling. Mohawk wanted to get deeper with it, though.

"I wasn't the fastest, strongest, or smoothest wrestler," Mohawk explained. "But I prided myself on being a great seller. That's partly what kept me on top for so long."

"Tell me more," Emily said.

Mohawk sat down in the middle of the ring and Emily did the same.

"Imagine me having a match," Mohawk said. "I'm facing the nastiest guy in the company. The worst heel imaginable..."

"...the baddest bad guy," Emily finished for him.

"Exactly. We're having a match and he's destroying me. And I'm acting like everything he hits me with is hurting me bad. I'm crying out in pain, I'm rolling around on the mat, my face is all scrunched up like this..."

Mohawk made a pained face and Emily laughed.

"How do you think the fans are going to react to this?" Mohawk asked.

"They're going to feel bad for you," Emily replied.

"Right. And then what?"

Emily pondered this. She then brightened, a realization hitting her.

"Then they're gonna start cheering!" she chuckled. "Because if they cheer and make some noise, they think they can get you going to fight back!"

Mohawk clapped his hands, very pleased that Emily was getting it.

"Which means they're invested in my comeback," he said. "We've drawn them into the story of the match, which is the underdog babyface good guy taking the bad guy heel's best shots and still coming forward."

"So when you win," Emily said. "The fans will be so happy because you won after taking a beating!"

"And sometimes, the good guy doesn't win," Mohawk added. "The bad guy might be just too much for him and that puts the heel over as a threat for the next guy to face him. It gets him heat because the fans'll recognize him as a killer because of the pain he put their hero through. And this is all because of..."

"...selling. Whoa."

"You become a great seller and you'll become a great wrestler. Guaranteed. Also, if you're a super-seller, your opponents will like working with you because you're making them look good. They'll respect you for this and in return, they'll try to make you look good, too."

Mohawk smiled.

"This is what wrestling is really about, Em," he said. "It's not just about the moves…it's about give-and-take and respect between wrestlers when you're in the ring together."

Emily's grin was ear-to-ear. She clearly enjoyed being under Mohawk's learning tree and he loved imparting his knowledge to her. They then practiced some very basic selling techniques, like if you're in a submission hold or right after taking a hard bump from a big move. Mohawk also taught Emily some timeless strategies about how to fire up the crowd during a comeback or when you're seemingly down and out.

"Every once in a while, you or your opponent might need a break," Mohawk continued. "Maybe you're actually hurt or winded or whatever. Then what you can do is take a bump or a shot and roll out of the ring. When you're selling like this, you're saying that the beating you're taking is so bad, you can't even stand up. So you take a breather outside. The fans will feel sorry for you as a babyface or hate you as a chicken-shit if you're a heel."

Father and daughter practiced some more selling techniques with Mohawk explaining as much as he could and as clearly as possible. He liked that Emily constantly asked him questions.

"Sometimes when I watch wrestling, I see guys who don't sell for other guys," she said. "What do I do in a situation like that? Like, what if I slam somebody and they don't sell my move?"

It was a good question and Mohawk thought hard for a minute before answering.

"In the past, we might pop a guy for that," he said. "Like a quick punch to the gut and then a word in their ear to stop being a jerk. But I don't think you can do that now."

"So what do I do?" Emily asked.

"There's no real answer," Mohawk replied. "Sometimes you just gotta do the best you can with what you got for the match. Not everybody's a good seller and some wrestlers don't want to be. They're selfish."

"What if somebody shoots on me?"

"Shooting" on someone meant if a wrestler actually tries to hurt their opponent with a real move or submission hold during a match. It didn't happen often but some wrestlers, like people in any vocation, could be assholes.

"We're going to show you how to protect yourself," Mohawk said. "Cobra will teach you some shoot holds and part of your training with Becca is learning how to take a punch."

"Okay," Emily said. "I guess I just gotta watch out for myself."

"All the time," Mohawk said.

The lesson went back to selling. Mohawk was wrapping up all he had to say on the matter for the day and hoped that it was getting through to Emily. It was something he would probably have to continually hammer her with.

"There's a fine line with selling," he said. "You don't want to be too over the top because then you're turning it into a comedy match. That's okay…if you want to be a comedy wrestler or underneath guy."

"I don't want to be that," Emily said. "I want to be the world champ."

"So don't overdo the selling like you're Yosemite Sam getting hit by an anvil."

"Who's Yosemite Sam?"

Mohawk let this slide and continued with his lecture.

"You don't want to be an under-seller, either," he said. "It's disrespectful to the opponent and also the match. If a guy is hitting you with everything but the kitchen sink and you just shrug it off, it makes him look weak and the match doesn't seem very competitive. It's just a bunch of moves."

"That makes sense," Emily said.

"Now let's talk about promos."

At this, Emily rubbed her hands together, a giddy expression on her face.

"Oh man," she said. "This is the good stuff!"

Mohawk laughed.

"I was a decent promo," he said. "And Cobra was really good. He could get the fans to hate him by screaming at them. 'You ignorant American scum!' was one of his big lines."

"I don't think I can get away with saying that," Emily smiled.

"Probably not. Tell me, though…what do you think is the purpose of being a good interview?"

Emily looked down at the mat, deep in thought.

"I guess," she began. "If you're a good interview and can do a great promo, the fans will want to see more of you."

"Good answer," Mohawk said. "That's part of it. You also want to be able to get them interested in whatever you're doing. So if you're in a feud, you want them to see you wrestle your opponent and if they do that…"

"…they'll buy a ticket to watch you," Emily finished.

"Bingo."

Emily then faced off with her father, surprising him.

"What are you doing?" Mohawk asked.

"I'm setting up," Emily said, in a combat-like pose. She then held her hand out like she was holding a microphone.

"Oh yeah? You've been practicing?"

"A little."

"With Becca?"

"Nah, just on my own."

Mohawk stepped back, allowing Emily some space. He leaned against the ropes and waited for her to begin.

"Let's see what you got," he said.

Mohawk watched as Emily changed gears. She began pacing back and forth, huffing and puffing, and sneering at the imaginary crowd.

"You think you all can stop me?!" she bellowed into the make-believe mic. "Everyone the brass has put in front of me, I've beaten!" Emily growled to emphasize her point. "And I'm not gonna stop beating on everyone until I get what I want! I want that championship gold! I want to be the most famous professional wrestler in the biz! And whoever the champ is when I finally get my title shot, I'm gonna pulverize and make them run back to their family...because I am EMILY!"

Emily stopped, out of breath, and looked to her dad for his reaction. Mohawk then burst into laughter.

"Good job!" he said, applauding. "That was a great comedy promo!"

"Huh?" Emily said. "I wasn't trying to be funny."

She frowned a little and Mohawk walked over to her. Time to share some more of his wisdom.

"Your passion is fine," he said. "You've got the energy...but was that really you? Didn't seem like it to me."

"I don't get what you're saying," Emily said.

Mohawk attempted to break it down further for his daughter.

"The top promos in pro wrestling are guys who aren't pretending," he explained. "Yeah, we're all playing characters and all that but the best talkers are those who truly become the character. It becomes real to them and the fans believe them. Ric Flair's gimmick was being a playboy who spent a ton of money, rode in limos, and bought expensive suits. And that's who he was in real life."

"So you're saying if I'm not authentic, the fans won't believe in me?" Emily asked.

"That's right."

"But who am I supposed to be in wrestling?"

"You tell me."

Emily suddenly became shy, looking away from her dad.

"Well, I've kinda been working on a character," she said.

"Oh yeah?" Mohawk said. "For a lot of wrestlers, it takes them years to find their character. I'm glad you've been thinking about it."

Emily brightened.

"You wanna hear about it?" she asked.

"Sure," Mohawk replied.

Emily became excited again, her eyes bright and wide.

"Okay, okay, okay," she said, trying to keep herself calm. "So you know how you're Mohawk Jones? I figure maybe I could do something like that?

I'll be...wait for it...TOMAHAWK JONES! I'll wear the headdress you did, paint my face, do the war dance! It'll be like the next gen of Joneses!"

Mohawk blanched. This was the last thing he wanted to hear.

"I'm not sure that's a good idea," he said.

Fortunately, Emily didn't look too crushed by this. She did appear a little disappointed, though.

"Why not?" she asked. "I thought it would be a great idea."

"Do you really want to be so associated with your old man's gimmick?" Mohawk asked.

"Yeah! You were awesome! I want to be awesome, too!"

Again, Mohawk didn't seem too enthused.

"I dunno, Em," he said. "These Native American characters...they seem out of date..."

"That's why I can bring it back!" Emily said. "It'll be old-school! Retro!" She scrunched up her face, as if remembering something. "By the way, I wanted to ask you...what tribe or band are we from anyway?"

Mohawk became alarmed. This wasn't a question he was expecting to be asked.

"I've been wondering for a long time," Emily said. "I know I'm only part Native American, right? Or is it 'indigenous' now? I should look it up..."

"I'm not sure," Mohawk said quietly.

"Since your name is Mohawk, are we Mohawk? Or Cree? Or Huron? You know what movie I watched right before I met you? Last Of The Mohicans...I really liked it!"

"I haven't seen it."

Emily giggled.

"Sorry, I'm just blabbering," she said. "So...what are we?"

Mohawk took a deep breath and looked away. He was ashamed to answer.

"I don't know," he said.

"You don't know?" Emily asked. "How can you not know?"

"It just wasn't a part of who I was growing up," Mohawk replied simply.

It was here that Mohawk and Emily actually had their first real talk about his upbringing. He explained to his daughter about how Ted and Barbara Jones had adopted him and how he came of age not knowing his roots. He knew he was an Indian but never delved into it any further than he had to, except with his wrestling gimmick. Mohawk also explained to Emily that he wasn't proud of himself, telling her about the incident at the downtown community center and how he had always meant to dig deeper into who he was.

"Thanks for sharing, Dad," Emily said.

"Thanks for listening," Mohawk said, feeling closer to his kid.

Emily gave her old man a hug.

"You know," she said. "We should do the research. Let's find out what our heritage is. Together."

"That sounds good," Mohawk said, relieved that Emily had not judged him at all. Her mother had raised her right and he wished Linda was still around so he could thank her for the job she did.

Mohawk broke the hug and held Emily at arms-length.

"Let's get you set up as a wrestler first, okay?" he said. "Then we'll go see what kind of Indian we are."

"Deal!" Emily said, smiling that goofy grin that melted Mohawk's heart every time.

CHAPTER 20

Cobra's heart attack came out of nowhere. Maybe Mohawk should have been more aware of the man's health and proactive with maintaining his diet but what more could he have done? The incident was especially hard for Emily since she was the one home with Cobra when it happened.

Mohawk had gone out to do some grocery shopping and other errands while Emily and Cobra practiced some submission wrestling in the garage. They didn't open the door because it was chilly out and then the garage got hot. Emily said that Cobra complained that he couldn't breathe and then he toppled over.

"You did good," Mohawk told the shaken Emily as they sat together in the hospital waiting room. She had called 911 immediately and did her best to keep Cobra comfortable. There was no need to perform CPR because Cobra had come out of it on his own. Mohawk had returned home in his jeep just as the ambulance had arrived and both he and Emily zipped to the hospital as fast as possible.

"I didn't even think we were going that hard," Emily said softly. "He had me in an armbar and I reversed out and then he started wheezing..."

Mohawk pulled Emily close to him and she seemed to appreciate the embrace, nestling against his chest.

"He better be okay," Emily whispered.

They waited a few hours for an update on Cobra and eventually, a young East Indian doctor, looking frazzled after a long day of seeing patients, came to speak with them. Mohawk couldn't help but think that Cobra would have appreciated being taken care of by one of his own.

Dr. Maini told Mohawk and Emily that Cobra had suffered a mild heart attack and he was going to be alright. Emily burst into tears at this and Mohawk listened to the doctor tell him that Cobra would need some dietary changes based on some of the tests that had come back and probably more exercise as well. They were going to keep Cobra for a night or two for observation, just to be certain, and then he could be released.

"Let's go see him," Emily said, following Dr. Maini down the hallway. Mohawk went after them and entered a recovery room where Cobra lay in bed, watching a game show on TV. He was dressed in a hospital gown and his turban was off, his sparse and stringy hair unwound. Cobra only allowed himself to look like this in private moments at home and for the first few weeks of her living with them, he didn't even allow Emily to see him without his turban.

"See? He's alright," Dr. Maini said to Emily. The young doctor smiled and Mohawk thought that maybe he was interested in his daughter. Emily didn't seem to pick up on the doc's cues and went straight to Cobra, holding his hand.

"You okay, Uncle Cobra?" she asked gently.

"A-okay!" Cobra said. He winced a little, still very much out of sorts. He did smile at Emily, happy to see her.

Dr. Maini was then called away, stepping past Mohawk to go confer with a nurse. Mohawk had stayed near the doorway, numbly staring at Cobra's weakened form, the man lying in bed with tubes coming out of him and his body attached to all kinds of apparatuses. It was uncomfortable to see Cobra Tara Singh like this and Mohawk wanted to leave.

"Let's let him get some rest," Mohawk suggested to Emily.

"No, no, no," Cobra said. "I am fine. I want to go home now."

"The doctor said you should just hang around a bit longer," Emily said. "Just to be sure."

Cobra took this in, nodding a little. He then took a deep breath.

"I was very scared," he said, which almost made Mohawk break down. He had never heard Cobra say anything like that before.

This was his best friend in the world. And he had almost lost him.

"Em," he said, after clearing his throat. "Can you give us a minute?"

"I don't want to leave Uncle Cobra," she said, holding the man's hand.

"Just a minute. I want to talk to him."

Emily stared at her father for a few seconds. She saw the graveness of his expression and kissed Cobra on the forehead, telling him that she would be right back. Mohawk watched her go and hoped Dr. Maini wasn't out there to hit on her some more.

Now alone in the room with Cobra, Mohawk made his way to the man's bedside. Cobra looked slightly nervous, as if expecting Mohawk to yell at him for having a heart attack.

Mohawk looked around and grabbed a chair. He sat next to Cobra, who had turned off the television.

"You dumb motherfucker," Mohawk said, shaking his head. "I should have taken you to your physical a few weeks ago. Maybe this wouldn't have happened."

"I will be better now," Cobra said. He then added, more firmly, "No more bad foods."

"Good. And we're gonna take a walk, every day, after dinner."

"Okay."

Mohawk coughed to quell some of the emotion welling up within him.

"You and me, we don't do the mushy stuff," he said quietly. "But this is the one time I'm gonna say it. I love you and don't you ever have a fucking heart attack again."

Cobra grinned.

"You are my best friend," he said.

He then reached for Mohawk's hand and Mohawk held the man's pencil-thin fingers. They sat quietly, not even looking at each other, until Emily returned. She didn't say a word herself, just standing behind her father and smiling gratefully at her uncle.

Family, Mohawk thought.

A couple of days later, Mohawk and Emily helped Cobra, who was walking gingerly as he regained his strength, back into the townhouse. They both fussed over the man for the next week, Mohawk even checking on Cobra a few times a night to make sure he was alright and still breathing. To his credit, Cobra stayed true to his word. He stopped eating junk food and took walks with Mohawk in the mornings as well as after supper.

"There is so much to live for," Cobra said happily during breakfast one morning. He pointed at Emily, who was dutifully eating some oatmeal with blueberries in it. "I must live to see this girl be a champion!"

Mohawk understood. Some people, after a health scare, might withdraw, frightened by their own mortality. Yet Cobra was so invested in Emily's pro wrestling journey, he wanted to survive. And thrive. The heart attack was just what he needed to make lifestyle changes. The man wished to be around for Emily. He even asked Betty for a cot at her training facility so he could take quick naps to rest up during Emily's training breaks. And when it was time for Emily to get in the ring, Cobra was right there, beside Mohawk, both watching their protégé with pride.

On this afternoon, Emily was about to have a simulated match with Becca. They weren't going at full speed or intensity but had some "spots", or sequences, mapped out. It was more to see how Emily would take to the ebb and flow of a match.

"Remember to keep yourself level," Mohawk called out from outside the ring, leaning on the ring apron. "It's okay to slow down and take your time."

"Yes!" Cobra agreed. "And you make her hurt!"

Becca burst out in laughter. She enjoyed having Cobra around during training sessions, finding him delightful.

"You're too much, old man," she said, shaking her head.

Emily wasn't in a smiling mood and Mohawk could tell she was anxious. He called her over.

"What did I just say to you?" he asked as Emily squatted down to hear him.

"Keep level," she replied.

"And what does that mean?"

Emily frowned.

"Be calm and don't freak out," she said.

"That's right. Remember...this is just training. Have fun out there."

"Yes, have fun," Cobra chimed in. He then grabbed Emily and pinched her hard on the ear.

"Owww!" she screeched. "Why the hell did you that for?"

Cobra grinned as Becca chuckled again, having seen the pinching.

"To relax you!" he said.

At this absurd remark, Emily laughed a little herself.

"You're lucky you just had a heart attack, Uncle Cobra," she said, turning away to face off with Becca. "Or else I'd fuck you up."

Betty Buxom, wearing a black and white striped t-shirt, was watching the match as well, sitting in the bleachers with a ring bell beside her. Her cousin nodded at her and Betty started the match by hitting the bell with a small hammer. She then slid into the ring to act as the referee.

The match began with a simple lock-up. Emily and Becca fought for position but Becca, as the stronger of the two, pushed her opponent into one of the ring's corners. She backed off and offered her hand to Emily, a show of sportsmanship. Emily went for it and then Becca pulled the hand away, laughing at her.

"Boo!" Cobra shouted from the sidelines. The lines were drawn. Emily was going to be the good guy of the match and Becca was playing heel.

The two women locked up again and this time, Emily dropped down, went behind, and took Becca down with a waist-lock takedown.

"Nice," Mohawk said, appreciating Emily's execution of the move.

"Very nice," Cobra agreed. "I taught her that."

"Uh huh."

The match continued with Becca reversing out of the takedown, getting Emily into a hammerlock, which Emily reversed into an armbar.

"Smooth," Mohawk said. These were very simple moves but he was pleased at how Emily was doing them. The foundation of professional wrestling was the basics.

Emily and Becca exchanged holds a few more times and Becca, playing the frustrated opponent, "poked" Emily in the eye to gain an advantage. Emily stumbled for a brief second but then continued on with the match. Mohawk made a mental note to bring this up with his daughter later on. She should have sold the eye poke more to give Becca some more time to get into position for the next series of moves.

Becca whipped Emily off the ropes, hitting her with a hard clothesline. This was sold much better by Emily as it looked like Becca took her head off. Becca then picked Emily off the canvas, sent her into a corner, bent down, and drove some shoulders into her midsection. Emily sold this like the wind was getting knocked out of her and then Becca picked her up for a body slam. Emily hit the mat hard but took the bump well, playing to the crowd that she was in agony.

"Boo!" Cobra yelled again as Becca mugged for the imaginary crowd. She turned her attention to Cobra, pretending to be angered by his heckling.

"You think you're tough?" she barked. "Come inside this ring and show me what you got!"

Cobra played up his role as the indignant fan and while Becca was "distracted", Emily snuck up from behind and pulled her backward, sending her to the mat for a quick roll-up pin.

"One...two..." Betty said, slapping her hand to the mat.

Becca kicked out of the pinning move before the three and was steamed. She started hitting Emily with forearms, barely grazing her temples but they looked like legit shots. Emily was now dazed and Becca whipped her into the ropes once more, readying to clothesline her with her muscular arm again.

However, this time, Emily ducked the attack, ran past Becca, and rebounded off the ropes, hitting Becca with the most perfect dropkick Mohawk had seen in a long time. It was a work of art and his jaw dropped in wonder.

"I had no idea she was learning how to dropkick," Mohawk said.

"It was a surprise," Cobra smiled. "You were the dropkick expert and now Emily is!"

Mohawk felt a ton of pride but didn't want to say or do anything to take Emily's focus away. She was in a zone now as she and Becca continued their match, picking up the pace. Emily nailed Becca with forearms and a clothesline of her own before going for the pin.

"One...two..." Betty said but Becca kicked out.

Becca, playing up her frustration, threw a wild haymaker punch that Emily ducked under. She rolled up Becca again.

"One...two..." Betty called out but Becca still kicked out.

Emily was so close to getting the win but just couldn't put Becca away. She lifted Becca up for a body slam herself, putting Becca down hard and then covering her for the pin.

"One...two..." Betty said...and Becca barely got her shoulder up, negating the pinfall.

Now Emily was the frustrated one, hitting the mat with her hand in dismay. She went after Becca, who was now backing off, playing coward, not wanting any piece of Emily anymore. Emily gave her hated opponent some kicks and whipped her off the ropes, dropping her head down for a back body drop, a move where Becca would run into her and Emily would flip her into the air. However, instead, Becca dropped to the mat, gave Emily a cheap-shot uppercut and rolled her up instead. Emily struggled mightily but Becca had her cinched up for the pin.

"One...two...three!" Betty yelled, her hand finally hitting the mat for the third time. Becca gloated and strutted around the ring to revel in her victory while the disappointed Emily agonized on the mat. Betty then held up her cousin's hand for the match announcement.

"Your winner...Wildcat Becca Stone!" she yelled.

"Boo!" Cobra hollered.

Everyone laughed and Becca pulled Emily to her feet. They hugged and Mohawk watched as Becca checked on Emily, making sure none of her forearms had hit her pupil too hard.

"Well?" Cobra said. "She is good, eh?"

Mohawk said nothing, keeping his eyes on his daughter. She was better than good. She was a natural.

"Dad!" Emily squealed, running over to Mohawk's side of the ring. "What did you think?"

"Not bad," Mohawk replied. "Your selling's getting better." He smiled. "Nice dropkick."

Emily beamed.

"We thought you'd like that spot," she said. "I had to practice it a lot. First time I did it, I was way too stiff and almost broke a trainee dude's face!"

Oh god, Mohawk thought. *She's starting to talk like a wrestler, too!*

"One of the sweetest dropkicks I've ever seen," Betty said, walking over to the group.

"Thanks, Betty!" Emily said. She then stared hard at her dad, looking nervous. "So...do you think I'm ready for my first real match?"

"It's not up to me," Mohawk said. "It's up to your trainer."

Everyone turned to Becca, who was resting in the far corner, wiping the sweat off with a towel and taking a swig of water. She was listening to the conversation and they all waited for her reply.

Becca simply nodded and Emily shrieked happily.

Cobra did some happy shrieking, too.

CHAPTER 21

With Mohawk and Cobra watching closely but not wanting to interject themselves, Betty and Becca argued, loudly, about where Emily's first match should be held. All four were standing outside the ring together.

Betty wanted the match to be at her school as the facility was equipped to host a small independent show. She believed it would be good publicity, especially if Mohawk and Cobra were around to sign autographs and take photos with fans. Mohawk couldn't help but admire the woman's hustle.

Becca rejected the idea, though.

"Wrestling here is too easy," she countered. "The girl knows the ring and she knows the environment. Let's take her out of her comfort zone and see how she does."

Emily was in the shower, cleaning up after her "match" with Becca. She had no say in the matter anyway.

"What do you two think?" Betty asked, turning to Mohawk and Cobra.

"I don't know," Mohawk said with a shrug. "I'm not crazy about making Em's first match a big thing, though. It's a lot of pressure for a rookie, especially with her background."

"She's going to have to face that stuff her whole career," Becca said testily. "She's the daughter of a world champion and her uncle is also a world champion. Better she starts to deal with it now so she's equipped to handle it when, sorry, *if* she makes the big-time."

Mohawk nodded. It was a good point.

"Cobra?" he asked. "What do you say?"

"Hmph!" Cobra replied. "I say hurry up and do whatever! She needs matches! Lots and lots of matches!"

Everyone agreed with this. Emily needed to get as much ring experience as she could get and as soon as possible.

In the end, Betty and Becca came to a compromise. Betty would promote the event, with Mohawk and Cobra as "guests", but do so in a larger venue than the training school. She had a connection at a local indoor sports center, a modest arena used for volleyball, badminton and martial arts tournaments, and the show would go down in a month's time. This would give Emily enough time to really amp up her training.

Which she did. Emily didn't even need Mohawk and Cobra to guide her through her exercises and wrestling training. She woke up early on her own, did her weight training and cardio work, and then drove Mohawk's jeep to go train with Becca and her other students. Mohawk and Cobra accompanied her most days but not as much as they did previously.

There really wasn't as much for Mohawk and Cobra to work on with Emily...until she had her first match. Then a whole new level of training would begin as the two men would work with Emily to improve and fine-tune her performances. Even so, Mohawk was extremely nervous for his daughter. He wished that the days would hurry up and pass by so they could get this damn match in the books and move forward.

Mohawk spent the afternoons with Cobra. They hardly squabbled anymore and Emily's training reignited Mohawk's love of professional wrestling. Emily had shown Cobra how to stream YouTube on the living room television and he and Mohawk watched all sorts of old-school matches as well as some of the newer stuff out there. Mohawk was especially focused on women's wrestling, wanting to know who all the top players were nowadays. Emily might find herself in the ring with them some day.

"That's a big girl," Mohawk said as he watched a match on the TV featuring a female wrestler named Toni Titan, a beefy gal over six feet tall and weighing two hundred and fifty pounds, absolutely terrorize a smaller opponent.

"Hmm," Cobra said. "But she is clumsy. Dangerous." He tut-tutted. "Badly trained."

Mohawk saw that Toni wasn't holding back on her strikes and when she dropped a legdrop, she didn't bend at the knee so her opponent's face was safely in the crook of her leg. Toni hit the young woman full-on with her heavy calf.

"Oof," he said, looking for blood but not seeing any. "Lucky that poor kid didn't get her nose broke."

"If that big girl does that to my Emily, I will jump in the ring!" Cobra snarled.

Mohawk smiled. Cobra had become very protective of Emily.

"Don't think we need to worry about that," Mohawk said. "Toni's up in Tom Victory's promotion. Emily's far away from that."

Cobra grunted and they continued watching some more matches. Eventually, Mohawk got up to stretch his legs.

"Gonna go check the mail," he said with a yawn.

Mohawk strolled over to the front door and opened it. The sun shined down on him and he felt...happy. Birds chirping and the laughter of children could be heard from somewhere in the neighborhood and the air felt fresh. Plus, his daughter, his beautiful warrior angel, was training to become a professional wrestler and she had the potential to be great.

Life was damn good.

Mohawk turned to the mailbox affixed to the side exterior wall beside the door and lifted the metal lid. He reached in and pulled out some assorted mail. Junk, some bills, coupons...

...and a thick, cream-colored envelope with ornate Indian scripture on it.

"Oh shit," Mohawk whispered. He knew what this piece of mail was.

"Mohawk!" Cobra called out from the living room. "I want to start to the next match, okay?"

Mohawk grimaced, stepping back inside and wondering what he should do. He looked at the envelope again and saw it was addressed to him only.

Mohawk slowly made his way back to the living room. He could have hidden the Kavita's wedding invitation from Cobra, maybe just chucked it in his bedroom and then come back downstairs, but he didn't want to. It would be better off if he was straight with his friend.

"Here," Mohawk said, handing the invitation to Cobra.

Cobra was puzzled at first, staring at the envelope and trying to make sense of the "Kavita weds Harvinder" lettering that was embossed on it. He then opened the invitation and Mohawk said nothing, letting the man read it. After a long time, Cobra put the invitation down on the coffee table.

"I am going with you," he said firmly. "To the wedding."

Mohawk shook his head.

"No way," he said. "I'm not taking you. I won't let you make a scene."

"I will make no scene," Cobra said indignantly. He then shrugged. "I want to make the peace. No funny stuff."

Mohawk stared hard at Cobra for a few seconds. It seemed like the man meant what he was saying.

"I don't have much time left in this life," Cobra explained further. "I want Kavita to be very happy."

This was good enough for Mohawk.

"She's still not going to give you her money," he said. "It doesn't matter how nice you are to her at her wedding."

Cobra laughed at this, appreciating the joke. He then got up and gently slapped Mohawk on the back.

"I want nap," he said, shuffling away.

To Mohawk, it seemed like Cobra needed some alone time to process things. He would have to call Kavita later and try to convince her to allow her ex-husband to attend the wedding ceremony, maybe the reception after as well.

Maybe it'll be okay, he thought. Kavita had visited Cobra briefly in the hospital after his heart attack, just to check up on him. There was still some coolness between them but it wasn't as bad as when he and Cobra had visited Kavita a few months back.

Emily got home a few minutes later and asked where her Uncle Cobra was. Mohawk then explained the Kavita situation. He hadn't really spoken to her about Cobra's family life before and Cobra himself wasn't one to talk about it, either. After showing Emily the wedding invitation, Mohawk was surprised by his daughter's reaction.

"I want to go, too," she said, almost adamantly.

"Why?" Mohawk asked.

"Because Uncle Cobra's my guy. It'll probably be a tough day for him. I want to be there."

Mohawk couldn't see why Emily shouldn't accompany them. It could be fun to be out with his daughter, all dressed-up and everything.

"Alright, I'll try to figure it out with Kavita," he said. "Should be fine, though."

The phone call with Kavita to RSVP was tense when Mohawk asked if Cobra could be his plus one. Mohawk feared that Kavita could even hang up on him. However, when he suggested Emily, who Kavita hadn't met (Emily was off at training when Kavita visited the hospital), attend the wedding as well, Cobra's ex-wife softened.

"Fine," Kavita said wearily. Mohawk felt terrible as the poor woman probably had enough stress in her life with all the wedding preparations. "Tara and your daughter can come to the wedding. And the reception after."

Mohawk thanked Kavita profusely, who did warn him to keep Cobra in check during the wedding. She even suggested an East Indian clothing boutique in the city where Emily could find proper attire for the ceremony and reception, on Kavita's dime since she had an account there. When the bleary-eyed Cobra stumbled into the kitchen after his nap, Mohawk told him that Kavita agreed to allow Cobra to attend the wedding and that

Emily would be coming along as well. This brightened the old man's spirits considerably.

"Very good!" he said cheerily, looking outside the window to see that Emily was doing some yoga, stretching her back and shoulders out in the backyard. "Very good!"

CHAPTER 22

The sports center was bigger than Mohawk expected it to be as he, Emily and Cobra snuck in through a back door to avoid being seen by fans. It looked like there might be a decent house tonight, maybe a few hundred or so in attendance, which was a good size for Emily's debut. Mohawk nodded at the "security guy" who let them in, a portly young man who was probably a fan himself and volunteered for the gig.

Mohawk could tell that Emily was nervous. She stayed quiet during the ride over to the venue, just staring out the window for most of the trip. Mohawk didn't want to disturb her as perhaps she was visualizing how the match would go like he used to do. Cobra was the one who was the nonstop chatterbox.

"If she shoot on you, you break her leg!" he barked, turning around in his seat to address Emily. "Like I show you!"

"I'm just wrestling another student at the school, unc," Emily said, rolling her eyes a little.

"Never mind student! You no take shit from no one!"

Once they got inside, the trio met up with Betty who steered them all to the locker room, which was co-ed. No one seemed to care, though. These were all wrestlers who mostly knew each other, having trained at Betty's school. After beating each other up so much, seeing your fellow trainee with their bare butt hanging out wasn't that big a deal.

Mohawk could see that Betty was giddy with delight, looking extremely alluring in a black cat-suit with a red pleather jacket.

"Near sell-out, Mo," she told him. "Got some IWC geeks in there, too."

Mohawk groaned inwardly. The "IWC" were the Internet Wrestling Community, a large group of wrestling hardcores who fancied themselves as journalists. They had a dedicated reader base and their opinions on their websites, YouTube videos, and social media apps could really affect how fans of pro wrestling perceive a performer. Mohawk was glad that grapplers like he and Cobra didn't have to deal with the IWC in their day but if Emily laid an egg tonight, these jerks would shit all over her on social media.

At the same time, Mohawk felt that this is what Emily had signed up for.

Sink or swim, kiddo.

Betty left them, leaving an aromatic cloud of her perfume all around Mohawk as he sat with Emily on a bench, watching closely as Cobra worked on her wrists with white athletic tape.

"This is the only time I do this," he said. "Next time you do yourself."

Cobra had said this to get a smile out of Emily but she just nodded at him. Mohawk took a closer look at her. She was dressed in his colors, red tights with white boots, kneepads and elbow-pads, and a white singlet to match.

Mohawk had bought his daughter her ring attire from Benita Alvarez, a seamstress he had a good relationship with who had made much of his gear when he was active. Emily had protested but he told her to consider it an early birthday gift.

"Let me buy your first boots, too," he had said. "It would mean a lot to me."

Cobra finished up taping Emily and the two went through some breathing exercises. Thankfully, Emily wasn't main-eventing the show, her match in the middle of the card. Mohawk could hear the murmurs of the fans filing in, the show starting soon. All around them were other trainees and some independent wrestlers getting their gear on, some of them stopping to respectfully introduce themselves to Mohawk and Cobra. Cobra sometimes dipped into his wrestling persona to mess with them but Mohawk told him to knock it off. These were just kids. No need to treat them poorly.

"Welcome!" Mohawk heard Betty bellow from a microphone in the arena section in the next room. "Tonight we've got some great action, some great debuts, and we hope ya'll enjoy the shit out of it!"

A big cheer erupted and Mohawk grinned. Betty knew how to put on a show and he wondered if he would get some alone time with her tonight...

"Dad?" Emily said, breaking into his thoughts.

Mohawk turned to Emily, who was now standing with Becca. Becca was wrestling in the main event but had a referee shirt on now.

"Yeah?" Mohawk said. "What's up?"

"My...my opponent didn't show," Emily said, eyes wide.

"Huh?"

"She no-showed," Becca said tiredly. "I always knew Meghan was gonna flake on us."

"What am I supposed to do now?" Emily asked. "Me and Meghan practiced our match for two weeks. We had it down!" She turned to Becca. "Do we cancel?"

"No!" Cobra shouted. "The show will go!"

"Cobra's right," Becca said. "I'll find someone else for you to wrestle."

She looked around the dressing room for potential opponents for Emily, maybe a wrestler with more experience who might have to perform twice tonight. Mohawk could see that Emily was freaking out.

"I can't just wrestle someone else, Dad," she said. "This is my first match...it has to go perfect!"

At this, Mohawk steered Emily away from everyone to a corner of the room. He gave her a stern look.

"This is pro wrestling," he said to her. "It's never going to go smooth. You gotta adjust on the fly."

"But you've only got one chance to make a first impression," Emily countered. "Betty said there's some internet dorks out there."

"So what? So what if you blow it out there? You gonna just retire if you do?"

Emily had nothing to say to this.

"It's just one match," Mohawk continued. "You're going to have thousands of them. Good or bad, there's always the next match." He smiled. "You'll be fine. You're trained, you're in good shape, and you're my kid."

Now Emily was the one who smiled, the first one Mohawk had seen from her all day, and it gladdened his heart. Being too tense might cause Emily to freeze up during her match, something he was definitely afraid of.

A few minutes later, Becca brought over Monica Shabazz, an African-American trainee in her mid-twenties who Mohawk had seen around Betty's school. Monica was tall, athletic and very fit, probably one of the few students who truly had a chance to make it to the big-time. Some of the other trainees, well, they sucked.

"Monica's volunteering to wrestle you," Becca said to Emily. Emily and Monica were friends and the teary-eyed Emily hugged her, thanking her for stepping up.

"No problem, girl," Monica said with a laugh. Becca mentioned she had about fifteen matches under her belt and Mohawk could see the young woman's confidence. A perfect replacement for Emily's opponent.

"Monica's playing heel," Becca told everyone. "And I'll be reffing. I'll talk you guys through the match."

Emily took a deep breath and Mohawk took one, too. This could work.

Becca went out to help Betty coordinate the show and Emily finished suiting up. She did some stretches with Cobra's help and Mohawk tried his best to "coach" her. He said stuff like, "Take your time", "Remember to sell", "Don't be nervous", and other nonsense, words that just felt empty at this particular moment, finally stopping when Cobra told him to shut up.

The three watched the early matches from behind the backstage curtain. It was some sad-ass professional wrestling. Sequences were blown, moves were missed or poorly executed, and some of the wrestlers looked just plain lost out there.

"Embarrassing," Cobra grumbled.

"They're just trainees," Mohawk said, not defending the kids beyond that.

"Not like my Emily. They are bums."

Emily said nothing. Those bums were her friends and teammates.

Then it was show-time.

"Ready?" Mohawk said, his armpits full of sweat.

"Ready!" Emily yelled.

And then she was off. Emily's theme music roared through the speakers, some Harry Styles song that she insisted on for her entrance, and she burst through the curtain. Emily got a loud pop as the audience knew who she was, one of the main draws for the night's show, and she excitedly slapped hands with the fans at ringside.

Emily rolled into the ring, waved to everyone in attendance, and then pointed down the aisle to the curtain. It was here that "Bad To The Bone" kicked in, which surprised Mohawk since neither he nor Cobra used that song for their entrance music in their careers. Still, Mohawk liked the tune and he and Cobra stepped into the lights to a gigantic reaction from the fans. They walked down the aisle to a standing ovation and Mohawk glanced over to his side where Cobra was grinning, struggling to keep up his heel persona.

"You're supposed to be bad!" Mohawk yelled to him over the cheers.

"I can't help!" Cobra chuckled.

Like Emily, Mohawk and Cobra walked all around ringside, giving high-fives or posing for selfies. It was a sizeable break in the action but seeing two professional wrestling legends together was the big draw of the show for these fans. Eventually, Mohawk was able to steer Cobra away from their adoring public to Emily's corner, nodding to Betty, still handling ring introductions, and Becca, standing by Emily in her referee attire, to get the match started.

Monica Shabazz then came out to the ring, getting polite applause from the fans at first but then boos when she started sneering at them. Mohawk had to stifle a laugh. Even after all these years, he was still happy to see when the audience recognized a heel wrestler's contempt for them.

Monica was a natural bad guy, cackling after she offered a high-five to a young fan and then pulling away at the last minute.

Monica slid into the ring and went right after Emily, shoving her hard, just as planned. Emily got fired-up, ready to retaliate, but Mohawk and Cobra held her back. Monica then turned her focus to Mohawk and Cobra.

"Get these old bastards out of my ring!" she yelled as loud as she could. Mohawk and Cobra looked indignant, as did Emily, and the early story of the match was working perfectly. Monica got the jeers she needed and the fans were hyped up, ready to see Emily teach this heel a lesson.

The bell rang and Mohawk and Cobra took their spots outside the ring to cheer Emily on. Whatever nerves she seemed to have before, when she had learned her original opponent was not going to be there, were now gone. Emily had a natural chemistry with Monica and with Becca pacing them, the match was starting off very well. Nothing extraordinary but just solid pro wrestling. They exchanged holds, ran the ropes and then things got feisty, the two exchanging punches and forearm shots, heightening the tension in the match. Eventually, Monica took the advantage, as the heel customarily does, pounding on Emily with a serious of devastating slams. Emily sold each one like it was close to crippling her with the fans moaning in dismay, and Mohawk beamed.

"That is how you sell!" Cobra said gleefully.

However, this is where things went off-track, something that Mohawk had feared would happen.

The fans started chanting but not for Emily, Monica or the match itself.

They began chanting for Mohawk and Cobra.

"Mo-hawk!" they started. Then it was, "Co-bra!"

Mo-hawk! Co-bra!

Mo-hawk! Co-bra!

Both Mohawk and Cobra saw that the fans weren't watching what was happening in the ring but rather what they were doing at ringside.

Mohawk looked at Emily, still selling one of Monica's power moves on the mat, and she seemed dumbfounded.

Mohawk felt awful. He was stealing a big moment from his daughter.

"We have to do something," he whispered to Cobra.

"What?" the man asked.

"Hit me!"

Mohawk was surprised that Cobra didn't ask a follow-up, instead just walloping Mohawk with a hard forearm smash to the chest. It winded Mohawk but he stayed on his feet, allowing Cobra to continue beating him up. The fans went unglued...the treacherous Cobra Tara Singh had turned on Mohawk Jones!

Becca, who understood the play Mohawk and Cobra were making, communicated this to Emily and Monica. Emily slid out of the ring and confronted Cobra, protecting her prone father.

"Leave my dad alone!" she shouted at Cobra, who threatened to knock her out with his gnarled fists.

The spectators were eating this up as Mohawk got back to his feet, egging Cobra on to continue to fight. The two began brawling all the way back up the aisle just as Monica snuck in behind Emily to attack her again. As much as the fight between Mohawk and Cobra got a reaction, Monica's cheap-shot got the biggest boos of the night. Mohawk and Cobra disappeared behind the curtain, no longer a distraction, and Emily and Monica were free to continue on with their match.

"Stiff," Mohawk winced, rubbing his chest.

"I had to make it look good!" Cobra laughed.

They watched the rest of Emily's match. Monica got more heat with a beat-down but then it was time for Emily to make her comeback. Monica missed an elbow-smash move and Emily took over. She hit Monica with three well-placed dropkicks and the fans were whipped into a frenzy. Finally, Emily picked Monica up and powerslammed her down, an homage to her father, for the pinfall.

The crowd erupted and Emily, exhausted and spent, had just finished her first-ever professional wrestling match.

"Your winner...Emily Jones!" Betty cried out on her microphone as Becca raised her arm in victory.

"You go," Cobra said, urging Mohawk to head back out there.

"No, this is her moment," Mohawk said.

"Go!"

Cobra pushed Mohawk through the curtain and the fans clapped when they saw him again. Emily beckoned for her dad to join her in the ring and the two hugged to great applause. Mohawk raised her arm as well and Emily blew kisses to the audience.

What a moment.

What a fucking moment…until Mohawk glanced back at the curtain and saw that Cobra was standing with Buddy Blaze, his old wrestling opponent and top talent scout for the UGF, who had an ear-to-ear grin on his face. And it wasn't for Mohawk. Buddy couldn't take his eyes off of Emily, who was now posing for selfies with ringside fans herself.

Shit.

CHAPTER 23

"I want to cut a promo before my next match," Emily declared from the backseat of Mohawk's jeep. She had just finished another show, her sixth match, wrestling in a high school gym two towns over. It was another bout against Monica Shabazz and Emily had lost this one, falling to Monica's dreaded sit-down piledriver, but she was still in high spirits.

Mohawk was pleased. He knew so many wrestlers who whined and complained when it came to taking losses, wanting to win all the time, and he was glad that his daughter didn't have that kind of ego.

"A good idea," Cobra chimed in. He was eating Haribo gummi bears for some reason, which a fan had gifted him during a pre-show autograph signing. Mohawk allowed him the junk food this one time.

"I want to be a well-rounded wrestler," Emily said. "So I need to be good on the mic, too. That means I gotta practice. In front of a crowd."

"You've been practicing by yourself like I told you to?" Mohawk asked. "In front of a mirror?"

"Yup."

Although Mohawk wouldn't admit it to anyone, he had been following wrestling social media to see what the early impressions were of Emily. After her first match, the IWC-types praised her for her skills and potential, some even posting clips of her match, as well as the shenanigans between Mohawk and Cobra. The initial buzz on Emily was good.

"I'll talk to Betty," he said. Emily's next show was back in the athletic center where she had her first match, this time going up against Becca in a student versus mentor match. "She'll probably okay it."

"Sweet," Emily grinned.

"What is your gimmick?" Cobra asked.

"Still working on it. It's gonna rock when I do it."

Mohawk grimaced. Was Emily getting too full of herself? Beyond the first match and the fans more interested in himself and Cobra, Emily's early career had been smooth-sailing. Simple, by-the-numbers matches with polite applause. Mohawk and Cobra also hadn't accompanied Emily to the ring since her debut, which was for the best.

Mohawk thought back to that night and how Buddy Blaze had been prancing around the locker room after the show, sweet-talking Emily about how he had never seen a first match go so well. Mohawk could tell the gears in his greasy head were turning. He asked Cobra what he and Buddy had been discussing while they stood at the curtain together but Cobra told him they were just basic questions, like Emily's age and athletic background. Nothing else.

"I can't wait to be a bad guy," Emily said giddily.

"Cobra will teach you all the tricks of the trade," Mohawk said, steering the jeep onto their block.

"Oh yes," Cobra said, rubbing his hands. "Emily will be a true villain!"

It wasn't too late, only about ten at night, as Emily's show started at around six and finished up after seven matches. The weather was cool but comfortable so Emily and Cobra sat outside in the backyard, the old man dropping evil pearls of wisdom on how to be a proper bad guy. Mohawk was with them, wondering how Cobra would break down lessons on heeldom.

"You must always believe!" Cobra said emphatically. "No matter what the heel do, he is right! If I hit with chair or punch in the privates, I am the right one!"

"I don't think I can hit Becca in the vagina," Emily smirked.

Cobra frowned, not liking the flippant answer.

"No jokes!" he snapped.

"Sorry," Emily said quickly.

Mohawk watched as Cobra relax, his coiled muscles becoming less tense. He was now in tremendous shape, for his age, as after his heart attack, he had a newfound respect for exercise. Cobra was working out and eating right, despite the odd bag of gummi bears. He knew he was fit, too. His confidence was back and the man often made his way through the neighborhood with a bit of a strut during his daily walks.

Mohawk still worried, though. He didn't want Cobra to entertain thoughts of an in-ring comeback.

"If you believe you are bad," Cobra continued, focusing hard on Emily. He then slapped his hand on the table several times to hammer home his point. "So. Will. The. People!"

This seemed to strike a chord with Emily. She pondered Cobra's words, nodding a little.

"So you're saying that to be real, and sell my badness to the fans, I gotta be bad," she said.

"You know it's about being authentic," Mohawk added. "Wrestling fans can spot a phony a mile away. The best gimmicks, like I told you before, are the ones where it feels the most real to them."

"Yes, you must be real," Cobra agreed.

Emily stood up.

"I want to go to my basement," she said. "And think on this stuff."

She headed off, leaving the two men by themselves.

"She is smart," Cobra said. "She says jokes but she wants to be good."

"Em wants to be great," Mohawk corrected. He then changed the subject. "How're you doing?"

"Tip top!" Cobra said, flexing his right bicep and showing an impressive knot of muscle. "Soon I will go back in ring and be a champion again!"

Mohawk was horrified but Cobra laughed hard, pointing at him.

"Your face!" he cried.

Mohawk frowned, letting Cobra chuckle himself out. It seemed to go on for a long time, the old bastard wiping tears from his eyes.

"I gots you!" he said, straightening up. Mohawk noted that even Cobra's posture had improved, too. "I do not want to wrestle. That is over."

"Glad to hear it," Mohawk said, relieved.

"Yes. I have other plans."

This piqued Mohawk's interest.

"Oh yeah?" he asked. "What do you got going on?"

"I want to get my wife back," Cobra replied calmly.

Mohawk groaned. He stared blankly at Cobra, who had a look of sheer determination on his face.

"Cobra…" Mohawk began, preparing himself to talk Cobra out of whatever stupid-ass scheme he was concocting in his crazy turbaned head.

However, once again, Cobra burst into the giggles.

"I got you again!" he squealed, laughing in Mohawk's face. Cobra then put his hands up and shook his head. "No, no, no…I do not want Kavita." He sighed. "She can marry her doctor man."

Cobra brushed his hands in a "finished" gesture before shrugging. Mohawk couldn't help but feel proud. His elderly roommate, his wrestling foe, his pain in the butt for life, was actually growing up.

Mohawk stepped inside, went to the refrigerator, and pulled out two beers. He returned to Cobra and passed him one.

"To Kavita," Mohawk said, lifting his beer.

"Kavita," Cobra said in return.

The two men took a swig and stayed quiet for a few seconds, savoring the taste. They didn't drink much nowadays but a cold beer every now and then wasn't so bad.

"I do not get my money but it is okay," Cobra said, shrugging his shoulders again. He took a sip and smiled at Mohawk. "I do not need…I have you for money."

"Great," Cobra said, rolling his eyes. They then raised their bottles again and, competitive as ever, had a contest to see who could down their beers the fastest.

The rest of the week was uneventful. Emily went to training every day, Cobra tutored her on the finer points of being a heel in the evenings, and

Mohawk became more of a spectator to everything. He didn't mind taking a backseat but now found himself with little to do.

And since he was idle now, Mohawk began to think of Betty Buxom a whole lot more. He would sometimes accompany Emily to training just to sit in Betty's office and shoot the shit, not even paying attention to whatever her daughter was doing since Becca was such a capable trainer. It seemed like Betty was enjoying Mohawk's company as well as she would ask him out for a drink every now and then. Every time, Mohawk would decline, though.

Why do I do that? Mohawk thought as he mowed the townhouse's back lawn. The neighborhood kid who usually did it was out of town with his family. *What's the big fucking deal? If she asks again, you're going to say yes. Or better yet, you're going to ask.*

Mohawk coughed. He knew he would never ask.

By the time Saturday rolled around, it was time for Emily's big match against Becca, the one where she would turn heel and finally do her first interview. Mohawk stood to the side of the locker room as Emily, Becca and Cobra put the match together. He didn't have much to add. When he was a wrestler, most of what he did was instinctual. Mohawk had left planning to the savvier performers.

The match was the main event of the show and Mohawk had noticed that crowds for Betty's little promotion were up since Emily's debut. She was easily getting the loudest reactions, even without Mohawk and Cobra "managing" her and staying in her corner. Mohawk could definitely say, with pride, that Emily was the brightest rising star on Betty's roster.

The match with Becca started out normally, a respectful technical exhibit of wrestling moves and countermoves. However, Becca was getting the best of Emily at every turn and Emily began to show little signs of frustration. This was planting the seed for what was to come.

"She is marvelous," Cobra said glowingly as he and Mohawk stood at the back curtain.

Emily and Becca continued wrestling and after Becca reversed out of Emily's powerslam, the switch happened. Emily reared back and sucker-punched Becca right in the face. The crowd "ooh"-ed in surprise and Emily then went on the attack, viciously kicking and stomping Becca, choking her and pulling her hair.

"Don't you ever embarrass me!" Emily shrieked, now wrestling as a full-on heel.

The fans were shocked by Emily's lack of sportsmanship and she stayed on Becca like a bloodthirsty animal. Finally, after the action had spilled to the outside, Emily hit Becca with a steel chair behind the referee's back, threw her in the ring, hoisted her up for her finishing move, and powerslammed Becca for the win.

A cascade of boos rained down from the stands and upon the satisfied Emily as the "injured" Becca was helped from the ring by the referee. Emily then gestured for someone to hand her a microphone.

"Here we go," Mohawk said. "Let's see what she's got."

He and Cobra watched as Emily, sweat-soaked and breathless, took in the boos and she, like Cobra had told her, took her time. There was no hurry. Cutting a promo after a hard match was tough since the adrenaline is still flowing and it's hard to remember what exactly you wanted to talk about. Taking a few moments was very much a necessity.

"C'mon," Mohawk said quietly from his spot backstage. "Deep breath and...go."

Even though Emily couldn't hear her dad, she did exactly what he said. Mohawk saw her do a big inhale...and come out of it with a sinister smile.

"Wildcat Becca Stone," she began, walking around the ring with a malevolent expression. "My trainer. The woman who taught me everything I know about being a pro wrestler...my mentor, my coach, my big sis, my everything." Emily shrugged playfully. "She really shouldn't have disrespected me today."

Loud boos aimed at Emily and Mohawk smiled. She hooked the audience, who, despite their new hate for her, were all leaning forward to hear what she said next.

"I didn't come into professional wrestling to make friends," Emily continued, her confidence growing as she spoke into the mic. "I came here for two things: make money and win championships. So thank you for your help so far, Becca...but I think we can all agree that the student has surpassed the teacher!"

More boos, these ones even more outraged.

"You suck, Emily!" a middle-aged guy with a Red Sox cap yelled. "You're only here because of your dad!"

"Oh no," Cobra said and Mohawk agreed. That was the kind of statement that could rattle Emily.

The fans all waited for her response.

And then she giggled.

"My dad?" Emily said, a harshness to her voice. "You wanna bring my dad into this?"

Mohawk and Cobra glanced at each other. Where was this going to go?

"MY DAD WASN'T SHIT!" Emily screamed at the top of her lungs, which immediately caused everyone in the athletic center to gasp. "That jerk wasn't there for me growing up! I'm the one who made myself who I am! I put in the work!" Emily's pacing around the ring picked up as she worked herself into a frenzy. "I don't need my dad or his legacy! I'm going to be better than him!"

Emily grinned at the stunned audience.

"Just watch me, losers...I'm gonna be a star," she said arrogantly before dropping the mic, jumping out of the ring and strolling to the back, double middle fingers held out for everyone.

"That was very real," Cobra said quietly to Mohawk. Mohawk said nothing but looked around the backstage area. Betty and the other wrestlers, including Becca, were wide-eyed and speechless.

A couple of minutes after she finished mocking the fans, Emily jubilantly leaped through the curtain and ran right over to Mohawk and Cobra. She was ecstatic and Mohawk had never seen his daughter so excited.

"Pretty good, huh?" she said, hopping up and down. "My first heel promo! It was so much fun!"

CHAPTER 24

"I don't get what you're so mad about," Emily said, a confused look on her face as she, Mohawk and Cobra headed out to the parking lot. They had waited for all the fans to head home so they could get to Mohawk's jeep without anyone coming up to them. That time was spent in the locker room, none of them saying much.

"I'm not mad," Mohawk said, trying to sound convincing.

"You're totally mad. And I don't know why. I just did what you taught me."

Emily turned to Cobra, who put his hands up in protest.

"I did not teach those words," he said nervously.

"Yeah, but you did teach me that to be a good heel, I had to be real," Emily fired back.

They arrived at the jeep and Mohawk felt true sadness in him.

"Is that how you feel about me?" he asked his daughter. "That I'm just some guy who wasn't there for you?"

"I think I should…not be here," Cobra said, stepping away so Mohawk and Emily could have it out.

Emily frowned at Mohawk, her eyes flashing with anger.

"Why would you ask me that?" she asked. "After all we've been through since we met?"

"That promo," Mohawk replied. "It came from somewhere."

Emily bit her lip, which she was prone to do when she was uncomfortable.

Then a black Cadillac SUV roared in, startling both Mohawk and his daughter, narrowly avoiding Emily.

"What the fuck?!" she yelled. It was night-time and even though the athletic center was well-lit, the Cadillac still caught them by surprise.

Mohawk went to the shaken Emily and Cobra jogged in to join them.

"Is everyone okay?" he asked.

"No!" Emily shouted. She then looked ahead at the Cadillac, which was parked a few feet away. "And whoever's in that fucking thing is not gonna be okay, either!"

Mohawk reached to pull Emily back from storming over to the idling SUV and they all watched as Buddy Blaze, dressed head-to-toe in a dark blue suit with black cowboy boots and a black Stetson hat, his wrists jingling with diamond bracelets and a Rolex, stepped out of his car.

"Like the new ride?" Buddy cackled. "Just got it. Drove it off the lot."

"What do you want, Buddy?" Mohawk asked tiredly. He really didn't want to deal with this jackass right now.

"It's not what I want, brother. It's what, or who, *he* wants..."

Tom Victory then stepped out of the backseat, dressed in a gray power suit with a blood-red tie, sporting an immaculate haircut, and wearing shoes so polished, they shone in the dark. A handsome and well-built man in his early fifties, Tom was the most powerful individual in professional wrestling.

"Mohawk Jones and Cobra Tara Singh!" Tom bellowed. "How the hell are ya?"

Mohawk wasn't intimidated by Tom, although most people were. He had known Tom as a boy and no amount of money or cosmetic sheen was going to impress him. Cobra and Emily were a different story, though. Both gaped at Tom with wide eyes.

"I'm good, Tom," Mohawk said. He shook the man's hand, Tom trying to crunch Mohawk's fingers to impress upon him his dominant nature. Mohawk wasn't some weakling off the street, though. He squeezed back, resulting in a stalemate.

The two broke off and Tom grinned at Mohawk.

"Is there somewhere we can chat?" he asked gently. "I want to talk business."

And right on cue, the man turned his gaze to Emily, who couldn't help but blush.

Mohawk had tried his best to mentally prepare for this moment. He knew that as soon as he spotted Buddy at Emily's first show, the man was going to scurry back to Tom Victory and implore the man to sign her to a UGF contract. Mohawk had certain feelings about this but out of respect for Tom's father, he felt he should at least hear the man out.

They all reconvened to the townhouse's kitchen, the five of them sitting at the table, Tom and Buddy on one side with Mohawk, Emily and Cobra on the other. Mohawk served coffee but no one really seemed that interested in a hot beverage.

Okay, Tom Victory, Mohawk thought. *Let's dance.*

"My people have been following Emily for a little while now," Tom began. There was no need for small talk. It was late and everyone wanted to get down to brass tacks. "We think she's one of the finest up-and-comers in the industry right now." Tom smiled at Emily, who blushed again. "Congratulations, young lady. You've done quite well for yourself."

"Thank you, sir," Emily said quietly. Mohawk could tell she was mush in Tom's presence. He was the man who could make every wrestling dream she ever had a reality.

"We trained her!" Cobra blurted out.

"Ya'll did a helluva job," Buddy said.

Mohawk knew that Buddy had a lot riding on this meeting. As the one who scouted Emily, a big win here would do wonders for his career.

Tom turned his attention back to Mohawk and it now felt like they were the only two in the room.

"We know that Emily has a lot of potential," Mohawk said. "She'd be an asset to any company she chooses to work for…when she's ready."

Even though Mohawk didn't see it, he could tell Emily didn't like hearing this. He hoped she would keep her mouth shut and let him handle this.

"We think she's ready now," Tom said emphatically. "So that's why we want to offer her a development deal."

Again, Mohawk could feel the excited energy emanating from his daughter. She would have yelped in joy if she could but something was holding her back. Mohawk hoped it was because of some kind of father-child connection they had.

"A development deal sounds like a good start for Emily," Mohawk said calmly.

"Yes, it would," Tom said. "We've already had our creative team working on how to progress her career, from in-ring to character ideas. If Emily signs with us, she'll have access to the best wrestling minds in the business."

"We don't make stars," Buddy added. "We make superstars."

"Money?" Cobra asked. He just couldn't help himself.

"Wrestlers in development don't make as much money as main roster wrestlers," Tom said. "We view them as projects. They work a smaller circuit while we prep them for the big show. But in Emily's case, we're prepared to make an offer that will be in the low six figures, which would make her among the highest-paid developmental wrestlers we have. Plus, we'll throw in a signing bonus."

This was quite a sizeable offer from the UGF. Mohawk pondered it and stood up. He then, without looking at Emily and Cobra, stuck out his hand to Tom Victory again. He thanked Tom and Buddy for their time and asked that they send in their offer in writing at their soonest convenience. Tom and Buddy seemed surprised that they weren't able to close the deal immediately.

"You'll have the offer tomorrow," Tom said, shaking Mohawk's hand a lot gentler now. He then added, confidently, to Emily. "I look forward to working with you."

Tom and Buddy left the townhouse and Emily clasped her hands in front of her chest in a beseeching manner.

"Dad, please," she said. "I want to take the deal!"

"Then take it," Mohawk said. "You don't need my permission."

"Yeah, but I want your blessing."

Emily looked at Cobra, who was looking starry-eyed.

"Both of your blessings," she said.

"You have it!" Cobra cried.

He and Emily stared at Mohawk, who sighed.

"Let's talk," he said to Emily. He then took her by the elbow and gently steered her to the backyard.

"What's there to talk about?" Emily asked, bewildered. When they stepped outside, they had startled a raccoon foraging around but it scampered off without incident.

"I want to talk about that promo," Mohawk replied.

"Seriously, Dad? After all that's just happened? It was just a promo!"

"Was it?"

Mohawk furrowed his brow at Emily, who leaned against the railing of the back porch. She threw her hands up.

"Okay, fine!" she said. "I used to be super pissed at you!"

"Used to be?"

"Yeah! When my mom told me about you before she died, I wanted to actually be your kid, like, have a relationship and all that, but I didn't know if it would ever happen. So sometimes I hated your guts because I thought you didn't care about me or whatever."

"I didn't know you existed."

"I know!"

Mohawk nodded, waiting for more. Emily went over to him and put her hands on his shoulders.

"Dad, believe me, I, like, love your old ass," she said emotionally. "What you've done for me…I'll never forget it. Ever. It makes up for everything." Emily sighed. "It really was just a promo. I was digging deep, looking for something that would make those people really hate me. And the best way to do it was to turn heel on you."

Mohawk was dumbfounded. Emily hadn't even been training for a full year yet she had already gotten a grasp on the hardest aspect of professional wrestling to master: psychology. The ability to manipulate the crowd's emotions to further storylines and enhance characters.

Mohawk felt so proud.

"You've got my blessing, Em," he said.

The next morning, a contract showed up at the house via courier. Tom Victory wanted Emily Jones under the UGF banner as quickly as possible. However, her deal was not the only offer that had come in. Large envelopes containing legal documents for Mohawk Jones and Cobra Tara Singh had arrived as well.

"What is this?" Cobra asked, mightily confused.

Mohawk smiled wryly.

"Tom wants to sign us, too," he said.

CHAPTER 25

Needless to say, Mohawk didn't want to go back to working full-time for the UGF or any other professional wrestling organization. Sure, he had been feeling aimless for the past few months but the prospect of being employed by Tom Victory didn't sit well with him.

Mohawk had no personal issues with Tom Victory. He was only wrestling sporadically, and rarely in North America beyond spot independent shows, when Tom took over from his father. Tom did more to grow the company than his dad, becoming a hands-on guy who oversaw all facets of UGF, from the live television to the merchandise they cranked out.

However, wrestlers talk and Tom was known as someone who could make you…or crush you. Even though UGF was a billion-dollar entity and Tom himself was worth close to that, wrestlers weren't treated much better now than they were in Mohawk and Cobra's day. There were no benefits, retirement plans, or guarantees of any kind if you were a UGF wrestler. You were an "independent contractor", a legal term that Tom and his lawyers frequently used to screw wrestlers over.

So why did wrestlers continue to want to ply their trade for such an unscrupulous promoter? Mostly because Tom was the only real game in town. There were smaller wrestling companies but the UGF was the place to make good money and become famous. The only comparative was maybe a top Japanese company but for a foreigner, living in Asia and so far away from home wasn't easy. So UGF remained the wrestling world's biggest stage.

As someone who had climbed the highest of heights in the business already, Mohawk wasn't eager to get back on that stage. He had earned his freedom after working his broken body to its upper limits for years. Why subject himself to the travel and anxiety of professional wrestling again?

Of course, Mohawk knew the answer to this.

His daughter and her dreams.

After the contracts were delivered, and a call was made to Buddy Blaze for some clarity on some of the legalese, Mohawk called everyone into the living room for a "family meeting". It was there that Mohawk explained to Emily that the creative plan Tom Victory had for them was for Mohawk and Cobra, two feudin' legends, to put aside their differences and act as onscreen "coaches" for Emily. Instead of just Emily coming into UGF, Tom wanted the trio as a unit.

Mohawk had thought Emily might not like this idea, wanting to make it on her own. To his surprise, and perhaps disappointment, she erupted with joy.

"Are you kidding me?" she squealed. "That sounds awesome! I'm so in!"

Mohawk kept a poker face on but his stomach dropped. Maybe Cobra would be on his side.

"Shabaash! Yes!" Cobra shrieked himself, high-fiving Emily and excitedly smacking his fists on the coffee table. "This is what I have been waiting for! My comeback!" He pointed at Emily. "We will be the world champion!"

Cobra and Emily hugged and Mohawk leaned back on the couch. He waited for them to finish their celebratory dancing around the room, Emily mimicking Cobra's Punjabi Bhangra-style.

Eventually, they tired themselves out. Out of breath, Emily knelt down in front of her father.

"Dad?" she said. "You haven't said anything."

Mohawk sighed.

"What's there to say?" he said. "The money's good and the opportunity's good. Let's sign."

More bellows of happiness from Emily and Cobra and they started dancing again. Cobra tried to pull Mohawk up to join them but was rebuked. That night, they ordered pizza and ate in the backyard, drinking beers together.

"This is just the beginning," Cobra said ominously to Emily, as a warning of sorts. He had calmed down a little. "The work is not done."

"I know that, Uncle Cobra," Emily said peevishly. She then grinned. "Those bitches at UGF don't know what's coming. I'm gonna out-train, outwork, and out-wrestle everyone one of those fuckers!"

She and Cobra clinked their bottles together. Mohawk had been generally quiet throughout dinner and after everyone headed off to bed, he stayed awake in his room for several hours. They had signed the contracts and sent them back but Mohawk couldn't help but have a bad feeling about what they were getting themselves into.

A few days later, Mohawk, Emily and Cobra flew out to Tampa to UGF's development facility. Tom and Buddy had put the three of them up in a condo, not much bigger than the townhouse's ground floor, but the place was tidy and the fridge was well-stocked with food and drink. The trio headed to the UGF headquarters in the morning for some medical testing, just to make sure everyone was in good shape to perform. Mohawk and Cobra weren't expected to wrestle or be physical at all on television but UGF officials still wanted to make sure none of their talent had any health issues, probably for liability reasons.

Emily aced every test and Mohawk did well enough, his cholesterol a little high. The real revelation was Cobra. The old bastard's health was stellar, to the point all the doctors were stunned by his results.

"This can't be right," Dr. Rosenbaum, the UGF's top doc, muttered as he sat with Mohawk, Emily and Cobra in his office and read the reports. He stared hard at Cobra, the man's beard immaculately groomed and his burgundy turban sitting proudly on his head.

"What's wrong, doc?" Mohawk asked.

"Mr. Singh's tests. It's as if he has the health of a man half his age. Some of our top wrestlers aren't as healthy."

Of course, Cobra accepted this with the regal humility of an Indian rajah. He took off his shirt and stood before Dr. Rosenbaum, showing off his bare torso. It was matted with white hair and the man was still thin...but absolutely ripped, his six-pack clearly defined and his chest muscles taut and veiny.

"You," Cobra said, pointing at the doctor. "Take all in."

Dr. Rosenbaum became flustered but ordered some more tests for Cobra, this time testing for steroids and other enhancement drugs. Cobra cockily took the pee test and came out clean.

Next up was enrolling Emily into the UGF Academy. It was a massive set-up compared to Betty and Becca's school with state-of-the-art training equipment, multiple rings to work out of, some of the best pro wrestling talents ever as coaches, and even video production facilities to practice promo and character work.

"Be cool," Mohawk whispered to Emily as they were taken on a tour of the place by Buddy Blaze, who ran the Academy, although he himself never got in the ring. He just oversaw everything, which he had said at least nine times in the first two and a half minutes of the tour.

"I am cool," Emily said, playfully squeezing her father on the arm. She certainly appeared calm but Mohawk wouldn't be surprised if she was feeling imposter syndrome, wondering if she actually belonged in the UGF or deserved the opportunity that she was given. However, if Emily felt this way, she didn't ever show it outwardly.

Within a week, Mohawk, Emily and Cobra had settled into their routines. Emily had joined a training cohort to get her primed for wrestling on television. This was meant to scrub some of the sloppy tendencies out of her ring work, tighten up her skills, and teach her to wrestle for the different cameras set up around the ring. The "hard camera" was always the one you needed to focus on, the perspective the fans at home would be watching on TV. It wasn't easy to wrestle towards one side of the ring and Emily had some frustrating moments at first, but she was a fast learner.

Mohawk and Cobra, who often sat in on her sessions, could see that out of the nine wrestlers in her group, she was one of the better athletes.

For Mohawk and Cobra, their days were spent mostly in the gym of the facility, pumping iron or getting their cardio work in. The UGF gym was the best Mohawk had ever been in and also had amenities like massage therapy, a swimming pool and steam rooms. It even had yoga classes and Brazilian Jiu-Jitsu seminars to participate in.

"We're just waiting," Buddy Blaze told Mohawk and Cobra while they lounged in his spacious office and watched some of their old matches together. "We gotta get Emily perfectly ready. Don't worry, it won't take long. A month. Maybe two."

It ended up being four and a half months but Mohawk and Cobra didn't mind. They enjoyed the Florida weather and while Emily was training, they explored Tampa, visiting the Sunshine Skyway Bridge, the Tampa Riverwalk in downtown Tampa, and even Busch Gardens. One weekend, they rented a fishing boat and took Emily out on the water with them. Neither Mohawk or Cobra could fish very well but it was a nice family outing, one that Mohawk cherished because they didn't talk about professional wrestling the entire time.

However, soon it was time for Emily's big debut...which was going to be a dark match.

"It's not gonna be on TV?" Emily asked as they drove their rental car to Orlando where their first show was going to be held.

"That's what Buddy said," Mohawk said. "They want to try out our gimmick and see how it does in front of a crowd. They do this for all new characters."

Mohawk was driving and checked out the rearview mirror. He could see the disappointment on Emily's face.

"It's a test," he continued. "There's going to be tons of them along the way. You're not going to get everything you want right away. Better prepare yourself for that."

Emily took a deep breath.

"You're right," she said, before adding with a big smile. "I'll just have to rock it tonight!"

She laughed, which caused Cobra, who had been taking a nap, to stir.

"What is the matter?" he asked sleepily.

"Nothing," Mohawk replied. "Go back to napping."

"Okay."

Cobra leaned to the side and was out like a light. Mohawk shook his head.

"No idea how he can snooze so easy," he said.

Mohawk waited for Emily to say something but she stayed silent. He glanced up at the rearview again and saw that Emily herself had zonked out.

"Someone else is driving home," Mohawk muttered to himself.

They arrived at the Amway Center, where the NBA's Orlando Magic play, about forty minutes later, and Mohawk showed their ID credentials to security, who allowed them to park in a restricted lot. Emily grabbed her gear out of the trunk and both Mohawk and Cobra had small satchels with their stuff. They rode up an elevator to the backstage area, which was a busy hive of workers prepping for the show. It was three in the afternoon and the show wouldn't be going live until eight. Emily's match was to be around seven-thirty, to help warm up the crowd.

An assistant came up to Emily to show where the locker room was. He suggested that Mohawk and Cobra go to catering and have a late lunch, maybe meet some of the wrestlers and crew. Both Mohawk and Cobra were hungry so they moseyed over to catering right away.

Immediately, Mohawk and Cobra were greeted warmly and respectfully by the young wrestlers. Neither man knew who these kids were beyond seeing them on television and were happy to be treated well by them. And what a spread at catering! Virtually every food you could ask for, including healthy options, as it seemed that Tom Victory spared no expense in this regard. Mohawk grabbed a serving of a delicious-looking chicken salad and Cobra had some lasagna...as well as a helping of some apple pie with vanilla ice cream.

Mohawk was disappointed that no one he knew from his in-ring days was working backstage. He had hoped to bump into an old-timer and shoot the shit. They did find Siniestro, who had been re-hired by the UGF recently. Siniestro invited Mohawk and Cobra to sit with him and the three dug into their lunches together.

"So nice to see you again," Siniestro said tiredly. He wasn't wearing his mask, dressed casually in jeans and a gray Adidas tee. Mohawk could see that the man was looking haggard and worn-out.

"We're glad you're back on TV," Mohawk said.

"Yes," Cobra added. "You are very, very talented."

Siniestro appreciated the compliments but kept his eyes on his steak wrap.

"You okay, brother?" Mohawk asked, sensing that something was wrong.

Siniestro mustered up a weak smile.

"I'm good," he said. "This life…it's tough. Lots of traveling. Don't see my son as much as I want. You know how it is."

Mohawk and Cobra nodded. They definitely knew that the wrestler's life was hard and unforgiving. It's why Mohawk didn't want Emily to be a part of this world. He could clearly see that it was taking a toll on Siniestro.

"How is your body?" Cobra asked. A weird question but Cobra was an eccentric man.

"I'm holding up alright," Siniestro replied. "Knee's a bit banged-up but I can deal. I might need it scoped next year." He smiled. "Then I can take a break for a few months."

Mohawk's stomach twisted. This young wrestler was looking forward to time off via healing up from surgery, like this was a good thing.

"Even if my knee's at seventy-five percent, I'm still better than most dudes on the roster," Siniestro said. "Not that management ever cares. I haven't had a good win on TV in months."

He said the last part bitterly and Mohawk again felt a pang of worry. He looked around at the other wrestlers in the room, all eating and chatting with each other. Many of them seemed fine but there were quite a few who appeared just as exhausted and frustrated as Siniestro.

"Don't trust the bosses," Siniestro warned, his voice a whisper. He left it at that.

Mohawk and Cobra then exchanged some small talk with Siniestro for a little longer, not talking about anything wrestling-related because the young wrestler didn't seem interested in doing so. After they finished eating, Siniestro shook both Mohawk's and Cobra's hands and was ushered away by a television producer to discuss his match on tonight's episode of Tuesday Night Massacre.

"What do you think?" Mohawk asked Cobra, both watching Siniestro limp away.

"I do not know," Cobra replied.

The two sat without speaking for the next few minutes.

"Mohawk?" Cobra said tentatively. "I do not think I want to eat my apple pie now."

"Then don't," Mohawk replied.

They tossed their food into the garbage. Mohawk felt bad for wasting something that tasted so good, and wondered what they should do next. Showtime wasn't for a while and the last thing Mohawk wanted to do was sit in catering all day.

"Mo! Co! Come over here!"

Mohawk and Cobra turned to see Buddy Blaze, dressed in a hot pink suit with sparkly boots, waving frantically at them.

"Got a meeting with Tom!" he shouted. "Let's skedaddle!"

Tom was their boss now so Mohawk and Cobra had no choice but to skedaddle. They followed Buddy down a corridor, walking past other wrestlers, referees, and backstage workers, waving and shaking hands along the way. They also saw Siniestro again, who didn't look happy at all, but still gave them a friendly nod.

They probably told him he's not winning tonight, Mohawk thought. At this stage of the game, wins and losses did matter to one's career. It was fine to take a loss when the story deemed it necessary but a wrestler who lost and lost and lost was someone that the top brass didn't see much of a future in and they were only kept around to make other wrestlers look good. Siniestro was a highly-skilled performer, proficient in all facets of the game, so that's probably what his role with the company was. Mohawk could understand that after years of honing his craft, this was a less than ideal position for Siniestro to find himself in. Any hope of becoming a top main event talent was likely a pipedream now.

This fucking business...

As they arrived at Tom Victory's office, Mohawk pushed thoughts like this out of his head. He was a contracted performer now and had to do his best for his daughter's future. He saw Tom sitting in a leather chair, his suit jacket off and sleeves rolled up while scrolling on an iPad. Tom also wore a pair of reading glasses and he looked up to see Buddy leading Mohawk and Cobra in.

"Here they are, sir," Buddy said, gesturing for the two older men to stand before Tom.

"Nice to see you both," Tom said simply. There was no enmity in his tone but no real warmth, either. A far cry from when the man was in Mohawk's house, performing a sales pitch to bring the family into the UGF fold. Then again, Tom had gotten what he wanted so why would he be kissing Mohawk and Cobra's butts now?

"Good to see you," Cobra said. He seemed intimidated, perhaps realizing for the first time that Tom was now his employer.

"Buddy's running the show tonight," Tom said. "At least before we go live. So he'll be producing Emily's match. I just wanted to wish you both luck before you go out there. I know you'll knock 'em dead."

He finally smiled and Mohawk felt disarmed. Not completely, though.

"Much appreciated," he said, offering his hand. Tom took it, squeezed it as hard as he could, and then went back to scrolling. It felt rude to Mohawk but he understood that the man had a lot to deal with. At least he found the time to chat a little with them before the show.

Mohawk and Cobra then went to the smaller room next door, which was Buddy's office. Emily arrived a few minutes later, looking wonderful in her new purple and white gear, make-up professionally done, and hair in wavy curls. Although Mohawk was disappointed she wasn't wearing his red and white colors, he was happy to see Emily looking like a true star.

"You like?" Emily asked. "Tom had a meeting with me and brought me the new gear."

Before Mohawk could speak, Buddy and Cobra burst forward.

"Goddamn, child!" Buddy said. "You look like ten million bucks!"

"My niece is a real wrestler!" Cobra exclaimed.

Emily grinned and turned to Mohawk. She was fighting back her emotions and so was he.

"You look perfect," he said softly.

Emily reached out and squeezed Mohawk's hand, the one that Tom had crushed, but Mohawk bit down his discomfort and smiled lovingly at his daughter.

"Should we wear purple and white?" Cobra asked Buddy. "To match?"

"Nah," Buddy said. "We're gonna go easy tonight." He turned to his assistant. "Take this down. Mo and Co will walk Emily down to the ring, wave and all that to the crowd to get some buzz, Emily will have her match, and then Mo and Co will go into the ring, congratulate Emily and then come back."

Mohawk was beginning to hate this "Mo and Co" thing and hoped it wouldn't make it to television.

Everyone agreed that Buddy's plan was straightforward enough although Cobra annoyingly asked if he could do some in-ring antics after the match for "heat". This was shot down fast by Buddy and after leaving the meeting, Mohawk, Cobra and Emily moved to a quiet corner of the arena to prepare.

"Who's your opponent?" Mohawk asked.

"Tom said it was some local veteran wrestler," Emily replied as Cobra ran her through some stretches. "Someone they use a lot with rookies. Tom said she would lead me through the match but I'd hit her with three big moves, like my dropkicks and a suplex, and finish her off with my powerslam."

Mohawk smiled.

"Your powerslam?" he asked teasingly.

"It's mine now," Emily replied with a giggle.

An hour later, it was time to wrestle. Mohawk, Emily and Cobra stood together at the curtain, Emily in the middle and holding both men's hands.

"Let's fucking go," she said as the curtain was pulled aside, the guitar riffs of Emily's new theme song began, and the trio took their first steps forward in front of a crowd of ten thousand people.

CHAPTER 26

It had been many years since Mohawk had been in front of a wrestling crowd like this. Legions of rabid fans proudly wearing their just-bought merchandise while holding up signs in support of not only their favorite wrestlers but the UGF as a whole. Equally impressive to Mohawk was the show set-up. He, Emily and Cobra walked down a ramp to the ring where dozens of bright lights shone upon them. Behind them was a huge video screen, displaying footage of Emily training at the UGF Academy as well as some clips of Mohawk and Cobra in action during their heydays.

Yet the reaction from the crowd was tepid. Mohawk had hoped for a rousing ovation but the fans only clapped politely for them. Mohawk had never considered that the UGF audience might not know who Mohawk Jones and Cobra Tara Singh were. It had been decades since they were prominent main-eventers and a lot of tonight's crowd hadn't even been born yet. Mohawk could see Cobra doing his best to mug for the fans but his antics were received with a bemused smile or two and that's it.

Mohawk glanced over to Emily, who was smiling and waving to the crowd like the consummate good guy. She didn't seem rattled and that's all that mattered. Mohawk watched as she slid in the ring, greeted the referee, and waited in the corner for her opponent. Mohawk and Cobra went around ringside, slapping hands with fans, and then stood near Emily.

"Why are they so quiet, eh?" Cobra asked, clearly confused.

"It's early in the show," Mohawk replied, trying to spare the man's feelings. It was true that some fans were still filing in but Mohawk didn't have the heart to tell Cobra that maybe they weren't the esteemed wrestling legends they thought they were.

Mohawk looked up at Emily, who was jogging on the spot to keep warm and loose.

"You good, kid?" he asked.

Emily winked at him. She opened her mouth to speak but was interrupted by the thunderous booms of drums followed by an electric guitar screech. Emily's opponent's theme music was starting up and the fans roared in delight.

"No, no, no…" Cobra said worriedly.

"What's wrong?" Mohawk asked.

"That is Toni Titan's music!"

Mohawk looked to the stage and saw the black leather-clad, heavily tattooed and black lipstick-ed Toni Titan tear out of the curtain and angrily stomp her way to the ring. She looked even more gigantic and fearsome in person.

"This isn't right!" Mohawk yelled at the referee. "She's not supposed to wrestle fucking Toni Titan!"

"Plans change," the referee said, shrugging his shoulders.

Mohawk remembered watching the match where Toni had completely decimated her opponent, doing so in a reckless and dangerous way and not protecting the other wrestler at all.

"Emily!" Mohawk yelled helplessly. What was he supposed to do now? His daughter was in the ring and he couldn't just drag her out of there.

"I got this, Dad!" Emily said as Toni went up the ring steps and charged into the ring. "It's just a…"

She was interrupted when Toni attacked her. The woman was twice Emily's size, clubbing her in the head and neck with forearms and then hitting her with a hard knee to the chin. Toni was "working", meaning her attacks weren't full force, but they were definitely hurting Emily.

"Ref! What the fuck?!" Mohawk yelled. It was hard to hear him because the fans were screaming, eating up the violence. Now Toni was stomping Emily in the corner with heavy kicks to the stomach and mugging to the crowd. Not once had Toni looked Mohawk and Cobra's way and Mohawk knew why. She had been told to lay in an introductory beating on Emily, a way to welcome her to the company.

Mohawk turned to Cobra, who stood watching in horror.

"What do we do?" Mohawk asked.

Cobra looked around at the crowd and shook his head helplessly.

"Nothing," he replied. "We do nothing."

Mohawk couldn't accept this. He ran around ringside to get closer to Emily, who was looking dazed but still aware of herself.

"She's shooting on you!" Mohawk shouted in his daughter's ear. "You gotta hit her back!"

Emily appeared confused by this and Mohawk could see she might be concussed. He looked around for the ringside doctor and gestured for him to do something but the man ignored his pleas.

This was a fucking set-up all the way, Mohawk thought.

He watched as Emily pulled herself to her feet, holding on to the ropes to keep upright. To a fan's eye, it looked like she was just selling Toni's attacks but any wrestler could see that Emily was in trouble. Toni then came at her again but Emily slipped away, smacking the woman in the face with a forearm of her own. There wasn't much behind it but it got Toni to reel back and give Emily some space.

"Try to tap her!" Mohawk screamed, not knowing what else to do. If Emily could get Toni into some kind of submission hold, it might end the match or at least get Toni to stop trying to kill her and start cooperating. However, Toni was a seasoned pro herself. She easily neutralized any choke or limb hold Emily attempted and countered with a serious of hard slams and more forearms to the head.

"End the fucking match!" Mohawk screamed at the ref. He was seconds away from climbing into the ring and Cobra was close by, ready to do the same. They were too late, though. Toni lifted Emily up in a dangerous high-angle powerbomb, flipping her up onto her shoulders and driving her hard into the mat, the impact in the neck and the back of the head. Emily was knocked out immediately and Toni pinned her for the win.

And then Toni was out of there, almost sprinting her way to the back and probably out of the arena so no one could confront her for what she did. Emily hadn't moved and Mohawk and Cobra were in the ring now, holding her hands as some UGF officials and the ringside doctor finally got their stupid asses in to help her.

"Em, can you hear me?" Mohawk asked, fighting back tears.

Emily's eyes were open as she had regained consciousness soon after the pin. She nodded slightly.

"Dad?" she said weakly.

"I'm here," Mohawk said.

"I am here, too," Cobra added softly.

To their credit, the fans were respectfully quiet as Emily was stretchered out, more of the medical staff rushing to the ring to help. Mohawk and Cobra followed as Emily was taken to the back, loaded into an ambulance, and sent off to the local hospital. Other wrestlers, including Siniestro, had come by to see what was happening, many of them looking worried for Emily.

Mohawk watched the ambulance go and then grabbed the referee for the match, a blond-haired man in his late forties named Ted, by the collar, spinning him around completely.

"What the fuck was that?" he shouted, shaking Ted fiercely. "You let that bitch destroy my kid!"

"I'm sorry!" Ted quailed, looking ready to shit his pants. "I just did what I was told to do!"

Mohawk tossed Ted aside in disgust and turned to Cobra, who was with Siniestro, a devout Catholic, kneeling down in prayer for Emily. The others had offered their condolences and best wishes for Emily but Mohawk was in no mood to hear them.

"Let's go," Mohawk said to Cobra, who nodded grimly.

The two men marched over to Tom Victory's office where he found Tom and Buddy. They were in great spirits and laughing it up.

"Hell of a debut!" Tom chuckled, smiling brightly at Mohawk. "That Toni Titan, eh?"

"Your girl could sure take a beating!" Buddy added gleefully.

Mohawk was so stunned by how cavalier Tom and Buddy were behaving, he momentarily forgot his rage.

"Why?" he asked simply.

"Because of a promise," Tom replied.

"What promise?"

Tom stood up and put his hands on his hips, staring hard at Mohawk.

"My dad always hated you," he said. "You almost killed his company."

Mohawk's head began to spin.

"What are you talking about?" he said.

Tom rolled his eyes, as if he was disgusted just being in the same room with Mohawk.

"My dad had big dreams," Tom said. "He put them on you. With Mohawk Jones at the top of the card, as world champion, the UGF would become a global sensation." He glared at Mohawk. "But you dropped the ball. You flopped as champ and Stan Victory almost lost everything. You nearly broke my dad, the best man I ever knew, and the greatest father a kid could have, and I promised if I ever had a chance to turn things around, I'd make Mohawk Jones pay."

Now Mohawk was the one rolling his eyes. This was too stupid.

"You nearly crippled my kid because I wasn't a good enough world champ for Stan Victory?" he said. "You know how fucking idiotic that sounds?"

Hearing this, Tom squared off with Mohawk. Although he was younger and in better shape, Tom wasn't ever known as a tough guy. Mohawk was a scarred and battle-tested warrior with decades of wrestling experience now in the best shape he had been in since he was an active performer. Mohawk could take an eye out in, well, a blink of an eye right now.

Tom seemed to recognize this. He backed off a few steps but still tried to project his authority.

"Emily's contract?" he said, deepening his voice. "Terminated. I never really wanted her here anyway. And your contract? Terminated. Cobra's contract? Terminated." He waved his hand dismissively. "Now get the fuck out of my sight, you old piece of shit."

"Or we'll get security to bounce your asses on out of here," Buddy added. He was taking much glee in this as Mohawk suspected the man had hated him for a long time, too.

That was it. There was nothing left to do now. Tom had gotten his revenge, killing Mohawk's daughter's dream and making him look like a pathetic fool. Mohawk didn't know what to do...until he turned and looked at Cobra, who stood near the grinning Buddy Blaze.

Cobra's expression was blank but Mohawk knew the man better than anyone. He was telling Mohawk that they couldn't let this stand.

And Mohawk agreed.

He turned back to Tom, who had appeared to already have forgotten about him, texting up a storm on his phone. Mohawk then glanced at Tom's workspace, which was littered with scripts for the night's show and other documents.

"Hey, Tom?" Mohawk said slowly. "That's a really nice desk."

From here, Mohawk stormed forward, grabbing Tom by the neck and hoisting him up in his arms. A few months ago, Mohawk wouldn't have been able to do this without his body crying out in pain. To his surprise, he found that Tom was quite easy to heft around.

Cobra was on the move, too. He grabbed Buddy in a chokehold from behind and, after the idiot gasped and flayed around, put him to sleep in seconds. Cobra then dropped the unconscious Buddy to the floor and nodded at Mohawk.

"Finish this," he said quietly.

Tom screeched in terror and screamed for help, but Mohawk promptly marched him over to the other side of the room. He then took a deep breath and knew he had to make this one count.

And so Mohawk Jones powerslammed Tom Victory, President and CEO of The Universal Grappling Federation and UGF Entertainment Inc., right through the man's desk, as hard as he fucking could.

CHAPTER 27

After laying waste to Tom Victory and Buddy Blaze, Mohawk and Cobra rushed to the hospital to see Emily. They bumped into some security guards on the way to their rental car but none of them, beefy young dudes with black t-shirts who looked big enough to be pro wrestlers themselves, seemed like they wanted to test them. The guys appeared happy enough that Mohawk and Cobra were leaving peacefully.

Mohawk and Cobra drove in silence, both processing what they had just done. Mohawk was surprisingly calm about it as his focus was on Emily and her well-being. Toni Titan had powerbombed her with such sickening impact and everything had happened so fast...he prayed that Emily was able to move her limbs and wasn't suffering from anything that would cause permanent damage.

Mohawk also wondered if Tom Victory would try to press assault charges but this was a minor concern.

Fuck him, Mohawk thought, his grip on the steering wheel tightening. The hospital was close, according to his phone, which Emily had taught him to use as a GPS. *If they want to arrest me, they can do it at the fucking hospital.*

Mohawk and Cobra hurried to Emily's room and to their relief, she was sitting up and watching Spongebob Squarepants on TV. Mohawk could have burst into tears right there but didn't when he saw that Emily had a spacy expression. She was also bruised up on her shoulders, arms and neck.

"I've got a minor concussion," Emily announced. "I shouldn't be watching TV but I'm more listening to it."

Both Mohawk and Cobra had both suffered concussions in their days so they knew that Emily would be a little out of it. She seemed surprisingly aware, though.

"How about the rest of you?" Mohawk asked, looking his daughter over and feeling a new wave of hate towards Tom Victory.

"I'm sore but okay," Emily said. She yawned. "Can someone turn Spongebob off?"

Mohawk gestured to Cobra, who found the remote and switched off the television. They stood on each side of the bed and Cobra brushed some hair out of Emily's face.

"You are a warrior," Cobra said.

"Thanks, unc," Emily said warmly. She turned to Mohawk. "Is Tom Victory mad at me for messing up my match? Can you tell him I'll do better next time? Should I call him?"

This knocked the wind out of Mohawk's sails. He saw Emily's words had a similar impact on Cobra. They watched as Emily started to cry.

"I fucked up," she whispered. Cobra put a comforting hand on her back but looked bewildered. He stared at Mohawk, who took a deep breath.

Time for Dad to step up.

"Em," he began. "You didn't fuck up anything. Like Cobra said, you were a fucking warrior. And you don't have to worry about Tom Victory anymore."

"What do you mean?" Emily asked.

Mohawk sat at the foot of his daughter's bed and took one of her hands in both of his.

"Those bastards set you up," he began. "Tom wanted payback for his dad, for something I did back in the day." Mohawk then explained that Tom Victory's grudge against him. Emily listened and then stared at her father in disbelief.

"That's fucked up," she said. "Tom had Toni Titan do that to me to punish you?"

"Yeah," Mohawk said. "I'm so sorry, Em. He killed our deals, too."

This was the part that Mohawk was most worried about telling Emily. That her dream to be a world famous UGF wrestler was over.

"This is so unfair," Emily said, her voice quivering. "That fucker is going to get away with this, isn't he?"

"Well," Mohawk said. "Not exactly."

"Huh?"

Cobra grinned.

"We fucked him," he said proudly.

"We fucked him up," Mohawk corrected.

He told Emily that they had kicked the shit out of Tom Victory and Buddy Blaze, leaving them both sprawled out in Tom's office. The story of the beat-down started out solemnly but as Emily grew more animated and excited hearing it, he put some more energy out of it.

"Your papa powerslammed Tom Victory to Hell!" Cobra said in delight.

"Holy shit, Dad!" Emily said, clapping her hands. "Do you know how fucking awesome that is? You, like, beat the fuck out of the top guy in wrestling because he messed with your daughter!" She smiled the widest smile Mohawk had ever seen. "Bad! Ass!"

"Yeah, I guess it was," Mohawk chuckled.

The three of them burst into laughter, no one harder and happier than Emily, and Mohawk knew that things, at least for now, were going to be okay.

The next day, Emily was discharged and the three of them packed up the condo and headed home to the townhouse. There was no interference from UGF officials and a week later, Mohawk had discovered, through Siniestro, that there weren't going to be any charges laid against him and Cobra, either.

"Tom doesn't want it to get out," Siniestro told him on a phone call. "He doesn't want to look bad in the wrestling media, getting beat up by two old guys."

This made sense to Mohawk as he had gone on the internet and hadn't heard any news about the fight, either. There were some reports about Emily's match with Toni but not really any buzz about it, which was good, as well as some "whispers" that something had gone down backstage after but it seemed Tom Victory had done a good job clamping down on the incident.

"Hey, Mohawk," Siniestro had said. "Just want to say...thank you from all the boys and girls in the locker room. We couldn't beat his ass but we're glad someone did. You're my hero, sir."

Despite the words, Mohawk didn't feel like a hero. He was worried about Emily. Concussions were tough to handle and although Emily's injury wasn't as severe as it could have been, she was still restricted in a lot of what she could do. She couldn't exercise or train and spent most of her first couple of weeks back at the townhouse curled up on the couch with Mohawk and Cobra tending to her. Mohawk was concerned that depression might set in because not only could Emily not wrestle right now but it was quite possible that Tom Victory would completely blackball her from the industry even if she got better. He did have that kind of power.

Gradually, the fog lifted. Mohawk and Cobra were constantly by Emily's side, taking walks around the neighborhood, starting some light training, and, after her doctor cleared her, progressing to more intense stuff, including wrestling work-outs.

"I'm not giving up, Dad," she told Mohawk. "I love this shit too much to stop."

What could Mohawk say to this? His daughter was young and had recovered well. If he was her, he wouldn't stop, either.

Eventually, Emily made her way back to Betty and Becca's school, wanting to improve her skills for her eventual return to the ring. Becca greeted her with a big hug and quickly whisked her and Cobra away to meet a new class of trainees, who were waiting in the ring.

"Coffee?" Betty offered Mohawk. He was surprised to see she was dressed in a more subdued way than usual, in relaxed jeans, Converse sneakers, a big black hoodie and no make-up. They went to Betty's office and sat down together.

"Thanks," Mohawk said, taking a mug from Betty. Her coffee was never any good but it did the job, something to sip on during a conversation.

"How's she doing?" Betty asked.

"Not bad. Getting back in shape."

"And now she's trying again."

"That's right."

Mohawk knew that Betty disapproved of this, having grown fond of Emily, but she also knew that wrestling was a tough habit to break.

"We've got a big show coming up next month," she said. "A tournament for ladies. Some international talent'll be there...you think Em'll be ready for it?"

"Definitely," Mohawk answered. This would be something good for Emily: a challenge to work towards.

"Good. I'll sign her up and let you tell her."

"Thanks."

They sipped their coffee.

"So," Betty said.

"So?" Mohawk said back.

"So what about us?"

This caught Mohawk completely off-guard. He wasn't expecting to have a flirt-fest with Betty today but something felt different. She wasn't looking at him with her usual lusty look. She seemed more like the regular Elizabeth, the girl who he held in his arms in a crummy hotel room after a show in Newark.

"You feel something for me," Betty said softly. "I know you do."

Mohawk couldn't lie here and didn't want to.

"I do," he admitted.

"So what are we gonna do about it?" Betty asked.

Mohawk looked down, collecting his thoughts.

"I'm always gonna love you, Betty," he said. "But Emily is my priority. I gotta be a good dad and set her up first." He sighed. "Can you wait?"

Betty smiled.

"Mohawk Jones loves me," she said, shaking her head. "Wow." She laughed, which was music to Mohawk's ears. "Set Emily up. But make it fast...I won't wait forever."

"I know," Mohawk said.

He then got up, stepped around Betty's desk, and kissed her. Betty tasted of coffee but Mohawk didn't mind at all. Her lips were still as sweet as ever.

"I'm gonna go see how Em is doing," Mohawk said, handing the mug to Betty, who seemed flustered by the kiss.

As he turned to leave, Betty clicked her tongue to get his attention. Mohawk looked back at Betty, who now struck a familiar seductive pose with her legs crossed and her smoky eyes fluttering.

"By the way," she said huskily. "Does it still work?"

Betty's eyes went to the front of Mohawk's pants, staring at the zipper. The woman just couldn't help herself.

Mohawk looked Betty over from top to bottom and back again.

"For you it will," he smiled.

CHAPTER 28

It was decided that Emily wouldn't wrestle in Betty's tournament. Coming off a head injury, it was too much to ask. If she had been booked to get to the finals, that would be three or four grueling matches. Mohawk, Cobra, Betty and Becca agreed that the best way to ease Emily back into wrestling was to take it nice and slow.

Unfortunately, Emily didn't agree.

"Fuck that!" she said. "Throw me into the fucking fire, Dad!"

And so they did.

Eri Takeda was one of the best female wrestlers in the world, maybe one of the best wrestlers, period, regardless of gender. Hailing from Japan, the forty-year-old had done it all and had inspired a generation of women wrestlers, many swiping Eri's moves or her style in the ring. And somehow, Betty was able to pull some strings to book her for an upcoming show during Eri's North American tour, where she would wrestle all over Canada and the United States for big paydays before heading back to Japan.

Eri needed an opponent for the tournament show as she was booked for an exhibition match. When Emily heard of this, she drove Mohawk's jeep right over to Betty and Becca's school.

"Give me Eri!" she demanded.

The match was set that day and a few weeks later, Emily was standing across the ring from the incomparable Eri Takeda.

Emily had asked Mohawk and Cobra not to accompany her to the ring this time. She wanted to do this match herself and succeed, or fail, on her own.

"Maybe wrestling isn't for me long-term," she explained to Mohawk back at the townhouse the night before. "But I just want one match to show everyone what I can really do."

Mohawk and Cobra stood silently by the back curtain, watching Emily and Eri circle each other. The athletic center was packed to capacity and the fans chanted for both competitors. Eri was the pro wrestling celebrity but Emily was the hometown girl, the one they had rooted for since her first match.

Mohawk had never met Eri Takeda before but could tell this was a seasoned performer. She dressed simply in a shiny blue outfit with kick-pads and blue amateur wrestling shoes, which made her red hair "pop". Eri wasn't muscular but had a lean frame, relying on martial arts and flexibility in her ring style.

This would be a good test for Emily to see if she could keep up with a top pro.

"No talking during match," Cobra said to Mohawk. Even though Cobra was one of the great characters of professional wrestling, he did love a technical masterpiece full of chain-wrestling and reversals. Cobra was as intent on watching the match as anyone else.

Becca was refereeing the match and signaled for the bell. Right away, Emily and Eri locked up and Eri kicked things off with some takedowns into an arm-lock. Emily countered with a reversal and a takedown of her own into a headlock.

Very smooth.

Eri fought back up and they initiated a running the ropes sequence. Emily rolled under an attempt by Eri to kick her head off with a roundhouse kick and countered with the Jones Special, a well-placed dropkick. Eri sold it like she got shot in the face and Emily preened for the crowd, who ate it up.

"Nice," Mohawk said.

"I said no talking!" Cobra snapped.

Emily followed up by hitting Eri with a snap suplex and a big elbowdrop off the ropes. She then put Eri in a camel clutch, one of Cobra's trademark moves, and Mohawk could see that Emily's uncle was very pleased.

Eri made a comeback, nailing Emily with a series of kicks, clotheslines, and a big tombstone piledriver. Emily looked to be done but kicked out before Becca's hand hit the mat a third time. The fans roared with approval.

"This is awesome! This is awesome!" the crowd cheered, followed by "Fight forever! Fight forever!"

Eri climbed the top rope and dove at Emily...but Emily rolled through into a pinning position! Eri barely kicked out and the fans were going crazy.

"This is awesome! Fight forever!" they screamed.

The match continued for another six minutes, Emily and Eri going back and forth, neither getting a full-on advantage over the other. Mohawk's respect for Eri grew exponentially. The woman could have easily just run over Emily like Toni Titan did but instead, she was giving Emily the match of her life and making her look like a superstar.

This was professional wrestling at its finest.

At the eighteen-minute mark, Emily and Eri went to the finish. Eri missed a spinning kick and Emily dropkicked her again before lifting her up for the big powerslam. However, Eri slipped out and rolled Emily up to surprise pin her...which Emily reversed...and then Eri reversed again. This time Emily was trapped and her shoulders were down for the pin.

The fans erupted and the exhausted Eri sold her victory like she had barely squeaked it out. A standing ovation of cheers and applause was given to both women, both having stolen the show, and they hugged before Becca raised both their hands, concluding one of the best matches Mohawk had ever seen.

"That is our girl!" Cobra said proudly.

Emily stuck around ringside to slap hands with fans and take selfies so Eri got to the backstage area first. She didn't speak English very well but recognized Mohawk and Cobra as legends of the sport.

"Thank you," Eri said simply, bowing to both men. Mohawk and Cobra were so touched, they bowed back.

Eri then walked over to her handlers as Emily came backstage herself. She ran over to Eri and hugged her so hard, she lifted her off her feet. Eri was confused at first but giggled nonetheless as she was put back down.

"You don't know what you did for me tonight," Emily said emotionally, her voice cracking. She couldn't help but cry and Eri tenderly wiped her tears away. Mohawk and Cobra watched as Emily and Eri chatted about the match together as best they could and then parted ways.

Emily then jogged over to Mohawk and hugged him, too. She also pulled the nearby Cobra into the embrace.

"I'm so fucking happy right now!" Emily cried. Mohawk and Cobra didn't say anything, just enjoying the moment with their kid.

Eventually, Emily broke the hug and she went off with Becca to go over the match, as was their custom. Mohawk and Cobra watched them go and took deep breaths.

"Hell of a match," Mohawk said.

"Emily is good, Mohawk," Cobra said. "She is very, very good."

They weren't the only ones to think this. A few minutes later, Betty brought over a well-dressed and handsome Japanese man in his fifties to them.

"This is Mr. Ishioka," Betty said, introducing Mr. Ishioka to Mohawk and Cobra, the gentlemen all shaking hands. "He's the president and booker of Dynamic Love Wrestling in Japan."

Mohawk had never heard of Dynamic Love Wrestling but knew that women's wrestling had a higher profile and deeper history in Japan than in North America. He also smiled at the strange names the Japanese gave their companies.

Dynamic...Love...Wrestling?

"Emily is a fine talent," Mr. Ishioka said in perfect English. "How long has she been training?"

"Almost a year," Cobra answered.

Mohawk could see that Mr. Ishioka was very impressed by this.

"And you two trained her?" he asked.

"We did," Mohawk replied. "Along with Wildcat Becca Stone."

Mr. Ishioka nodded and smiled knowingly at Mohawk.

"You're one of Mr. Sanada's students," he said.

"My mentor," Mohawk said.

"A very good man and wrestling legend. I knew him well. My father was one of his tag team partners in Japan."

Mohawk tried to recall a wrestler with the last name Ishioka but his knowledge of Mr. Sanada's career was limited.

"I would like to extend an invitation to Emily to come to Japan for the next year," Mr. Ishioka said. "We would like her to wrestle exclusively for Dynamic Love Wrestling. I have spoken to Eri Takeda and she is interested in taking Emily under her wing as a protégé."

Mohawk and Cobra were blown away. This was the opportunity of a lifetime for Emily, to train and wrestle under the guidance of a legendary wrestler in a country where professional wrestling was revered and respected.

Even so, Mohawk couldn't help but feel saddened by Mr. Ishioka's offer.

Emily would be gone.

For a whole year.

CHAPTER 29

Mohawk, Cobra and Emily didn't go to Kavita's wedding ceremony to the venerable Dr. Harvinder Rai. It was to be held in a Sikh temple and for the sake of keeping the drama to a minimum, it was decided that Cobra shouldn't show up, although the trio were planning to attend the reception later that day. Emily was a little bummed about it as she wanted to experience a Sikh wedding.

Mohawk had bought a new suit for the reception, a charcoal number with a navy blue tie. He felt he looked like a mafia don or an old lawyer but Emily assured him that he looked "dope". She herself was wearing a purple dress and a matching flower in her hair, politely turning down Kavita's earlier offer for an Indian sari at the downtown boutique.

"Never seen you wear a dress before," Mohawk laughed.

"I'm just worried people'll see the wrestling bruises on my legs," Emily said, struggling in her high-heeled shoes.

The two waited in the kitchen for Cobra to make his grand entrance and he didn't disappoint. He wore a full Indian kurta, a cream-colored and sparkly outfit with his typical red turban. On his feet, Cobra wore pointy Indian slippers. Cobra's beard was also trimmed and combed and he looked healthy and full of energy.

"You look awesome, Uncle Cobra," Emily said.

"I feel the awesome," Cobra smiled.

He walked over to Mohawk and began to adjust his tie.

"Almost right," Cobra said. He finished and both men stared hard at each other.

"No funny business, Cobra," Mohawk warned. "This is Kavita's night."

Cobra bowed his head solemnly.

"I will not be funny," he said.

The drive to the banquet hall was about thirty minutes and the party had already begun when they arrived. The place was packed and gaily decorated with red and white balloons, elegant tablecloths and cutlery for the seated guests, a DJ playing Bhangra beats for the young people on the dance floor with some of the older men happily enjoying each other's company at the open bar.

Mohawk spotted Kavita and her new husband seated at a table on a stage above the dance floor, the grim-faced Mama-Ji beside them glowering at everyone with the cool-as-fuck Michael standing nearby. Kavita looked beautiful in a pink sari. Indian bridal jewelry adorned her ears, neck and wrists and Kavita's hands were done up in gorgeous henna designs.

She looks like a queen, Mohawk thought. He turned to Cobra, who was staring at Kavita with wide eyes. Mohawk knew this moment must have been difficult for his friend, especially when Kavita's husband was no slouch, either. Dr. Rai was a very handsome turbaned Sikh man, dressed in a dignified black suit and gray and black striped tie.

"I want to go to her," Cobra said to Mohawk, which alarmed him.

"I told you no funny business," Mohawk reminded Cobra.

"I know. No funny."

And no funny business happened. Cobra courteously walked over to Kavita and Dr. Rai and congratulated them on their wedding, wish them the best of luck on their marriage. It happened quickly and Mohawk was there when Cobra sadly walked away from the bride and groom's table.

"You good?" Mohawk said, putting his arm around Cobra's shoulders.

"I am good," came the reply. Cobra smiled. "I am happy for my ex-love."

He chuckled at the term he used for Kavita as Emily sidled up to them.

"It's really an open bar?" she asked hopefully.

Mohawk rolled his eyes.

"Let's all get something to eat first," he suggested.

Mohawk expected Kavita to put up a great spread and she did not disappoint. Mohawk, Emily and Cobra loaded up their plates with kebabs, tandoori chicken, samosas and pakoras, found a table, and chowed down. The food was spicy for Emily but it was delicious and she tucked in as heartily as her father and uncle. As they ate, some of Cobra's relatives, including his cousins and some friends he grew up with, made their way to their table. Cobra greatly enjoyed re-connecting with his family members, having been estranged from them for so long.

Soon after, Cobra dragged Emily and Mohawk to the dance floor. Bhangra was Punjabi dance music that was full of heavy drum beats and contemporary Bhangra mixed a traditional style with hip hop and pop flavors. The young people at the reception ate this up and the older folks surprisingly did as well. Cobra was an excellent dancer, getting down with his cousins, the males dancing with the males and females with females. Mohawk wasn't a dancer at all but he did try a little, mostly standing to the side and clapping as he watched Cobra's fancy footwork.

Mohawk also saw that Emily was very much enjoying herself. She had downed a couple of drinks before she kicked off her heels and made her way to the floor, dancing quite close with one particular Punjabi woman, a pretty girl close to Emily's age with thick black eyebrows, a dangling nose ring and jingling anklets. This was the first time Mohawk had wondered about Emily's romantic preference and he smiled, finding that it didn't matter to him what kind of person she was interested in.

As long as she's happy, right?

The party raged on but Mohawk needed a breather. He went outside to the front of the banquet hall to take in the fresh night air, making sure he was away from the smokers hurriedly puffing away before they returned to the dance floor. Not long after, Emily joined him.

"Damn, these Punjabis know how to party," she said, favoring her feet. "Feel like I should have trained for this thing."

"Where's Cobra?" Mohawk asked.

"He's dancing on top of the bar now."

"Oh lord..."

Emily laughed and it was still the best sound in the world to Mohawk. He said nothing more, not wanting to ruin this moment of him standing side by side with his brave and incredible daughter.

"It's amazing how much they love their culture," Emily said. It seemed like dancing had sobered her up a little. "It'd be nice for us to have that feeling."

"What do you mean?" Mohawk asked.

Emily sighed.

"Dad, I've learned that wrestling isn't everything," she said. "I want us to trace our roots. For real. Let's find out what tribe or band we're a part of. Maybe go visit our people. You up for it?"

Mohawk nodded.

"That sounds good," he said. "We'll do it together."

"You promise?" Emily said.

"Yeah. But first...you gotta go to Japan."

CHAPTER 30

To Mohawk's surprise, Emily wasn't as enthusiastic about going to Japan as he expected her to be. Maybe it was the prospect of being in a foreign country for up to a year and doing it all by herself. Mohawk and Cobra weren't going along and that might have been a frightening prospect for Emily.

"You can do it," Mohawk said the day after Kavita's wedding reception during yet another family meeting. "Actually, you *have* to do it, Em."

"Yes," Cobra said. "In Japan, you will be great…and then, some day, you will be the champion."

Mohawk and Cobra worked on Emily for the rest of the meeting and by the end, she had made her decision.

"Alright," Emily said. "I'm going to Japan."

A few weeks later, Emily was packed and ready to go. She would be staying with Eri Takeda at the Dynamic Love Wrestling dojo and had even downloaded a language app on her phone to start learning Japanese.

Mohawk was so proud of his daughter, ready to embark on a new adventure where she could make a name for herself away from her father and uncle.

He, Cobra and Emily stood outside the townhouse as the Uber driver pulled up to the curb. Emily signaled for him to wait a second and she turned to Mohawk and Cobra.

"I love you guys," she said, jumping into a hug with them.

"We love you," Cobra said, choking up a little. "You are the very best of us."

Cobra stayed by the front door as Mohawk walked Emily to the driver's sedan. They put her luggage in the trunk and Mohawk struggled to find some sage wisdom to impart to his departing daughter.

"Be safe," Mohawk said softly. "And know that we're always here for you, Em. You want to come home, you come home, okay?"

"Okay, Dad," Emily said, looking to the ground, the tears streaming down her face.

"And remember this most of all...don't take shit from anyone. They try to break you, you break'em first. And you keep breakin'em until they can't get up."

Father and daughter burst into laughter and shared one last hug that Mohawk wished would never end. A few minutes later, Emily was on her way to the airport to catch her flight to Tokyo.

Mohawk and Cobra stayed outside for some time, looking out at the neighborhood together. Mohawk glanced at Cobra and saw that he was wiping his eyes.

"You crying?" he asked.

"You shut up," Cobra replied.

He then patted Mohawk on the shoulder and went inside to watch a Bollywood movie. Mohawk lingered, seeing Karen coming by with her kid, who was now walking. The child was giggling uncontrollably, picking up speed as he waddled, and Karen dashed after him when he almost wandered into the street. She directed her son back to the sidewalk and then turned to the watching Mohawk, shaking her head.

"They grow up too fast!" she yelled good-naturedly, chasing after the little boy, who had escaped her once more.

Mohawk smiled.

Yeah, they do, he thought. *Way too fucking fast.*

THE END

ABOUT THE AUTHOR

Jagjiwan Sohal is a South Asian screenwriter and author and has worked with prolific film and TV production companies with a focus on diversity, comedy, and children's entertainment. Jagjiwan has written scripts for *Nina's World* (NBC Sprout), *Opie's Home* (TVO), and *Addison* (CBC Kids) and has acted as writer/script editor for the hit kids' series *Dino Dana* (Amazon/TVO) and *Endlings* (HULU/CBC/BBC). Recently, he has written for Netflix's *Action Pack*, *Deepa and Anoop*, and *Team Zenko Go* as well as the upcoming *Caillou*, *Press Start*, *Ghee Happy*, and *Late Bloomer*. He also has several film and TV projects in development. Also, a published novelist, Jagjiwan's middle-grade horror/comedy novel *Smorgasbord* was published in 2014.

NOTE FROM JAGJIWAN SOHAL

Word-of-mouth is crucial for any author to succeed. If you enjoyed *Two Old Indians*, please leave a review online—anywhere you are able. Even if it's just a sentence or two. It would make all the difference and would be very much appreciated.

Thanks!
Jagjiwan Sohal

We hope you enjoyed reading this title from:

www.blackrosewriting.com

Subscribe to our mailing list – *The Rosevine* – and receive **FREE** books, daily deals, and stay current with news about upcoming releases and our hottest authors.
Scan the QR code below to sign up.

Already a subscriber? Please accept a sincere thank you for being a fan of Black Rose Writing authors.

View other Black Rose Writing titles at www.blackrosewriting.com/books and use promo code **PRINT** to receive a **20% discount** when purchasing.

www.ingramcontent.com/pod-product-compliance
Lightning Source LLC
Chambersburg PA
CBHW072152070526
44585CB00015B/1104